DISRAELI AND THE ART OF VICTORIAN POLITICS

DISRAELI AND THE ART OF VICTORIAN POLITICS

SECOND EDITION

Ian St John

ANTHEM PRESS
LONDON · NEW YORK · DELHI

Anthem Press
An imprint of Wimbledon Publishing Company
www.anthempress.com

This edition first published in UK and USA 2010
by ANTHEM PRESS
75-76 Blackfriars Road, London SE1 8HA, UK
or PO Box 9779, London SW19 7ZG, UK
and
244 Madison Ave. #116, New York, NY 10016, USA

British Library Cataloguing in Publication Data
A catalogue record for this book is available from the British Library.

Library of Congress Cataloging in Publication Data
A catalog record for this book has been requested.

ISBN-13: 978 1 84331 873 6 (Pbk)
ISBN-10: 1 84331 873 3 (Pbk)

This title is also available as an eBook.

To Jean, Chandrika, Lawrence,
and the memory of my father, Roy.

CONTENTS

Timeline		ix
Introduction		xi
I.	Disraeli's Political Career, 1804–1846	1
II.	The Politics of Opposition, 1846–1866	35
III.	The 1867 Reform Act	73
IV.	Disraeli's Political Ideology	97
V.	Opposition Again, 1868–1874	131
VI.	Prime Minister, 1874–1880: Domestic Policy	143
VII.	Prime Minister: Foreign and Imperial Policy	165
VIII.	Disraeli and the Art of Politics	209
	Notes	223
	Bibliography	233
	Index	237

TIMELINE OF DISRAELI'S CAREER

1804   Benjamin Disraeli enters this earth

1817   Disraeli converts from Judaism to Christianity

1819   Leaves Higham Hall school

1821   Commences training as a solicitor

1825   Failed share speculations leave him in debt

1826   Failure of *Representative* newspaper
Publishes first novel, *Vivian Grey*

1827–30 Disraeli depressed

1830–31 Tours the Middle East

1832   Reform Act. Disraeli enters politics, professing radicalism

1835   Publishes *Vindication of the English Constitution* in defence of House of Lords

1837   Elected to parliament

1839   Marries Mary Anne

1841   Peel forms Conservative government. No place for Disraeli

1842–45 Disraeli works with Young England colleagues

1844   Publishes *Conningsby*

1845   Publishes *Sybil*

1845–46 Corn Law crisis. Disraeli attacks Peel

1846   Corn Laws repealed. Fall of Peel. Break up of Conservative party

1847–49 Disraeli emerges as deputy Conservative leader to Lord Derby

1847   Publishes *Tancred*

1848   Takes up residence at Hughenden Manor

1852   Conservative government. Disraeli Chancellor of Exchequer and Leader of Commons. Government resigns on defeat of budget

1854–56 Crimean War. Palmerston ascendant

1858–59 Conservative government. Disraeli Chancellor and Leader of Commons

1859   Government resigns on failure of Reform Bill

1861   Death of Prince Albert

1864   Disraeli's 'Ape or Angel' speech at Oxford

1865   Death of Palmerston

1866	Liberal Reform Bill brought forward by Russell and Gladstone. (June) Defeat of Liberal Bill. Government resigns (July) Hyde Park pro-reform riots
1866–68	Conservative government
1867	Conservatives pass the Second Reform Act, introducing household suffrage in boroughs
1868	(February) Retirement of Derby. Disraeli becomes Prime Minister. (November) Gladstone's Liberals win election
1870	Disraeli publishes *Lothair* John Gorst placed in charge of Conservative Central Office
1872	Manchester (April) and Crystal Palace (June) speeches (December) Death of Disraeli's wife
1873	Disraeli declines Victoria's invitation to form a government
1874	Conservatives win general election. Disraeli Prime Minister
1875	The year of social reform legislation (July) Uprising against Turkish rule in Bosnia-Herzegovina (November) British government purchases 44 per cent stake in Suez Canal company
1876	(May) Disraeli refuses to sign the Berlin Memorandum on Turkish reform (May) Turkish massacre of Bulgarian Christians (August) Disraeli becomes Earl Beaconsfield (September) Gladstone's pamphlet on 'Bulgarian atrocities'
1877	(January) Victoria declared Empress of India (April) Transvaal annexed to British South Africa (April) Russia declares war on Turkey
1878	(March) Russia forces Treaty of San Stefano on defeated Turks (March) Britain begins preparations for war. Derby resigns as Foreign Secretary (June–July) Disraeli attends Congress of Berlin. Achieves 'peace with honour' (November) British force enters Afghanistan
1879	(January) British South Africa declares war on Zulus (January) Zulus destroy British force at Ishandhlwana (September) British mission to Afghanistan massacred
1880	(March) General election defeat for Conservatives. Disraeli publishes *Endymion*
1881	(March) Last speech to House of Lords (April) Disraeli departs this earth

INTRODUCTION

There were many lives of Benjamin Disraeli. There was Disraeli the novelist, whose career spanned more than fifty years, comfortably enveloping that of his contemporary, Dickens; the 'man of the press', who was involved in the founding of two unsuccessful newspapers; the political thinker, who assailed utilitarianism and 'educated' the Conservative party to think in terms of One Nation and see that a Democracy might be Tory; the exotic outsider, boasting variously of his 'revolutionary' and 'continental' mind and his ability to plumb the depths of the Great Asian Mystery; the Sephardic Jew, convinced of the indestructible virtues of the pure Semitic race; the parliamentarian, who over-threw Robert Peel, the foremost statesman of his age, and commanded the opposition forces in the Commons for a longer period than any other individ-ual in history; the socialite, whose brilliant wit gained him admission to the most exclusive salons; the Prime Minister who awakened Britain to its impe-rial estates and dominated Europe's premier leaders at the Congress of Berlin; and the courtier, who turned the suspicions of the Widow of Windsor into affectionate regard. Such a list might almost be extended indefinitely. Even then, it would probably be exceeded by a catalogue of the published *Lives* of Disraeli, which, in 1998, was already estimated at more than eighty.

So what of *this* life? The following pages offer an analytical interpretation of the political life of Disraeli. Admittedly only one amongst many possible lives, it happens to be the most important for it supplies the organizing principle that *makes sense* of, if it does not wholly coincide with, the others. What then was Disraeli's political life? It was the sphere of public action, set within such environs as the Commons Chamber, the Cabinet room, and the town and country houses of other leading politicians, within which Disraeli sought to realize his personal needs for adulation, status, excitement and creative expression. Yet politics, for Disraeli, could never be a mere instrument; to fulfil his purpose it had also to be an art. He regarded it, from the begin-ning, as a dramatic stage upon which an individual of vision, imagination, courage and audacity could manipulate events, ideas, and men so as to realize ends that he defined. And it was in the achievement of these ends that Disraeli deployed the breadth of his talent – whether as writer, wit, thinker, debater or courtier.

As an outsider, Disraeli was not born to a political position or set of social or familial expectations. Initially, this was a handicap and never ceased to bring significant disadvantages. Yet, it was to prove, paradoxically, the key to his most prominent achievements. For Disraeli possessed a degree of autonomy rare in 19th century politics. It was, for example, *his* decision to enter politics at all, instead of, say, working full time as a writer or journalist; to ally with the Tories and not the Whigs or the Radicals; to lead a backbench assault upon Peel, rather than support the Conservative leader, as he had previously done and some former members of the Young England group continued to do; to persist through the laborious years of opposition, when members of his own party would have welcomed his departure; to seek to outbid Gladstone on parliamentary reform in 1867, as opposed to pursuing cross-party support for a more moderate reform bill; to set a sceptical Conservative party upon a social reform agenda; and to choose, in 1872, to associate Conservatives with the cause of the Empire. Of course, Disraeli was subject to constraints, often quite rigid ones that chaffed and frustrated – most obviously, his need to defer to Lord Derby, the Conservative leader, during most of the 1850s and 1860s. Also, he operated within a parliamentary and national context whose logic dictated certain courses of action. Even so, at crucial stages of his career, Disraeli *did* make decisions that were neither necessary, nor inevitable, nor even likely, and he made these decisions in the light of his own calculus of costs and benefits. It was precisely because of this scope for taking his own initiatives from a position of relative autonomy that his career has so often been labelled opportunist, which in this context is another word for self-willed. It is, accordingly, the core intention of this study to explain how, why and with what results Disraeli acted as he did at each defining moment of his political life.

Whatever autonomy Disraeli may have possessed, a political life cannot be lived alone. Disraeli operated amidst the world of mid-Victorian Westminster parliamentary politics. What, specifically, was the art of Victorian politics? It was the art of forming, out of diverse groups and individuals, sufficiently sustained political connections in order to make a realistic bid for power or influence. In the 19th century, the weakness of the party system, the financial and psychological independence of MPs, the territorial loyalties of electors and elected, and class and religious differences within and outside parliament, all meant that governing majorities were never ready to hand – they had to be *made* and, what was equally difficult, *sustained*. This was an exercise in compromise, tact, strategy, timely concession, manipulation, deference, ideological positioning, speech making, country house visiting and so forth. This is, to be sure, what politics is about at all times, but the characteristics of the Victorian political world meant that it was peculiarly all-consuming.

The essential reason for this was that the Victorians' political life was so intimately bound up with their social life. There were two aspects to this. First, Westminster politics was conducted by a wealthy social elite for whom political activity was really an extension of social activity. The decision to enter parliament, the connections they formed, the parliamentary timetable (with its long recesses when the political world took leave of London for its country estates), the linked network of clubs and dining societies, the jostling for place and patronage and titles – all exemplified the seamlessness of the join between the world of politics and the social life of the propertied elite. Politics was a consuming passion of the upper class. To operate politically, therefore, someone like Disraeli had to operate socially. If you left the office it was simply to carry on with politics at the club, or ball, or country house. Second, the world of Westminster politics was finding itself increasingly under pressure from major changes occurring within wider British society. These changes are familiar – industrialization, the shift from rural to urban living, transformations in the speed of communications and transport, agricultural change, population growth, scientific discoveries, the extension of popular education and the emergence of new intellectual currents, notably political economy and Benthamite utilitarianism. The challenge confronting the politicians of the period was to formulate responses to the pressing issues thrown up by such changes whilst maintaining the parameters of the constitution and the privileged position they occupied within it. In this sense, nearly all leading politicians were students of Burke, regarding themselves as making the minimum of changes necessary to conserve the whole. What was in dispute was not the necessity, but the extent, of change. Here, too, Disraeli was actively engaged. To a degree that is highly unusual of British politicians, he reflected intellectually upon the meaning of the social trends he observed and engaged in the battle of ideas over issues such as the Condition of England question of the 1840s – though it ought to be borne in mind that his interventions were never disinterested, being motivated chiefly by the exigencies of his struggle for place within parliament. Later, as Prime Minister, he took the initiative, again for reasons of party advantage, in confronting social issues arising out of urbanization and the changing character of capital-labour relations, whilst simultaneously seeking for Britain a meaningful place within a world of developing continental powers. To comprehend the art of Disraelian politics is thus not merely absorbing in itself; it provides a peculiarly informative insight into the world of Victorian politics as a whole.

The subject, then, of this study is the political activity of Disraeli – the motives behind his political decisions, the considerations that shaped his attitudes to policy issues, the strategies he deployed to negotiate the convolutions of Victorian political society, and his intellectual response to the more profound questions posed by the seismic shifts occurring within the social and economic foundations of the exclusive milieu to which he was so irresistibly drawn. As such, it will meet the needs of students of Disraeli and Victorian politics, whether at undergraduate or sixth form level. It will also, hopefully, be appreciated by anyone wishing to better understand Britain's uniquely evolved political heritage in general, and the meaning and practice of Conservative politics in particular.

The author would like to express his appreciation to Mr Alex Keenlyside for undertaking the thankless task of reading through the proofs, and Mr Jamie Day for his help in compiling the index. Professor Michael Bentley made insightful comments upon the chapter on Disraeli's ideology. All remaining errors of fact or judgment are the responsibility of the author alone.

Preface to the Second Edition

The appearance of a Second Edition of this book has provided an opportunity to take account of some recent studies of Disraeli's career, notably those by Parry and Aldous. In preparing it for publication the author was fortunate to have the invaluable assistance of Kirti Shah, who removed several errors in the old index and updated it in the light of the newly incorporated material.

Ian St John
Haberdashers' Aske's School
October 2010

I

DISRAELI'S POLITICAL CAREER, 1804–1846

To understand Benjamin Disraeli, we need to take seriously the intensity of his ambition. Contemporaries did; it was one reason why so many disliked him. He was a supreme egoist who was convinced that his abilities would elevate him to the highest social position, carry him through the portals of power, and ensure that he left a permanent mark on his age. 'There were,' he later recalled, 'days when, on waking, I felt I could move dynasties and governments…' It is tempting to see such remarks as the product of a playful and ironic character. They were, but they contained an essential kernel of self-belief which he did little to disguise. In 1844, he told his constituents:

> There is no doubt, gentleman, that all men who offer themselves as candidates for public favour have motives of some sort. I candidly acknowledge that I have and I will tell you what they are: I love fame; I love public reputation; I love to live in the eyes of the country.

Disraeli felt himself to possess unique talents. 'To enter into high society, a man must possess either blood, a million, or a genius' he wrote, aged 21. Deficient in social connections and wealth, he trusted his talents to set him at the pinnacle of 19th century society. Few aspirant politicians, when asked by a senior political figure (Lord Melbourne) 'what do you want to be?' could have had the presumption to reply, 'I want to be Prime Minister'. At this point he did not possess a seat, or even a Party. Yet, Disraeli believed this and he did not merely make his own myth: he lived it. He really did go on to move governments, make Emperors and, of course, become Prime Minister. We must take Disraeli's egotism and ambition seriously.

Where did this ambition come from? The inner springs of human psychology are beyond the gaze of the historian. We naturally shape our explanations within the context of observable circumstances. Fortunately, in Disraeli's case these go some way to providing a convincing explanation. The key factor here was the ambiguity of Disraeli's position. It was sometimes said that Disraeli rose to the Premiership from a socially disadvantaged background. This was not the case. Disraeli's father, Isaac, inherited a fortune of £2 million in our values and used this to fund the life of the gentleman scholar, producing books on literature and history which brought him into contact with many of the foremost writers of his day, including Byron. It was in his Bloomsbury house in 1804 that Disraeli was born. Later Isaac moved to a country house in Buckinghamshire, where Disraeli spent much of his early twenties. So Disraeli's origins – like Peel's and Gladstone's – were middle class, though metropolitan-literary rather than northern-commercial. Yet there were a series of distinctive features. If Disraeli later summed up his politics as 'England', he could hardly say as much of his family background. Both his mother and father came from Italian families. On his father's side, Disraeli was only a second generation Englishman, his grandfather having arrived in England from Italy in 1748 to make his fortune. Similarly, though reasonably well-educated in a private school, Disraeli did not experience the public school and Oxbridge education increasingly customary for the upper and middle classes. He was one of only two 19th century Prime Ministers not to have attended university and always regretted this fact and the entrée into upper class society he had missed.

Most important, though Disraeli was a baptised member of the Church of England, he was raised as a Jew till the age of 12. That he became a Christian was due to the accident that his father quarrelled with the local synagogue, resigned from it in 1817 and had his children baptised. It was a crucial decision. If Disraeli had remained a Jew, his political career would have been impossible since Jews were not allowed to enter the House of Commons until 1858. Of course, as far as Victorian society was concerned, a Jew he always remained. One of the issues Disraeli had to confront in his life was how to deal with this fact. It is an interesting facet of his career that he celebrated rather than denied his Jewish heritage – albeit in an idiosyncratic way.

Disraeli, then, was a paradoxical and ambiguous character, and this was the mainspring of his ambition, since it was by striving for recognition and prestige that Disraeli sought to reconcile his ambiguities by transcending them. Through the sheer force of his ego, he would construct a unique and exotic personality in which potential liabilities, such as his Italian origins, unconventional education, and Jewish ancestry, were transmuted into strengths. In this sense Disraeli's life was a work of art – it was his own creation in a way that was not true of most of those who followed the well-worn tramlines of conventional upper middle class society.

The intellectual framework within which Disraeli embarked on this project to fashion his destiny was provided by the Romantic milieu of his youth. Romanticism was not merely a fashionable literary attitude when

Disraeli was a young man. 'It presented,' writes Paul Smith, 'a natural affinity with his deepest needs and purposes.'[1] For what Romanticism taught was the power of the individual to mould reality through the creative power of the imagination. To achieve this transformation was the work of the spirit of genius, an innate quality exemplified in men such as Byron, Beethoven and Rousseau. Interestingly, Isaac Disraeli had delineated the personality of the man of genius in his 1795 *Essay on the Literary Character*. In 1820, a re-issued copy of the book found its way into the hands of the sixteen-year-old Disraeli. 'Geniuses,' wrote Isaac, 'were born and not made and rarely excelled academically.' 'He is a daydreaming dawdling child, often delicate and some-times physically clumsy. He takes no part in the sports of his school mates; his parents find him difficult and sullen and his teachers find him slow and dull.' As Ridley remarks:

> It was almost as if Benjamin's childhood and schooldays had been formed on the template of genius… He had felt different from the other boys at first because he was Jewish; now he knew that he was different because he was a genius.'[2]

Disraeli's ambition and egotism had now acquired a justifying ideology. His restless desire to make his mark was the striving of the man of genius to realize his capabilities within the stultifying constraints of commonplace society. His role model was Byron, who was at the peak of his infamy when Disraeli was a teenager. Disraeli idolized Byron, whom he considered to be a 'master spirit', and 'wished to be thought the new Byron'.[3] He affected Byronic poses, dressed in black in the manner of his hero, had himself rowed on Lake Geneva during a thunderstorm by Byron's boatman Maurice and eventually acquired the services of Byron's servant Tita, in whose arms the poet had died at Missolongi.[4]

Defining and realizing his 'genius' now became Disraeli's preoccupation. His father had arranged for him to enter a solicitor's office in London, but the legal profession was never going to satisfy the restive longings of such a man of destiny:

> I passed my evenings at home, alone and always deep in study… I became pensive and restless and before I was 20, I was obliged to terminate the dream of my father… Nothing would satisfy me but travel…the hour of adventure had arrived.

Years of Adventure, 1824–1831

We now enter what were, for Disraeli, eventful but frustrating years. The objective was simple – to make his mark on his age. Yet the methods adopted were unfocused and frequently unconventional and the reputation he acquired remained with him for the rest of his life.

Disraeli first endeavoured to become rich. In the early 1820s, the stock market had been booming, with shares in South American mining companies doing particularly well. Disraeli and his partners bought in November 1824 – at precisely the moment the shares began losing value. Attempting to revive interest in the shares Disraeli produced his first publication, An Enquiry into the Plans, Progress and Policy of the American Mining Companies. But it was to no avail and by June 1825, Disraeli (aged only 20) had incurred debts of around £2,000, almost £120,000 in today's prices.

Another disaster soon followed. In 1825, Disraeli became involved with the publisher John Murray, a friend of his father's, in a project to commence a new newspaper called The Representative. Its politics were to be Liberal Tory. Disraeli was to provide one-quarter of the capital. But the project did not proceed smoothly. The editor chosen was Lockhart, a Scottish Tory and son-in-law of Sir Walter Scott. Disraeli travelled north to interview both men. Unfortunately, Scott objected strongly to Lockhart becoming involved in anything so vulgar as newspaper journalism. The paper, when it finally appeared in January 1826, was a failure. By the time it ceased publication in July, Murray's debts stood at £26,000. Disraeli, already indebted, was in no position to bear his share.

Out of work and in debt, Disraeli turned for salvation to his pen. The result was his first published novel, Vivian Grey (1826). Like most first novels, it was autobiographical, relating the story of the failed Representative but in the guise of the formation of a new political party. The young Vivian is Disraeli, while the old and ineffectual aristocrat behind the new party is Murray. The book was a 'Society Novel', affecting to describe the lives of the rich and famous, and at first the author was simply known as a 'man of fashion'. But when Disraeli's authorship emerged and the fact that he was far from intimate with the privileged world he described, the reviewers were fierce in their criticism. Murray was particularly hurt by his caricature as the frequently inebriated Marquis and broke off his relations with the Disraeli family.

Thus, although Disraeli emerged from the Vivian Grey episode with £700 and some of the notoriety he craved, he had also acquired a number of enemies and, what was more damaging, they were to be found in the very levels of society in which he wished to move. To his debts he had added, says Blake, 'a reputation for cynicism, double dealing, recklessness and insincerity which it took him years to live down'.[5]

The strain of the period 1824–1826 took its toll on Disraeli and he spent much of the following three years under a cloud of poor health, low spirits and debts. Richmond and Post believe he was suffering from a 'major clinical depression', brought on by a series of rebuffs to his highly sensitive, narcissistic personality.[6] He now doubted 'whether I shall ever do anything which may mark me out from the crowd. I am one of those to whom moderate reputation can give no pleasure and who, in all probability, am incapable of achieving a great one.' However in 1830, his health revived. His dress became increasingly dandified. Henry Bulwer described how he came to one dinner wearing green velvet trousers, a yellow waistcoat, shoes with silver buckles, lace at his wrists and his hair in ringlets.

The recovery of his spirits was completed by an extensive tour of the Mediterranean and Middle East in 1830–1831, including Constantinople, Jerusalem, Spain and Egypt. This was one of the turning points in Disraeli's life. He revelled in the atmosphere of the East – its colours, smells, indulgences, ideas and social mores. He felt instantly at home and engaged with the people on their own terms – there was none of the judgmental reproach of the Englishman abroad. 'I am quite the Turk,' he wrote during his stay at Navarina, 'wear a turban, smoke a pipe six feet long and squat on a Divan… I find the habits of this calm and luxurious people entirely agree with my own preconceived opinions of propriety and enjoyment…'[7] For Edward Said, Disraeli exemplifies the mentality of the 19th century Orientalist, believing that Orientals live in the Orient, live lives of Oriental ease, subject to Oriental despotism and imbued with Oriental fatalism.[8] But Brantlinger qualifies Said's characterization, pointing out that Disraeli, as a Jew, was able to think of himself as an Oriental – he Orientalized himself.[9] As a consequence, he evolved a positive Orientalism which, while stereotyping the East, did so in ways that evoked a vision of its spiritual and cultural superiority to the West. Indeed, for Disraeli, Eastern travel represented a return to the birthplace of his people. Romanticism and latent Judaism thus converged. The result was 'the Great Asian Mystery' – that insight Disraeli believed he possessed into the Oriental mind and manner of life. Like all Oriental truths, it defied verbal articulation. When a clergyman later wrote to request an explanation of the Asiatic Mystery, Disraeli could only suggest that he read his novels.

Thus, by the early 1830s, Disraeli presented a striking, if affected, character. He was an individualist. He possessed a self-proclaimed, if not altogether apparent, genius. He had penetrated the profundities of the Eastern consciousness. For such a young man to fail to be ambitious would be a denial of his essence. Even so, the problem remained of finding the appropriate vehicle for this potential. The obvious medium was literature. Turned to first as an economic necessity, novels, journalism and poetry became, for Disraeli, a means of working out his ideas, reflecting upon his psychology, and making his mark. A succession of novels (eight in all by 1837) sought to do this with varying degrees of success, both literary and financial. *The Young Duke*, *Contarini Fleming*, *Alroy* – all revisited the theme of *Vivian Grey*, that of the young man seeking to work out his place in the world and realize his capacities.

Unfortunately, none established the literary recognition he craved and the financial dividends provided little compensation. In 1833, he produced the first instalment of his *Revolutionary Epic* – a poem designed to capture the spirit of the French Revolution. It was, he believed, the best thing he had ever done and when this, too, failed to elicit a response, Disraeli, writes Smith, 'must have known the game was up'.

> Supreme literary talent was not his and he lacked the patience and application to go on trying to cultivate it... Action was better for the system than the sedentary musings of authorship, its rapid results more suited to his nature than the grinding disciplines of literary development...the full exhibition of his genius must take place elsewhere.[10]

Into Politics, 1832–1837

From 1832, Disraeli began to see the political world as the most appropriate sphere for the realization of his genius. For Disraeli, politics was from the beginning, and remained, a game, in the sense of a complex social activity played for the 'only real object for a man' – power. And it really was the greatest of all games, for its raw material was the psychology of individuals and nations as shaped by countless influences, great and small, open and hidden, class allegiances, party strategies, race, prestige, ideas, secret societies, international diplomacy, money, family loyalties, monarchs, newspaper editorials, rhetoric and ambition. The list of relevant variables was endless, yet at any given moment a pattern was formed, rather in the manner of the images formed by a kaleidoscope. These images were always changing: as old patterns dissolved, new ones replaced them. All this was fascinating enough. But more alluring still was the fact that it appeared to be within the power of certain individuals to form and break these patterns, to hold the diverse threads in their hands. These were the men of power, the leaders of societies and the shapers of national destinies. To aspire to be such a man was a worthy ambition for a genius such as Disraeli. If he could not shape the character of his age through his literary genius, he might realize the same end through his political genius. As he wrote in one of his first purely political works:

> Let us not forget also an influence too much underrated in this age of bustling mediocrity – the influence of individual character. Great spirits may yet arise to guide the groaning helm through the world of troubled waters – spirits whose proud destiny it may still be at the same time to maintain the glory of the Empire and the happiness of the People.[11]

Where was a Britain, besieged by bustling mediocrity, to find such a spirit? There can be little doubt that Disraeli had in mind a candidate close at hand – himself.

From this perspective, party-political labels were of minimal importance. Great spirits make and use parties, but they are not bound by them. One need only think of the careers of men like Pitt the Younger, Robert Peel, Lloyd George and Churchill to see what Disraeli was driving at. It was a measure of his precocity and naivety that he thought he could fulfil this role from the beginning, affecting an open disdain for party categorization. In only his second electoral campaign, he called upon the voters to rid themselves 'of all that political jargon and factious slang of Whig and Tory – two names with one meaning, used only to delude you...' In an earlier novel, *The Young Duke*, his detached perspective on Party was brilliantly expressed:

> Am I a Whig or Tory? I forget. As for the Tories, I admire antiquity, particularly a ruin; even the relics of the Temple of Intolerance have a charm. I think I am a Tory. But then the Whigs have such good dinners and are the most amusing. I think I am a Whig. But then the Tories are so moral and morality is my forte; I must be a Tory. But the Whigs dress so much better; and an ill-dressed Party, like an ill-dressed man, must be wrong. Yes, I am a decided Whig! And yet – I feel like Garrick between Tragedy and Comedy.

What we see, therefore, in Disraeli's first political moves is not a career politician seeking to ascend the rungs of party preferment but a self-confessed outsider seeking to storm the citadels of power with more in the way of vanity than ammunition.

What brought Disraeli into active politics was the Whig Reform Bill, introduced in 1830. Disraeli supported the Bill, writing to Murray in March 1832: 'It is quite impossible that anything adverse to the general measure of Reform can issue from my pen...' He supported it because it created a dynamic political situation – challenging entrenched political interests, throwing the country into turmoil and extending the franchise to the middle class. It was precisely in such circumstances that a man like Disraeli, possessing talent and vision, but lacking wealth and connections to the landed elite, could rise. Previously, Britain had seemed 'too uneventful for a man of genius'. Now 'all was stirring' and he 'intended to ride the storm, if the hurricane did occur'. Disraeli's support for the Reform Bill, in other words, owed little to principle and everything to his determination to enter upon the great game of politics, a game he was convinced he could win. Having attended a Commons debate in 1833, he wrote to his sister that 'between ourselves, I could floor them all... I was never more confident of anything than that I could carry everything before me in that House'.[12]

But Disraeli had first to find a seat. By chance, a vacancy for the borough of High Wycombe, close to his father's house in Buckinghamshire, arose in June 1832 while the Reform Bill crisis was still in progress. Disraeli decided to stand – but as what? Without connections with either main party, his options were limited. The Tories would have had little time for a literary Jew, recently returned from an engagement with the mysteries of the East and Disraeli had, in any case, little reason to associate himself with what was then a losing cause – especially in a Whig-controlled borough like High Wycombe. Yet, Disraeli was certainly not a Whig. He had no connections with the local Whig grandees, who neither needed nor wanted him and he always expressed a basic antipathy towards the social exclusivity of the leading Whig families. 'Toryism is worn out,' he remarked at the beginning of his campaign, 'and I cannot condescend to be a Whig.' In any case, the Whigs had a candidate in the shape of Charles Grey, the son of the Prime Minister. Disraeli did, however, support the Reform Bill and the Reform Bill was popular. He decided, therefore, to stand as a pro-Reform Bill Radical, hoping to pick up the votes of those supportive of Reform but hostile to the Whigs' aristocratic exclusiveness. He hoped, also, to pick up some Tory support as there was no Tory candidate. In this context, Smith writes that Radicalism was a natural 'holding position'[13] and he raised the traditional Radical demands for parliaments to be limited to a period of three years, the secret ballot, the repeal of taxes on newspapers and books and measures to improve the condition of the lower orders. Unfortunately, the 'people' had few votes and Disraeli was defeated 20 votes to 12.

In October 1832, after the Reform Bill had passed and an election was called, Disraeli contested High Wycombe again. Once more he stood as a Radical and promised to be a champion of the people: 'I shall withhold my support from every Ministry which will not originate some great measure to ameliorate the condition of the lower orders…' This time he was more explicit in his attacks on the Whigs – describing them as a 'rapacious, tyrannical and incapable faction' and made a bolder attempt to pick up Tory votes, seeking to associate his Radicalism with the old 'country' Tory tradition of Wyndham and Bolingbroke.[14] He was 'a Conservative to preserve all that is good in our constitution, a Radical to remove all that is bad.' One of the things to be preserved were the Corn Laws. As long as taxes remained high, farming needed high prices if it was to survive – 'better to have dear bread than no bread at all.'

Several basic themes of Disraeli's subsequent politics thus emerged during these High Wycombe campaigns – first, the conviction that the Whigs were an exclusive caste that represented a barrier to his advancement; second, that the way to prevail over the Whigs was to link up with others who were excluded from the charmed circles of Whig power; third, that this meant, in practice, coming to a rapprochement with the Tories; fourth, that the problem of how to reconcile Toryism with a declared Radical platform was to argue that true Toryism, the Toryism not of the narrow and complacent post-Napoleonic Wars period, but of the 18th century, had a natural affinity with populist Radicalism. This attempt to build an anti-Whig majority by uniting Radicalism and Toryism was to be a recurring theme of Disraeli's politics in the 1830s and 1840s.

With the extended franchise, Disraeli was hopeful of victory, but was again disappointed, coming third with 119 votes, behind two Whigs – Grey (140) and Smith (179). Another chance to contest High Wycombe came in late 1834 when the Tories, who had been put in power by William IV, dissolved Parliament in search of a majority. Though Disraeli stood as an Independent, he received £500 towards his expenses from the Tory party and the old Radical demands were not heard. He declared himself a supporter of the Duke of Wellington and an opponent of both the malt tax and the Whigs' proposals for municipal reform. It was, writes Ridley, 'a stoutly Tory platform, rather to the right of Peel [the Tory party leader]'.[15] It was to no avail – he still came third behind the Whigs.

Joining the Conservatives

It was apparent that Disraeli's political stance would have to be more conventional if he were to secure a seat. Over the next few years he definitely allied himself to the Tory party. There were two factors at work here – personality and political ideas.

Personality

In the career of most successful young politicians, there is usually a mentor figure or patron, someone who will make introductions, offer employment and provide advice. Disraeli had briefly looked to the Radical Whig politician Lord Durham to fulfil this role. But Durham had resigned from the Whig government in 1833 in protest at its moderation and his influence counted for little after 1834 when the cautious and sceptical Lord Melbourne replaced Lord Grey as Prime Minister. That same year, Disraeli formed a close friendship with the former Tory Lord Chancellor, Lord Lyndhurst and it was he who smoothed Disraeli's entry into the Tory party. Like Disraeli, Lyndhurst was something of an outsider, being the son of an American painter and having risen to high position through the law. Though in his early sixties, Lyndhurst retained a passion for women and in late 1834 commenced an affair with Disraeli's mistress, Henrietta Sykes, who pressed Disraeli's claims to preferment. Lyndhurst's conversation was notably racy and for the first time Disraeli felt himself privy to the secrets of high politics. He was also on the High Tory wing of the party, which was then under pressure as the new leader, Robert Peel, pursued a pragmatic reforming agenda that would shortly see the Tories re-branded the 'Conservatives'. According to Ridley, Lyndhurst looked to Disraeli, with his quick wit and impressive rhetoric, to inject fresh thinking into the High Tory cause. Disraeli did his best to satisfy his patron in his one sustained piece of political writing – his 1835 *Vindication of the English Constitution in a Letter to a Noble and Learned Lord by Disraeli, the Younger*. This pamphlet, which was essentially a defence of the powers of the House of Lords, brings us to the role of ideas in Disraeli's conversion to the Tory cause.

Political Ideas

In intellectual terms, Disraeli's move to the Tory party was less remarkable than is often suggested. From the beginning of his active political career, Disraeli was a *Tory Radical*. He was a Radical in the sense that he welcomed the Reform Act and wanted to push beyond it towards a 'democratic principle' of government with triennial elections and the secret ballot. He made frequent references to 'the people'. Yet the reasoning behind his radicalism ran directly in a Tory direction. His basic argument against the Whigs was that they were pursuing a selfish agenda in the interests of a narrow elite – a collection of wealthy aristocrats whom Disraeli dubbed the 'Whig Oligarchy'. This group of 200 or so landed families, the Russells, Cavendishes, Spencers and Greys, had dominated politics since the early 18th century and were determined to retain control over government. To do this, Disraeli argued, they had adopted the clever stratagem of posing as the enemies of privilege and the friends of democracy. By this means, they had attracted the support of the rising business class and middle class intellectuals who favoured institutional reform. The result was the formidable coalition which had pushed through the Reform Act and was now in the process of centralizing power in Westminster. Yet, although the rhetoric and methods used were apparently democratic, the objective throughout, Disraeli contended, was the maintenance of the power of the Whig elite.

How could this winning formula be countered? That was the question Disraeli encountered at High Wycombe and which dominated his entire political career. And the solution he came to at High Wycombe was equally to inform all his subsequent political manoeuvres. To the narrow Whig oligarchy, Disraeli counter-posed the idea of the English *nation* – of the great majority who were outside of the exclusive networks of the Whigs and their middle class allies. 'My politics,' he once declared, can be 'summed up in one word – England.' As John Vincent remarks, he had seized upon the truth that 'politics is inherently oligarchical' and that whoever is in power, there is always a majority made up of those who, for various reasons, feel themselves disaffected and excluded from power. 'Bring that sense to life,' writes Vincent, 'and you have a natural majority.' That was what Disraeli endeavoured to do throughout his career. 'Faced with an established Whig supremacy…he retorted with an anti-elitist or popular doctrine of national solidarity: "trust the people" was code for "distrust the Whigs".'[16]

The challenge was to mobilize this implicit 'anti-Whig' majority. In the context of 1832, that meant associating with the idea of reform and downplaying traditional Toryism, which was discredited in the manner of post-Thatcherite Conservatism in the later 20th century. Yet beyond these tactical considerations, his basic reasoning was Tory. In pamphlets such as *What Is He?*, *The Spirit of Whiggism* and *The Vindication*, he argued that the welfare of the mass of the English people was tied up with their history and traditions. These traditions and customary usages were not encumbrances to the advance of the many, they were the main support not only of countless individuals but of the civilization of England, without which the country would descend into disorder – its property, culture and status as a great power all being put at risk. That, he argued, was where the Whigs had begun to take England. The Reform Bill in itself was not a revolutionary measure. That, indeed, was the point. It professed to be a democratic measure, bringing power to a wider electorate, when in practice, it was a limited measure designed to 'destroy Toryism' and consolidate the rule of the Whig elite. Its ethos was not democratic but exclusive. Yet the *method* by which the Bill was passed *was* revolutionary, as the House of Lords was intimidated by the threat of popular violence into passing it. The House of Lords, a key part of the balanced constitution, had been 'as completely abrogated and extinguished as if its members had torn off their robes and coronets and flung them in the river and, stalking in silence to their palaces, had never returned to that Chamber…'[17] With the power of the monarchy also a shadow, the House of Commons had centralized power in itself, which meant in practice the dominant Whig elite which controlled the majority of constituencies. In 1832 and 1833, Disraeli seems to have believed that the power of the monarchy and House of Lords could not be revived – that the only way by which the Whig elite could be checked was by pushing the Reform Bill through to a genuinely democratic conclusion. It was this more radical dimension to Disraeli's thinking that diminished after 1834, not surprising, perhaps, given that he was now writing pamphlets for Lord Lyndhurst. He began to argue that there was life in the old institutions yet; that what they needed was a champion and that this was something the Tories could still be. Less and less was heard of 'the people'. In 1834, he described 'the people' as a species, not a real political entity. What was important was the 'nation' and this was the sum total of a community's institutions, religion, myths, history and laws: it was a construct – a work of the imagination. This British nation could yet be preserved if it found an articulate advocate – and such Disraeli considered himself to be.

The problem with this line of reasoning was that it was hard to get beyond already tired clichés. A national myth tends, inevitably, to sound complacent and rather commonplace – useful in times of national crisis, as Churchill demonstrated in 1940, but of limited relevance to everyday politics. Consider a passage like the following:

> A nation is not a mere mass of bipeds with no strength but their animal vigour… There is required to constitute that great creation, a people, some higher endowments and some rarer – honour and faith and justice; a national spirit fostered by national exploits; a solemn creed expounded by a pure and learned priesthood; a jurisprudence which is the aggregate wisdom of the ages; the spirit of chivalry, the inspiration of religion, the supremacy of law; that free order and that natural graduation of ranks which are but a type and image of the economy of the universe; a love of home and country, fostered by traditionary manners and consecrated by customs that embalm ancestral deeds… these are some of the incidents and qualifications of a great nation like the people of England.[18]

This is laboured rhetoric with minimal operational value outside the assumptions of its own inflated language. There was little here that was dynamic, which looked to the future. By the later 1830s, Disraeli's ideological development had thus placed him squarely within the Tory camp; but it had also brought him perilously close to becoming merely the hired advocate of the landed elite. He had entered an ideological *cul-de-sac* in which he was to spend several decades.

Member of Parliament at Last

In 1835, the Whigs returned to power and this necessitated a series of by-elections as those taking government office were required to submit themselves for re-election. Disraeli stood as the Conservative candidate for Taunton. Although defeated, this was a big step forward. It was only a matter of time before the Conservatives found him a winnable seat. In 1837, Disraeli's chance finally came. With the death of William IV, a general election was held. Disraeli secured the nomination for Maidstone and he and the existing MP Wyndham Lewis were returned as Conservatives against Radical opposition. Shortly afterwards, Wyndham Lewis died and Disraeli married his relatively wealthy widow, Mary Anne.

Disraeli, Peel and the Crisis of Conservatism, 1837–1846

Within a month of parliament opening, Disraeli delivered the most notorious maiden speech in history. The subject of debate was Ireland and Disraeli, by the extravagance of his manner and language, sought to take the House by storm. It was not a success. Greville recorded in his diary:

> D'Israeli made his first exhibition last night, beginning with florid assurance, speedily degenerating into ludicrous absurdity and being at last put down with inextinguishable shouts of laughter.

He was barracked by Irish MPs, who saw him as an enemy following an earlier exchange of insults with their leader Daniel O'Connell and he was finally forced to sit down after 20 minutes. His final words were, 'I have begun several things many times and I have often succeeded at the last. I will sit down now, but the time will come when you will hear me!' Disraeli was disconsolate at his 'failure', but Peel, the Conservative leader, was more complimentary, remarking that 'he did all that he could do under the circumstances. I say anything but failure; he must make his way.'[19]

Disraeli's moment of entry into the Commons was propitious. The Whig majority was now slender and with the Prime Minister Lord Melbourne, preoccupied with educating the young Queen Victoria, the government gradually subsided, finally falling in 1841. During these years Disraeli could broadly be called a Tory Radical, developing his theme that the Tories were the true friends of the nation – and hence the people. The Whigs were the anti-national party, who governed in the interests of sectional minorities without reference to the feelings and needs of the majority. From this perspective, he condemned the New Poor Law, which instituted a centralized system of poverty relief based around the workhouse. He also expressed sympathy with the sufferings of the working class that had produced the Chartist movement, although he did not believe universal suffrage was the correct solution. He outlined his views in an interesting letter to the Birmingham Radical, Charles Attwood.

> I entirely agree with you, that 'an union between the Conservative Party and the Radical Masses' offers the only means by which we can preserve the Empire. Their interests are identical; united they form the Nation; and their division has only permitted a miserable minority, under the specious name of the People, to spoil all rights of property and person.'
>
> Since I first entered public life, now eight years ago, I have worked for no other object and no other end, than to aid the formation of a National Party... None but those devoid of the sense and spirit of Englishmen can be blind to the perils that are impending over our

country. Our Empire is assailed in every quarter; while a domestic oligarchy, under the guise of Liberalism, is denationalising England.

However, Disraeli's ability to pursue these themes was constrained by his need to establish relations with the Conservative front bench. At this period, he considered himself a loyal follower of Peel. In 1838, he wrote to Peel offering to produce a manifesto of Conservative principles and he usually tried to sit behind the Conservative leader.[20] Even so, Disraeli's views rendered him out of step with the direction in which Peel was trying to take the Conservative party. While Disraeli wished to unite the range of different social classes – from landed gentry to the urban working class – in the defence of traditional social structures and institutions against the corrosive effects of Whig reforms, Peel was engaged in a very different strategy, seeking to out-bid the Whigs by appealing to the expanding middle class with a more reformist and liberal brand of Conservatism, supporting, for instance, the New Poor Law. While Disraeli considered himself to be a loyalist, this was not the view of the Conservative leadership, which regarded him as an eccentric and potential troublemaker.

Conservative Government, 1841

In the general election of 1841, the Whigs were decisively beaten by Peel's revitalized Conservative party – with Disraeli being returned for the comparatively safe seat of Shrewsbury. On 30 August 1841, Peel became Prime Minister with a majority of around 80. The moment for ambitious Conservatives had arrived – but not for Disraeli. Soon most government offices had been filled, yet still no summons had come. In desperation Disraeli wrote to Peel:

> I have tried to struggle against a storm of political hate and malice which few men ever experienced, from the moment, at the instigation of a member of your Cabinet [Lyndhurst – again Lord Chancellor], I enrolled myself under your banner and I have only been sustained under these trials by the conviction that the day would come when the foremost man of the country would publicly testify that he had some respect for my ability and character.
>
> I confess to be unrecognized at this moment by you appears to me to be overwhelming and I appeal to your own heart – to that justice and to that magnanimity which I feel are your characteristics – to save me from an intolerable humiliation.

In understanding Disraeli's desire for office one should remember, not only the intensity of his ambition, but the precarious state of his finances (his debts standing at about £30,000, around £1 million in present day values).[21] In the 19th century, a seat in Parliament carried no income and brought many costs. Only government office brought a salary.

Unfortunately Peel declined to reconsider. This is not surprising. As Blake has argued, it would have been remarkable if Peel *had* appointed him to government.[22] He was a newcomer with no experience and no social or landed position. Peel's Cabinet consisted almost wholly of Lords and Knights – there was only one plain 'Mr'. Only four men included in the government had entered Parliament since 1835. Disraeli remained something of an oddity with a less than consistent political record and no influence within the party.

Nevertheless, Peel's failure to give Disraeli office had momentous consequences. Disraeli was greatly offended by the rebuff. He later remarked that 'we came here for fame'. If Peel would not provide a route to this, he must, as he had done throughout his life, make his own. How was not clear, but he now felt free to take a more openly critical attitude towards Peel and the direction in which he was leading the Conservative Party. He wrote to his wife in February 1842:

> You cannot conceive how solitary I feel: utterly isolated. Before the change of Government, political party was a tie among men, but now it is only a tie among men who are in office. The supporter of administrations, who is not in place and power himself, is a solitary animal. He has neither hope nor fear.[23]

Disraeli and Young England

Disraeli's feelings of isolation were partly overcome when, in early 1842, he formed an alliance with a group of young aristocrats newly elected to parliament which became known as Young England. Its leading figures were George Smythe, eldest son of Lord Strangford; Lord John Manners, second son of the Duke of Rutland; and Alexander Ballie-Cochrane, whose father was an Admiral. These men had been friends at Eton and Cambridge and had developed an ideology of revived Toryism with the object of restoring the ordered cohesion of English society and the moral and physical health of the people.[24] Their preoccupation with these issues arose out of two observed tendencies:

1. The disintegration of society as the forces of 'democracy' and economic change undermined the old forms of social control.
2. The deteriorating condition of the poor as traditional mechanisms of social protection broke down and the factory system brutalized both working and living environments.

These two developments, Young England believed, were linked. The poverty and hardships of the working people generated the popular demands for radical reform that would, in the long-term, threaten social stability and the position of the propertied classes. These problems were perceived by others, including Robert Peel. Peel's solution was to embrace economic modernity. Economic growth, rising living standards and cheap imports would all improve the material condition of the masses and thereby ensure social peace. This was the essential conservatism that underlay his reforms – liberal reform in the short run would sustain established social hierarchies in the long run.

It was this reformist-conservatism that Young England rejected. Their solution was to revive traditional forms of social organization and control. Social disintegration was to be overcome by promoting social *integration* on the basis of a return to the kinder and closer links between the classes which, they fondly believed, had existed in the Middle Ages. If the privileged classes could only be prevailed upon to take seriously their responsibility for the wellbeing of the poor, then the poor would reciprocate with their loyalty. The responsibility for initiating this process lay with the landed aristocracy. If the aristocracy acted as a *real* aristocracy, using their wealth, education and prestige for the benefit of the people, then social conditions would improve and class harmony prevail. Parliament had a role too, in legislating to limit working hours, oversee the provision of urban sanitation and adequate housing and putting in place a humane system of poverty relief. But something more than administrative efficiency was required of government. It had to appeal, also, to the *imagination* of the people. Imagination and faith, not utilitarian calculation and rational principles, were the true foundation of a successful community. Only by engaging the hearts and minds of a people would real loyalty be evoked. A central role here fell to monarchy, which could generate loyalty in a way that parliamentary proceedings and party manoeuvring could not – an idea later developed by Bagehot in his distinction between the 'dignified' and 'efficient' portions of the Constitution.[25]

Put briefly, then, the Young England group believed that the key to the strength of England and the well being of its people was the provision of inspiring and concerned leadership by the traditional elites – the monarchy, government, Church and aristocracy. Young England sought, in the years 1842–1845, to make these elites appreciate their role.

From 1842, Disraeli formed a close connection with the Young England group, becoming, in effect, its political leader. There were obvious affinities between the doctrines espoused by Young England and the kind of Tory radicalism Disraeli had been advocating since the early 1830s. As we have seen, Disraeli had come to argue that the wellbeing of the English people was bound up with the defence of traditional customs and institutions from the attacks of the selfish Whig oligarchy and their intellectual allies – the utilitarians and economists. What had made England a great and free nation was the complex fabric of classes, organizations, institutions and customs which had evolved over history – its Church, its ancient universities and schools, its House of Lords, its monarchy, its system of local government centred on the parish and the squire. He would later describe this system as 'the territorial constitution'. It was, he contended, the role of the Conservative party to uphold this system in the interests of the whole nation, for the poor as well as the rich benefited from the stability and liberty it provided. This was, in its essentials, the programme of Young England and Disraeli, who had a longstanding fascination with young aristocrats, was bound to wish to associate with their cause.

Yet, Young England made its own mark on Disraeli. Under the impetus of his new friends, Disraeli advocated his ideas in a more elaborate form, affecting, for a time, something of Young England's reverence for things medieval. The most important result was his trilogy of novels – *Coningsby* (1844), *Sybil* (1845) and *Tancred* (1847). For the first time, politics and ideas occupied centre stage in Disraeli's fiction. The first named was explicitly about the Young England group. It was subtitled *The New Generation* and Coningsby, the young aristocrat who was the nominal hero of the story, was modelled on Smythe. In these novels, Disraeli developed in clever, witty form his Tory interpretation of history, this time tracing the subversion of the traditional fabric of English society to the Tudors and the dissolution of the monasteries. The complacency and posturing of the aristocracy was ruthlessly exposed. In *Sybil*, Disraeli described a society sharply divided between rich and poor, a division so complete as to warrant the book's subtitle, *The Two Nations*:

> Two nations; between whom there is no intercourse and no sympathy; who are as ignorant of each other's habits, thoughts and feelings, as if they were dwellers in different zones, or inhabitants of different planets; who are formed by a different breeding, are fed by a different food, are ordered by different manners and are not governed by the same laws...THE RICH AND THE POOR.[26]

The basic problem was that 'there is no community in England', only 'aggregation'. The aristocracy, who should have given the lead, were too busy idling their time away in selfish pleasures, ignorant of the real condition of the people. Indeed, there was no longer a true working 'aristocracy in England' for the superiority of the 'animal man' that was its basis had been destroyed by 'the chains of convention, an external life grown out of all proportion with that of the heart and mind...' These were exactly the issues that preoccupied Young England and the solutions, also, owed much to Young England thinking. The monarchy is exalted as the one power in the state able to stand outside

of the faction and consider the interests of the nation as a whole. This it had
not been able to do since the 17th century, as the powers of the monarch had
been gradually taken over by parliament, which meant, from Disraeli's view-
point, its subordination to the Whig oligarchy. 'In the selfish strife of factions,
two great existences have been blotted out of the history of England – the
Monarch and the Multitude; as the power of the Crown has diminished, the
privileges of the People have disappeared; till at length the sceptre has
become a pageant and its subject has degenerated again into a serf.'[27] Disraeli's
'prayer' was to 'see England once more possess a free Monarchy and a privileged and prosperous people...' For this result, Disraeli looked to 'the energy
and devotion of our Youth...', where there were grounds for hope:

> There is a dayspring in the history of this nation, which perhaps those
> only who are on the mountain tops can as yet recognize... The new
> generation of the aristocracy of England are not tyrants, not oppres-
> sors... Their intelligence, better than that, their hearts, are open to
> the responsibility of their position... They are the natural leaders of
> the people...believe me they are the only ones.

Again we have the basic Young England refrain. What divides rich and poor
is not so much wealth as a lack of sympathy and understanding. Social stability will only be ensured when the aristocracy, still the natural leaders of society, take seriously their responsibilities to the poor, finding out about their
lives, undertaking constructive reforms and generally demonstrating a sense
of fellow feeling with those less privileged. It was through the union of hearts
and minds, rather than specific measures of social reform, that class peace
and social harmony was to be secured.

Though Disraeli never took too seriously the more romantic feudalism of
Young England, he sympathized with its basic principles and it left its mark on
his thinking. Even so, this was not the most important role it fulfilled during
the years 1842–1845. For what Young England provided above all was a context within which he could operate politically. Instead of being an isolated
maverick, sulking on the backbenches, Disraeli was at the centre of a group of
privileged young men cooperating in a common cause, a cause which provided
ideological coherence for his developing critique of Peel. By 1843, the Young
Englanders were sitting together and coordinating their speeches, which were
frequently critical of the government's liberal-reformist policies. Indeed,
Disraeli began to see the possibility of building up support amongst a broader
section of landed Tory backbenchers and so exert influence over government
policy. The extent of some of his schemes disconcerted Ballie-Cochrane:

> Disraeli's head is full of great movements, vast combinations, the
> importance of numbers, Cabinet dinners, the practice of dissimulation!

In fact of the vaguest speculations, the mere phantasmagoria of politique legerdemain...

They attacked the working of the Whig's New Poor Law, which Peel had left unchanged. They criticized the government's handling of Irish problems and supported a proposed committee of inquiry into the condition of Ireland. They voted, against Peel's opposition, for Lord Ashley's amendment to the Factory Bill, reducing the maximum hours of work for boys under eighteen from twelve to ten. They voted, too, for an amendment to Peel's Sugar Duties Bill, which proposed to reduce the tariff on foreign (i.e. non-British Empire) sugar down to the level set for sugar from the colonies. What made this issue so controversial was the fact that, since slavery had been abolished within the British Empire, colonial sugar was cultivated by free labour while foreign sugar was generally cut by slaves. Disraeli and Young England voted for the Opposition amendment, which proposed to lower the duties on *both* colonial and foreign sugar, thereby maintaining the differential between them. The government was defeated and Peel called an emergency meeting of the Conservative party, threatening to resign if the vote were not rescinded. The vote was indeed overturned – though Disraeli continued to support the amendment on the grounds that he would not change his vote within 48 hours 'at the menace of a Minister'.

Disraeli, Young England and the Developing Crisis of Conservatism

For a government with an 80-seat majority and under the commanding leadership of a great administrator like Peel, the attacks by a minority of idealistic young aristocrats might not have been expected to occasion much concern. Yet the conditions for rebellion within the Conservative party were, in fact, propitious. Three points need to be grasped.

1. *The dominant political personality of Peel.* Since the later 1830s, Peel had been the dominant figure in British politics. He was not merely a great parliamentarian but a skilled administrator and commanding party leader. From the devastation of the Tories in 1832, Peel had reconstructed a new Tory Party – the Conservatives – with a new ideology of reformist conservatism as embodied in the Tamworth Manifesto. These efforts appeared to be triumphantly vindicated in 1841 when Peel formed a powerful and talented administration with a large majority. All seemed set fair for the full realization of his political abilities.

2. *The incompleteness of the change among backbench Tories.* However, although leading figures in the Conservative party had absorbed the message of the new Conservatism, this was less true of the country gentry who formed the bulk of Tory backbenchers. Notwithstanding Peel's apparent

victory in 1841, it was, ironically, in the unreconstructed county seats that the party did best. The Toryism of the gentry still revolved around such 'core' issues as defence of the landed interest, support for the Church of England and resistance to the reformist doctrines of middle class liberals. Moreover, Peel's own views were evolving. He was increasingly persuaded, on Conservative grounds, of the benefits accruing from the doctrines of free trade and economic liberalism being advanced by the political econ-omists and the Manchester Radicals, notably MPs Richard Cobden and John Bright. Free trade, he had come to believe, would mean economic prosperity and low prices and hence, social stability.

3. *Peel's personal manner was haughty and rigid.* With his abilities and experience, he increasingly felt contempt for the ill-informed and preju-diced members of his own party. He had no time for the backbench Tories and made little effort to explain his policies or consult them for their views. He was totally devoid of 'people management' skills. At times he could be brutally frank. 'How,' he asked, 'can those who spend their time in hunting and shooting and eating and drinking know what were the motives of those who are responsible for the public security, who have access to the best information and who have no other object under heaven but to provide against danger and consult the general interest of all classes?'

As a result of these factors, a gap increasingly emerged between the Conservative leadership and the bulk of the party rank and file. This gap was Disraeli's window of opportunity and he took it. The majority of back-benchers were men of the country, firm in their prejudices, but little practised in the arts of debate. They needed a champion and found one in Disraeli, who from 1844 increasingly brought Peel within the focus of his critical scrutiny. The result was one of the ironies of history, as a dandified, literary Jew of Radical Tory opinions came to lead a body of men distinguished by their Anglicanism, their rustic simplicity and their rejection of all that was exotic and alien. Young England had been his launching point, but this grad-ually subsided after 1844 as Disraeli pursued his duel with Peel and the enthusiasm of the other members waned. It finally expired in the crisis period of 1845–1846 as its members took diverging attitudes towards the character of Robert Peel and his proposal to repeal the Corn Laws.

The mounting battles within the Conservative party took place over a number of issues. In 1844, Peel twice threatened to resign the leadership if defeats sustained by his government after Conservative backbenchers sided with the opposition were not reversed. On both occasions, the sullen back-benchers, unable to face life without Peel, backed down. A greater crisis occurred in April 1845 when Peel proposed to increase and make permanent the annual government grant to Maynooth College in Ireland, a Catholic institution dedicated to the education of priests. The move caused uproar, not just on the Tory backbenches, but amongst the wider forces of conservatism within the country. For the British government to be subsidising Catholicism caused widespread indignation – especially when that government was ostensibly dedicated to the defence of the Church of England and led by the one-time 'Orange Peel' who had, in 1829, argued that Maynooth's charter be revoked.[28] Disraeli took a prominent part in the attack on Peel. His speech of November 1845 was scathingly sarcastic and introduced a theme which was to figure prominently in his later attacks on Peel's proposal to repeal the Corn Laws, namely, the importance of consistency to party principles.

> If you are to have a popular Government, if you are to have a Parliamentary administration, the conditions antecedent are, that you should have a Government which declares the principles upon which its policy is founded and then you can have on them the wholesome check of a constitutional Opposition. What have we got instead? Something has risen up in this country as fatal in the political world as it has been in the landed world of Ireland – we have a great Parliamentary middleman [immense cheering]. It is well known what a middleman is; he is a man who bamboozles one party and plunders the other [great laughter]…

He concluded by reminding the 'people in high places that cunning is not caution and that habitual perfidy is not high policy of state' and calling upon the House of Commons to dethrone 'this dynasty of deception, by putting an end to the intolerable yoke of official despotism and Parliamentary imposture'.

Maynooth was a traumatic experience for the Conservative party. It prompted Gladstone's resignation from the Cabinet. It also marked the effective end of Young England. While Disraeli attacked the measure, Manners and Smythe, with more consistency to their nostalgia for the pre-Reformation church (in which Disraeli himself had indulged in Sybil), supported it. This must raise questions about Disraeli's loyalty to Young England principles. At this critical juncture he was clearly not prepared to allow youthful idealism to stand in the way of his personal vendetta against Peel's government. As Blake writes, he 'was not really concerned with the merits of the case. He wished to have another hit at Peel and this was an opportunity not to be missed'.[29]

What Motivated Disraeli's Attack on Peel?

Why did Disraeli launch a sustained and increasingly personal attack on Peel? The basic motive was self-interest. It is both unlikely and out of keeping with his subsequent career that he should have embarked on such a course if it would have damaged his political prospects. The fact was that, as things stood, he had no political prospects. He had been excluded from office in 1841 and nothing that had happened since had made entry into government any more likely. There was no personal warmth between Peel and Disraeli and the evolution of Peel's government in a pragmatic-liberal direction was at variance with Disraeli's romantic character and expressed opinions. With Peel set to remain in place for possibly a decade, Disraeli was likely to languish in the parliamentary sidings. This was, in the 19th century, the fate of the majority of MPs, yet most had little ambition and, unlike Disraeli, had the wealth to sustain such a lifestyle for social reasons. This Disraeli lacked. Politics drained his rickety finances and distracted him from the novels that brought him at least some income. So Disraeli had powerful reasons for hoping to displace Peel and very few for supporting him. This was the underlying motive for his opposition.

What, then, were the arguments Disraeli advanced in his criticisms of Peel? The answer is less explicit or convincing than one might expect. Disraeli's criticisms were three-fold.

1. *That Peel's Conservatism, as articulated in the Tamworth Manifesto of 1834, lacked substance and represented merely a pragmatic concession to the forces of Liberalism.* Far from resisting the dissolving effects of commerce and utilitarian thinking on the social fabric of England, Peel's reformism was reinforcing them. This takes us back to the Young England objections outlined earlier. Disraeli made this case against Peel with great literary skill in *Coningsby*, famously defining Peelite Conservatism as 'Tory men and Whig measures'.

> The Tamworth Manifesto of 1834 was an attempt to construct a Party without principles: its basis therefore was necessarily Latitudinarianism; and its inevitable consequence has been Political Infidelity... There was indeed considerable shouting about what they called Conservative principles; but the awkward question naturally arose, what will you conserve? The prerogatives of the Crown, provided they are not exercised; the independence of the House of Lords, provided it is not asserted; the Ecclesiastical estate, provided it is regulated by a commission of laymen. Everything in short that is established, as long as it is a phrase and not a fact.[30]

The Whigs at least had an intelligible principle: 'They seek a specific for the evils of our social system in the general suffrage of the population.' The Conservatives merely wished 'to keep things as they find them for as long as they can'.

> Whenever public opinion, which this party never attempts to form, to educate, or to lead, falls into some violent perplexity, passion, or

caprice, this party yields without a struggle to the impulse and, when the storm has passed, attempts to obstruct and obviate the logical and, ultimately, the inevitable results of the very measures they have themselves originated, or to which they have consented.

Disraeli recognized Peel's achievement in reconstructing the old Tory Party, after its exclusive principle had been shattered in 1830–1832. But it was his basic criticism that Peel had failed to construct the lasting national party that was needed. For Peel adopted an opportunist policy guided by momentary expediency and formulated no great principle for the party. As a result, he ended up espousing the principles of the enemy. His role was to 'create public opinion instead of following it; to lead the public instead of always lagging after and watching others'.

The problem with this argument is that Disraeli had originally supported Peel and sought office under him in 1841. He had welcomed Peel's free trade budgets, claiming that free trade was the true Tory policy. More generally, Disraeli had advocated uniting the country against the Whig elite and this is precisely what Peel had done, building a winning coalition for the Conservatives and seemingly establishing them as the 'natural party of government'. Of course, this had meant appealing to the growing middle class, but this was electorally unavoidable. The middle class possessed votes and Young England's loyal poor did not. In later years, Disraeli was to himself seek to attract middle class votes. Finally, Disraeli was mainly concerned to sustain the existing influence of the aristocracy of England, not revive some lost medieval idyll. This was Peel's objective too. The dispute was largely over tactics and even here, the Young England prescription of good feeling between rich and poor hardly represented a tangible programme to take to the country.

2. *That Peel lacked imagination and charisma.* The Young England group believed that governments must appeal to the emotions of the people in order to win their loyalty. Disraeli shared this view and it was a genuine criticism of Peel that he was an aloof administrator who did little to inspire the Tory party or the country. The parliamentary leader, he wrote in *Coningsby* in an obvious dig at Peel, who has the faculty of inspiring enthusiasm 'doubles his majority; and he who has it not may shroud himself in artificial reserve and study with undignified arrogance an awkward haughtiness, but he will nevertheless be as far from controlling the spirit as from captivating the hearts of his sullen followers'.

Whether, of course, this deficiency was sufficient to justify overthrowing a man of so many other qualities is another matter. Certainly, when Gladstone later combined Peelism with charisma, the result was far from Disraeli's liking. Disraeli was to spend the middle years of his career loyally following

Lord Derby, a man who made no impression on the general public and was soon forgotten by his own party.

3. *That Peel failed to respect the wishes and beliefs of the Conservative party.* As Prime Minister, Peel thought himself free to pursue whatever policy he considered best for the country, even if this caused him to diverge from traditional Conservative thinking. His proposals for Maynooth illustrate this. Disraeli attacked this approach as destructive of the principles of party government. Peel, he believed, had risen to power through the Conservative party and relied on its votes to sustain him in office. It was his duty, therefore, to respect the traditions and opinions of its members. If he did not do this he would be acting, in effect, as an arbitrary ruler. The party system, which provided stability and allowed electors to vote for principles and not merely personalities, would break down. On these grounds, Disraeli told his constituents in 1844, he had no compunction in voting against the government. 'I supported the Conservative party as long as they kept to their principles and when they deserted those principles I voted against them.'

This was Disraeli's most consistent and formidable argument and it was the only one that really resonated with the backbenchers. Peel was indeed contemptuous of his own followers and treated them as 'lobby fodder', petulantly threatening to resign if they did not follow his lead. For such men, neglected and ignored, one can only imagine the appeal of rhetoric like the following:

> There is no doubt a difference in the right honourable gentleman's demeanour as Leader of the Opposition as Minister of the Crown... I remember him making his Protection speeches. They were the best speeches I ever heard. It was a great thing to hear the right honourable gentlemen say: 'I would rather be the leader of the gentlemen of England than possess the confidence of sovereigns.' That was a great thing. We don't hear much of 'the gentleman of England' now [great cheering]. But what of that? They have the pleasures of memory – the charms of reminiscence. They were his first love and though he may not kneel to them now as in the hour of his passion, still they can recall the past... For me there remains this at least – the opportunity of expressing thus publicly my belief that a Conservative Government is an organized hypocrisy.

Even so, there are problems with this argument too. Disraeli himself had never been a conventional 'Party man' and never became one. As Machin argues, Disraeli realized as well as Peel the need to develop Conservatism in a liberal direction and his criticisms of Peel on this ground were 'spurious'.[31] More importantly, the idea that Party was something which should constrain the actions of the King's ministers was a relatively new one and did not become the conventional wisdom until late in the 19th century – and since then has operated only partially. It was not explicitly stated what a party's principles were – there were no party election manifestos, no policy documents, no statements of objectives. The Conservative's great victory of 1841 was seen as a personal triumph for Peel – not the endorsement of some party manifesto. Party policy was, in effect, what the parliamentary leaders said it was. Nevertheless, it was this issue that formed the basis of Disraeli's sarcastic assaults on Peel. It was always the usefulness, rather than truthfulness, of an idea that concerned Disraeli.

Corn Law Repeal, 1846, and the Fall of Peel

In 1845, Peel's Conservative government entered its last phase. The issue which broke up the party was the repeal of the duties on wheat imports – the famous Corn Laws.

Peel had been converted to the merits of free trade by 1841 and in a series of historic budgets had removed import duties on a wide range of manufactured imports and raw materials. These measures reduced the cost of living and landowners had been pleased to vote for them, as had Disraeli. However, these reforms left the duties on imported corn as an increasingly irksome anomaly and they were the subject of sustained attack by the most successful pressure group in British history, the Anti-Corn Law League. Peel himself was convinced that the Corn Laws would have to go. For a parliament of landowners to seek to artificially raise the price of corn, and hence bread, whilst removing the protective duties on the articles they consumed, smacked too blatantly of 'class legislation' and was provoking social dissension, which could easily spill over into a general denunciation of the landed interest. Peel's formula for class peace was economic prosperity and low prices and this logic dictated that the corn duties be abolished. Yet Peel was awkwardly placed since the Conservative party, as the party of the agricultural interest, was strongly wedded to the duties and in 1841 had fought the election on a policy of upholding the Corn Laws against the attacks of the Whigs. He himself declared in August 1841 his support for 'the principle of protection in agriculture'. Peel therefore decided to delay moving against the Corn Laws until *after* the next general election had given him a fresh mandate.

However in 1845, potato blight struck Ireland, destroying the staple crop of the country. Serious famine resulted, ultimately leading to a million deaths. Peel believed the only solution was to open the ports to cheap foreign grain and decided to proceed immediately with his plan to repeal the Corn Laws. At this point, it is necessary to understand that it was possible to import grain freely by *suspending* the Corn Laws. They did not have to be permanently abolished. Indeed, suspension would take effect immediately, whereas abolition would take months – and even then, Peel was proposing to phase out the Corn Laws over a period of three years. In other words, Peel was using the Irish crisis as a lever to push through his policy of complete repeal, rather than proposing repeal as the most relevant response to the emergency. 'Moral Right' was not wholly on Peel's side and his critics, who were prepared to accept immediate suspension, believed they had a just and defensible case.

For much of the Conservative party, Peel's proposal to abolish the Corn Laws represented a betrayal. The Corn Laws did not have to be repealed. And even if they did, then surely the Whigs should take responsibility for this measure since they had long advocated a thorough revision of the Corn duties and their leader, Lord John Russell, had recently put the case for repeal onto the political agenda. In seeking to move even on this issue, Peel was going too far and stretching party loyalty to breaking point. The Conservative back-benchers needed a spokesman and it was now that they found in Disraeli the man who could articulate their sense of outrage. Disraeli seized the opportunity with gusto and in a series of speeches did much to bring down, not merely a government, but the dominant political figure of his age. The tone of his speeches was brilliantly judged, deploying, comments Bentley, 'a style of limp-wristed discourse with a playful eloquence designed to score Peel's cheek with blades of grass'.[32] Whatever his debating strengths, Peel was a rather self-righteous, pompous and humourless individual. He found it hard to respond to the ridicule and sarcasm Disraeli heaped upon him.

> *Peel the burglar of others' intellects*
> When I examine the career of this Minister... I find that for between 30 and 40 years...that Right Honourable gentleman has traded on the ideas and intelligence of others. His life has been a great appropriation clause [laughter]. He is a burglar of others' intellect...there is no other statesman who has committed political petty larceny on so great a scale [renewed laughter].

> *Peel and the Turkish Admiral*
> Sir, there is a difficulty in finding a parallel to the position of the Right Honourable gentleman in any part of history. The only parallel I can find is an incident in the late war in the Levant... The late Sultan, a man of great energy and fertile in resources, was determined to fit out an immense fleet to maintain his empire... Away went the fleet, but what was the Sultan's consternation when the Lord High Admiral steered at once into the enemy's port [loud laughter and cheers]. Now, sir, the Lord High Admiral on that occasion was very much

misrepresented. He, too, was called a traitor and he, too, vindicated himself. 'True it is' he said 'I did place myself at the head of this valiant Armada; true it is that my Sovereign embraced me. But I have an objection to war. I see no use in prolonging the struggle and the only reason I had for accepting the command was that I might terminate the contest by betraying my master.' [tremendous Tory cheering]

These attacks caused delight amongst the backbench Tories and uproar in the House. Peel was stunned and outraged but found it hard to respond. A series of long and passionate debates followed, in which the Protectionist Conservatives, led by a previously reticent backbencher, Lord George Bentinck, and ably assisted by Disraeli, fought a guerrilla campaign against Peel in the Commons. After many weeks of debate, the third and final reading of the Corn Law Bill was carried, on 16 May 1846, by 98 votes. But what was important about this figure was that Peel's majority rested chiefly on the votes of the opposition Whigs. Of the 354 Conservatives who voted, 242 voted against the measure; only 112 supported it. The repeal of the Corn Laws had been carried, but the Conservative party had split irrevocably.[33] Five weeks later, the measure became law and the following day, Peel's government was defeated in the Commons as his Conservative opponents joined forces with the Whigs on a matter of Irish policy. Peel's government resigned. He never held office again and died, four years later, following a fall from a horse in Hyde Park.

Explaining Disraeli's Role in the Corn Law Crisis

Why was Disraeli such a vocal critic of Peel's decision to repeal the Corn Laws? The natural answer would be that Disraeli, like the majority of the Protectionists, disapproved of Peel's action on principle. It would have been quite easy for him to make a consistent case on such grounds. As we have seen, Disraeli believed in an aristocratic social settlement based on land. It was this that provided the structure for a stable society and guaranteed Britain's traditional freedom from an over-powerful centralized state. This hierarchical landed system would be imperilled by the opening of British agriculture to cheap food imports. There could thus have been a powerful ideological dimension to Disraeli's opposition to Corn Law repeal and one which would have fitted comfortably into the wider conflict between the ideas of Young England and the managerial reformism represented by Peel.[34]

Now, Disraeli *did* argue that, by giving in to the agitation of the Anti-Corn Law League and its radical supporters, Peel was compromising the long-term interests of the landed class, opening the way to yet more challenges to the status of landed wealth. The Corn Laws were thus of *symbolic* importance – 'the outwork of a great system fixed and established upon your territorial property and the only object the Leaguers have in making themselves masters of the outwork is that they may more easily overcome the citadel.'[35] The Corn Laws, then, were only a defensive position and Disraeli never really contended that they were necessary for the maintenance of the rural society he so revered. They were an expedient and not a principle. In a speech to his Shrewsbury constituents in 1843 he remarked:

> I will never commit myself on this great question to petty economical details; I will not pledge myself to miserable questions of 6d. in 7s. 6d. or 8s. of duties about corn; I do not care whether your corn sells for this sum or that, or whether it is under a sliding scale or a fixed duty; but what I want and what I wish to secure…is the preponderance of the landed interest.[36]

Like Peel, he seems to have believed that the status and prosperity of the landed interest owed little to the Corn Laws and was not materially threatened by their repeal. As with his critique of the 1832 Reform Bill, it was not the measure itself that was revolutionary but the manner of its passing – the fact that, in this instance, a Conservative Prime Minister was giving way to the agitation of the radical Anti-Corn Law League. Once again Peel had demonstrated the latitudinarianism of his 'Conservatism', once more 'the rule of practice' was being bent 'to the passion or combination of the hour'. This helps explain why he was prepared, very soon after 1846, to see the Conservatives abandon any commitment to restore the corn duties. 'Search my speeches through,' he later said, 'and you will not find one word of Protection in them.'[37] True enough, but Disraeli seemed typically insensitive to the paradox that he had helped to destroy Peel's Conservative party in the service of a Protectionist cause in which he did not believe. It was just such fleet-footed, almost sophistical, manoeuvring that got Disraeli his reputation for self-serving opportunism.

The key to explaining Disraeli's behaviour in 1845–1846 must be found in the context of his bid for influence within the Conservative party and his deteriorating relationship with Peel. Disraeli knew all too well that with Peel in place he would never gain admission to the closed world of the Conservative elite. As Blake observes:

> Time was against him. He was 40, old in those days for first entry into office. A whole group of able, hardworking and younger men were ahead of him in the official hierarchy: Gladstone, Sidney Herbert, Lincoln, Dalhousie, Cardwell, Canning; all members of the Government…all Oxonians – mostly products of Eton and Christ Church. How could he hope to displace these distinguished figures, who represented the very cream of the upper class English political world?[38]

But Disraeli was nothing if not fertile in his ambition. In 1845–1846 he saw that a fissure had opened between that confident ruling elite and the bulk of the excluded backbenchers and he deployed all his energies to widen it. His tool was the concept of party, which he drove, like a stake, into the fault line. It was, in a way, a re-run of that dichotomy he had previously exposed between the Whig oligarchy and the excluded nation. His tactic was the same – to rouse the excluded majority against the governing elite. Where the Whigs had ignored the people in the pursuit of their own agenda, Disraeli accused Peel of ignoring his party. It was his basic theme in these weeks that Peel had systematically betrayed the principles of the Conservative party. He had betrayed them in 1829 on the issue of Catholic Emancipation, in 1844 over the sugar duties, in 1845 on the matter of Maynooth and now, in 1846, on the Corn Laws. Peel's executive arrogance was dissolving the very bonds of the old Tory party. 'He is so vain,' wrote Disraeli in a letter to Lord John Manners, 'that he wants to figure in history as the settler of all the great questions; but a Parliamentary constitution is not favourable to such ambitions: things must be done by parties, not by persons using parties as tools – especially men without imagination or any inspiring qualities...'[39] There were, for Peel, no sacred principles or debts of loyalty to the party which had nurtured and sustained him. On that basis, modern Conservatism as practised by Peel, was indeed an 'organized hypocrisy'. The Conservative party, as an organized political connection, could not survive on such a basis. This was the substance of Disraeli's attack.

There was, of course, an understandable difference here. Peel had matured in a political environment where the concept of 'Party' was much less firmly entrenched. He saw his first responsibility as that of providing strong executive government in the national interest. He regarded himself as a *national* rather than a *party* leader. It was the job of the Conservative party – and in effect the Commons more generally – to support him in this. Disraeli's view was the opposite. He argued that Peel owed his position to party support and that his first duty was loyalty to his party. The difference is easy to explain. Peel had spent nearly all his adult life in government and had imbibed the doctrine that there existed in government an original power, derived from the king, to initiate and execute policy. As early as 1835 he had warned of 'the great public evil in permitting the House of Commons' to act independently of the government and thereby usurp its functions.[40] Disraeli had never held an executive position. With his hopes in 1841 dashed, he saw the Conservative party as the only vehicle for his advancement. He recognized that it lacked a spokesman for its grievances. In the Corn Law crisis, Disraeli stepped forward as the spokesman of the party against the leadership. Whether he actually believed in the importance of loyalty to party is rather doubtful. The sometime author of *What is He?* had only formally allied himself with the Conservatives in 1835 and had, throughout, demonstrated a strong independent streak in his Conservative thinking. Since 1843 he had been in more or less open rebellion against the party leaders. And when, in the aftermath of the Corn Law crisis, he found himself at the head of the Protectionist Conservatives, he was quick to cast aside the very principle of protection as an electoral liability.

The early weeks of 1846 were vital ones in Disraeli's life. His eloquent, witty and personal attack on Peel rallied the forces of protection and gave hope to the backbench country gentlemen. In the process, he confirmed his reputation as a formidable orator, divided the government front bench from its back bench followers and helped set in motion the events leading to the splitting of the Conservative party and the loss of most of its executive talent – clearing a path through which he himself could advance to occupy a high place in the Conservative party. At this moment, Disraeli exemplified the true spirit of the *entrepreneur*. As defined by Joseph Schumpeter, the entrepreneur is someone who does not accept the constraints in which he is placed but overturns them through an act of 'creative destruction' – creating a new set of conditions from which he can profit. This is precisely what Disraeli did. Of course, the risks as well as the potential gains were high and the outcomes in 1846 did not all work in Disraeli's favour. In terms of Disraeli's future career, three key negative consequences should be noted:

1. According to John Vincent, Disraeli did not intend to split the Conservatives so irrevocably. He expected the repeal to be carried by only a narrow majority, with the Conservatives largely voting against. Peel and the foremost leaders of the party would then resign, leaving the way for a reconstructed Conservative party in which he could play a leading part. The split which occurred was much deeper than he expected, depriving the party of most of its talent. This was to handicap the Conservatives throughout the middle decades of the century. Disraeli had become a bigger fish, but in a much smaller pond.

2. By conducting his case against Peel in such a bitter and personalized manner, Disraeli made many enemies amongst the senior politicians who supported Peel. He became, thereby, the biggest single obstacle to the reunion of the Conservative forces which many expected once the dust thrown up by the Corn Law debates had died down. Gladstone, in particular, never forgave him his treatment of Peel.

3. Most fundamentally, Disraeli always wanted to make the Conservative party a genuinely national party, one which could reach out beyond the narrow landed interest to unite the people of England as a whole, in contrast to the closed oligarchy of the Whigs. Yet this was precisely what Peel had begun to do. He had rebuilt the Conservative party from the collapse of 1832, had given it a new rationale with the Tamworth Manifesto and

had begun the process of attracting a broader range of social support which was reflected in the large electoral victory of 1841. It seemed that the Conservatives could become the national party of government with policies of moderate and cautious reform to remove abuses and grievances. But this project now lay in ruins and much of the responsibility for this rested with Disraeli. By helping to break up Peel's government it was not the Conservatives who dominated the next 30 years but the Whigs and Liberals. It took 28 years before Disraeli finally brought the Conservatives back to the kind of position they had occupied in 1841 and he did so largely by pursuing Peel's liberal-conservative strategy.[41] The only consolation for Disraeli was that when the wheel did finally turn full circle, he became Prime Minister – an event unthinkable if Peel's Conservative party had not disintegrated.

Historians' Debate: **What motivated Disraeli's attack on Peel and the Corn Laws – was his behaviour purely opportunistic, or was there some underlying principle at stake?**

Some historians have argued that Disraeli's attack on Peel reflected a fundamental divergence of political principle.

Feuchtwanger
[Disraeli's philosophy] was not the philosophy of Peel and of the Tamworth manifesto. Peel wanted to fashion a moderate Conservative block appealing to all the men of substance, the commercial middle classes as well as the territorial squirearchy and aristocracy... Disraeli envisaged a union between the landholding classes and the dispossessed masses held together by a bond of mutual obligation. Peel had a realistic strategy for the immediate future; Disraeli's imagery was a long-term vision.[42]

Walton
[Although] it is difficult to imagine Disraeli having become involved in this fuzzily romantic aristocratic cabal if Peel had given him the minor ministerial place he craved in 1841...the aristocratic revivalism of Young England represented a lot of what Disraeli actually believed in, even though he might seek to distance himself from some of its excesses and we need not assume that his espousal of 'One Nation' Toryism was at all insincere, even if we also suspect that his principles might have been vulnerable to the temptations of office.[43]

Others, however, have seen Disraeli's conduct as driven far more by personal ambition for office.

O'Connor
As long as Mr Disraeli had anything to hope from Sir Robert Peel, he poured upon him the most abject flattery... On the other hand... Mr Disraeli, when

he had lost all hope from Peel, was as lavish in abuse as he had formerly been in praise… I believe that I am justified in saying that never was any opposition to any minister conducted with less scruple… Mr Disraeli did play for high stakes and Mr Disraeli played well. But I have shown the motives with which he entered the game. The sublimity of the stakes cannot exalt the meanness of his passions.[44]

Earl of Cromer
Now all the circumstantial evidence goes to show that from 1841 onwards Disraeli's conduct, culminating in his violent attacks on Peel in 1845–1846, was the result of personal resentment due to his exclusion from office in 1841 and that these attacks would never have been made had he been able to climb the ladder of advancement by other means.[45]

Jenkins
It would be naïve to suppose that Disraeli's attachment to Young England and its ideals was not primarily motivated by his need for a vehicle with which to publicize himself and, with luck, to further his political career.[46]

It is certainly the consensus that Disraeli was not a protectionist and that the Corn Laws represented an opportunity for him to displace Peel.

Smith
Disraeli could be virtually certain by 1843 or 1844 that he was not going to be taken up by the neo-Pittite meritocracy of middle class origin represented by Peel and the rising W.E. Gladstone… His future in the Conservative party must depend on their displacement by other forces… The fulcrum from which to move them was supplied by Peel's decision at the end of 1845 to repeal the Corn Laws. Disraeli had little independent weight to apply to the lever. The Conservative backbench revolt against Peel in the Corn Law debates of 1846…could perfectly well have proceeded without him. His real significance was to bring to a crescendo the work he had begun in 1845 of undermining Peel's hitherto commanding authority in the house, partly by ridicule to which Peel was unduly sensitive, partly by pressing home…the charge of betrayal to which he was more sensitive still… It did not matter that he did not believe in protection. Party was the stirrup he must mount.[47]

Machin
Disraeli's stand in 1846 was…essentially political rather than economic. He currently appeared a firm defender of Protection, but this matter was secondary to him whereas the removal of Peel was of primary importance. His later willingness, indeed eagerness, to abandon Protection testified to the absence of any decided and long-term commitment to it on his own part…[48]

Aldous

For Disraeli there was little or no principle involved at all. Later he would drop protectionism almost as quickly as he adopted it. His interest in 1845/6 was one of simple ambition. Here was an opportunity to confront a prime minister who would not promote him.[49]

II

THE POLITICS OF OPPOSITION, 1846–1866

Although the protectionists were the majority of the Conservative party, the men of proven executive ability such as Aberdeen, Gladstone, Lincoln and Graham followed Peel and left the party. They became known as the 'Peelites', a small but significant force in British politics which gradually merged with the Whigs to help form the modern Liberal party. The Leader of the remaining Conservatives was Lord Stanley – the only man of significant executive experience not to follow Peel. Stanley was a considerable orator who had held the Secretaryships of Ireland and the Colonies. As the future 14th Earl of Derby, he also happened to be one of the richest and most socially eminent individuals in England. He had wide interests, producing a translation of Homer's *Iliad* and devoting much of his time to winning the horse race that bore his family's name. He had originally been a Whig. Indeed when, in 1834, Disraeli had expressed to Melbourne his ambition to be Prime Minister, Melbourne replied: 'No chance of that in our time. It is all arranged and settled... Stanley will be the next Prime Minister, you will see.' However, there was something unpredictable about Stanley's politics. In 1834, he resigned from the Whig government over Irish policy and, after joining Peel's government in 1841, resigned from that too in opposition to the Corn Law repeal. These actions highlight an essential negativity. He was a pessimist by political temperament, admitting to his son that he knew that 'the game was lost, but I think that it ought to be played and I would play it out to the last'. By this he meant, added his son, resistance to the advance of the democratic levelling principle in society. It was an understandable position for an Earl to adopt. Yet, it implied a fatalism that was alien to Disraeli, who did not see his role as that of overseeing a dignified retreat before the forces of modernity. The Conservatives could still win the future. Quite how this was to be achieved was less clear and his personal resolution of this question would have to await the demise of Derby in 1869.

Disraeli could not have survived politically without Derby; yet with Derby he could never succeed on his own terms.

But the fact that Derby was in the House of Lords left the question of who should lead the party in the Commons. Until 1847 this was Lord George Bentinck. Though Bentinck entered the Commons in 1827, his passion was horse racing and during his first eight years in the House, he did not speak at all. It was Peel's betrayal of the party over the Corn Laws that prompted him to sell his horses and devote the next three years to the cause of protection and the Conservative party, forming an unlikely partnership with Disraeli. Unfortunately, the stress of this transition hastened his end, for Bentinck died in 1848, aged only 46. Fittingly, it was Disraeli who did most to preserve his memory in his biography, *Lord George Bentinck* (1851). This is unquestionably Disraeli's best book. Notwithstanding its title, it is in no sense a conventional biography of an 'English worthy'. Beginning in 1845 it is, in fact, a sophisticated account of the political events surrounding the fall of Peel and the conduct of Russell's Whig government up to 1848. Many pages are devoted to reflections upon the problems of Ireland and there is a curious chapter in which Disraeli outlines his own idiosyncratic views regarding the Jewish race and religion. Taken together with the historical sections of his political novels, *Lord George Bentinck* reminds us that Disraeli could have been a considerable historian had so much of his energy not been lavished upon the pursuit of a literary career for which he had limited calling.

Disraeli's connection with Bentinck had another important result, for it led to his establishment at Hughenden Manor. Disraeli's friends felt that the leader of the country gentry should himself be a country gentleman, an idea which appealed equally strongly to Disraeli. It would also enable him to stand for a more prestigious county constituency. At this point, Hughenden Manor, an 18th century house set amongst 750 acres, became available only a couple of miles from his father's house near High Wycombe. Unfortunately, the price was £35,000 and Disraeli still had debts of £20,000. Bentinck now intervened to make the purchase possible by promising a loan of £25,000. His death shortly afterwards threw the scheme into crisis, but his brothers agreed to make up the sum and Disraeli moved into the house in the winter of 1848 – by which time he had already been elected MP for Buckinghamshire. In effect, the Bentinck family were financing a champion of their aristocratic order at a time when most of the Parliamentary talent was with the Whigs and Peelites.

The resignation and death of Bentinck raised again the question of the leadership in the Commons. Disraeli was the obvious candidate. But while the Conservatives had grown to tolerate him as the destroyer of Peel, neither the backbenchers nor Stanley were yet reconciled to the idea of a middle class, Jewish adventurer leading a Party of landed gentlemen.

Disraeli had himself made his position within the Party weaker by his advocacy of the removal of Jewish Disabilities. In 1847, the Jew, Baron Lionel de Rothschild, was elected MP for the City of London. As he could not swear his oath on the 'true faith of a Christian' he was barred from taking his seat. A controversy was created and a motion was introduced by the Whig Prime Minister to allow Jews to enter the Commons. This was a difficult issue for Disraeli since backbench Tories disliked Jews at least as much as Catholics. Nevertheless, Disraeli spoke at length in favour of the Bill, arguing not on the conventional (and respectable) grounds of religious toleration, but because of the close relationship between Judaism and Christianity. The Christian religion, Disraeli argued, was the logical fulfilment of Judaism. Just as he could not understand Jews who refused to accept the divinity of Jesus, so he urged Christians to acknowledge the Judaic origins of their faith. Were not Jesus and Mary both Jews? On this basis, Jews ought to be admitted to parliament as there was really no essential difference between the two faiths.

These are unconventional arguments even today. Disraeli once described himself as the blank page between the Old and New Testaments and for a leading member of the Conservative party to admit to occupying such a position in the 1840s was paradoxical to the point of perverse. The back-benchers of the country party were violently hostile to such reasoning and by speaking out in this manner Disraeli risked his rise to the Conservative leadership. Why, then, did he take such a controversial line?

For Blake, his consistent support for the removal of Jewish Disabilities (until they were rescinded in 1858) provides an example of fidelity to conscience at a time when his 'career was in the balance' and 'a great deal depended upon his presenting to the Tory squires with their belief in Church and State the appearance of a "sound man"'.[1] Vincent, however, suggests less disinterested motives. Disraeli was a friend of the Rothschild family, which he held in high regard and had made Lionel de Rothschild the model for the multilingual polymath Sidonia in his novel, *Coningsby*. He may well have hoped to act as their political advocate in return for financial assistance – though the evidence is not available to confirm this suggestion. Alternatively, Disraeli may have intended to remind the Tories that he retained his old independence of mind and, hints Vincent, could even have been looking for an issue which would permit him to break with the Tories and link up instead with Lord Palmerston, the Whig Foreign Secretary with whom Disraeli was on good terms and who he may have approached in search of a diplomatic posting at this time.[2] As late as 1859, Stanley records, Disraeli appeared keen to distinguish between his own private position and that of the Tory party, acting rather 'like a skilful counsel...defending some clients whose actions cannot be justified...'[3]

In the event, Disraeli's conduct over the Jewish vote confirmed the view that he could not succeed Bentinck as leader in the Commons and a compromise was arrived at according to which the leadership was to be shared between a triumvirate of Lord Granby, John Herries and Disraeli. The very fact that neither Granby nor Herries are particularly well-known to history highlights the fact that Disraeli remained the dominant figure and gradually assumed an unrivalled position.

Disraeli's Problem

With the fall of Peel, the Whigs, led by Lord John Russell, formed a government and a general election in 1847 yielded the following result:

> Whigs, Radicals and Irish 325
> Tory Protectionists 226
> Peelites 105

Thus, although the Whigs and their allies were the biggest grouping, they relied on Peelite support for their overall majority. The Conservatives remained a sizeable force but were unable to command an overall majority. This was the basic problem that Disraeli, as leader of the Opposition in the Commons, faced. Underlying it was a deeper fact. As a result of the schism of 1846, the Conservative party reverted to something like the old Tory party which Peel had reconstructed from the 1830s. That is to say, *it was essentially a party of the country gentry*. In some ways, this was a source of strength. They were an important and sizeable group. For much of the 1850s and early 1860s they were the largest single party, the number of MPs reaching as high as 300 in 1859. Their strength rested on their domination of the county seats – they took two-thirds of the English and Welsh counties and one-half of the Scottish and Irish counties. But there were important limitations:

1. *The country interest could not yield a majority for the Conservatives*. They were weak in the boroughs, where the party was unable to take more than a third of the seats. Of the 45 constituencies in the 29 major manufacturing towns, the Conservatives never took more than 13 in the period 1847 to 1865.
2. *The Conservative party had become more agrarian at a time when the country was becoming ever more urban and industrial*. They were going against the tide of social change. The only thing which kept the Conservatives in the running was the continuing electoral under-representation of the urban population as compared to the rural.

3. *The country gentry did not take politics seriously as a profession.* They produced few talented debaters or administrators and could not be relied upon to turn up at the Commons and vote. Disraeli gave vent to his frustration to Stanley in 1853, complaining 'loudly of the apathy of the party: they could not be got to attend business while the hunting season lasted...they never read: their leisure time was passed in field sports: the wretched school and university system was in fault: they learned nothing useful and did not understand the ideas of their own time'.[4]

This was the foundation from which Disraeli had to build. But he was determined to do so as effectively as possible. For Disraeli, the object of politics was power and if the Conservatives were not in power it was necessary to attack the government until they were. The situation was not an unfamiliar one. Ever since he had first sought election to parliament he had been confronted with the problem of overcoming a natural Whig majority and, as we have seen, his response had been to seek to build up a coalition of anti-Whig forces, appealing to all those – from Tories to populist radicals – who felt themselves excluded from the Whig elite. Those early battles to win High Wycombe were now played out on a national scale. By themselves the landed gentlemen did not constitute a majority and if they were to get power, they needed to gain support from other anti-Liberal groups inside and outside parliament.

This was not a necessarily insurmountable task. For much of the 19th century no single party commanded a stable majority. There was no 'two-party' system of the post-1945 variety. All governing majorities were compounded out of coalitions made up of shifting patterns of Whigs, Radicals, Peelites, Irish representatives, Liberals, protectionist Tories and so on. Even the nominal parties were badly organized. Individual MPs were not signed-up members of political parties; rather, they chose to stand for election in the Tory, Whig, or Radical interest but did not thereby feel themselves bound to some specified party policy. There were, after all, no such explicit party programmes and individuals considered that they were free to vote as their consciences, interests, or constituents dictated. This is well illustrated from the careers of the leading politicians of the day. Palmerston had been an indolent Tory minister. He became a vigorous Whig Foreign Secretary and ended his days as leader of the Liberal party. Gladstone was an earnest young Tory, became a Peelite and was the greatest Liberal Prime Minister of the 19th century. Lord Derby, who led the Protectionist Conservatives, had once been a Whig. And so on. In this fluid environment, in which between 1841 and 1868 only one government retained its majority throughout a parliament, there was good reason to believe that the Conservatives could construct a governing majority. This attempt to construct an anti-Liberal majority was the basic theme of

Disraeli's years as opposition leader. To this end, he sought to win the support of key groups and individuals; attacked the government whenever possible; tried to develop popular policies; and oversaw the rebuilding of Conservative party organization. He exhibited great tactical skill and flexibility – he was, says Vincent, 'the greatest leader of the opposition modern Britain has known.'[5] But the fact remains that he failed. There was no Tory majority between 1846 and 1868 and the party only gained brief tenures of office when the Liberals fell out amongst themselves. Even in 1874, when Disraeli did gain a sizeable majority, the electorate were voting against Gladstone, not for Disraeli, and that the majority was lost in 1880. This inability to build a working Tory majority was the great disappointment of Disraeli's career and was the price he and the backbench Tories paid for their destruction of Peel in 1846.

Disraeli as Chancellor of the Exchequer

The indeterminate nature of mid-19th century politics is indicated by the fact that, though the Conservatives were unable to build a governing majority, they were asked by the Queen to form a government on five occasions in the period 1847 to 1868 and accepted on three of them – 1852, 1858, and 1866. On each occasion, Disraeli served as Chancellor of the Exchequer and Leader of the House of Commons. This, therefore, will be a useful point to assess Disraeli's performance as Chancellor in a period in which fiscal policy became one of the great battle grounds of Victorian politics. It is symptomatic that both Disraeli and Gladstone spent the bulk of their pre-prime ministerial careers at the Exchequer.

The 1852 Conservative Government

Russell's 1847 Whig government was not a strong one and when, in February 1851, it was defeated in the Commons, Russell resigned. The Queen sent for Stanley, who at first agreed to form a Government, hoping to secure the services of Gladstone and the other Peelites. Disraeli's position was potentially awkward – as he himself described in a subsequent memorandum:

> Stanley told me Her Majesty had enquired of him to whom he proposed to entrust the Leadership of the House of Commons and he had mentioned my name. The Queen said: 'I always felt that, if there were a Protectionist Government, Mr Disraeli must be the Leader of the House of Commons: but I do not approve of Mr Disraeli. I do not approve of his conduct to Sir Robert Peel.' Lord Derby said: 'Madam, Mr Disraeli has had to make his position and men who make their positions will say and do things which are not necessary to be said or

done by those for whom positions are provided.' 'That is true,' said the Queen, 'and all I can now hope is that having attained this great position, he will be temperate. I accept Mr Disraeli on your guarantee.'

But if the way was cleared for Disraeli, it was not for the government. Gladstone and the Peelites refused to join after Stanley went against Disraeli's advice to drop agricultural protection and told Gladstone he intended to re-impose a moderate duty on corn imports.[6] Stanley was thus restricted to the inexperienced ranks of the Protectionists. The frustrating business of forming a government culminated in a meeting at Stanley's house on 27 February 1851. After several of those present declined to take office, Stanley announced that they could not go on and the Queen was forced to call upon Russell to return as Prime Minister.

A year later, the Conservatives had their chance again. Relations between Russell and his Foreign Secretary, Lord Palmerston, were increasingly strained and in December 1851 Palmerston was sacked from the Cabinet. This spelt the ministry's doom as Palmerston had a strong personal following which he used to bring down the government by voting with the Conservatives in February 1852. Again the Queen asked Stanley (now Lord Derby) to form a government and this time he accepted. Derby, with Disraeli's approval, asked Palmerston to join the government. Palmerston said he could not do so unless the government rejected any idea of a reintroduction of protection. This Derby was not prepared to do and the result was a purely Tory administration. Disraeli was appointed Leader of the House of Commons and Chancellor of the Exchequer. He was not pleased with the latter appointment, preferring to be Foreign Secretary. However, Monypenny and Buckle note, neither Derby nor the Queen would have assented to such a high profile and sensitive appointment.[7] In any case, Derby had positive reasons for making Disraeli Chancellor – financial policy and the issue of protection were likely to be the main challenges facing the government and it was vital that they be dealt with deftly. Disraeli was the obvious man to do this. When Disraeli cited his ignorance of financial matters, Derby reassured him: 'You know as much as Canning did; they give you the figures.' Most of the other members of the Government were equally inexperienced (only three had sat in a Cabinet before) and it was soon known as the 'Who? Who?' Government.

Disraeli was elated to have attained high office at the age of 47. However, it was accepted that an election would be called in late 1852 and this first period in government was essentially a holding operation until the end of the session. Disraeli's first budget was thus a routine affair and involved no changes in taxation, though he pointedly praised the consequences of the Whig government's 1851 free trade budget. It was a characteristically Peelite scenario Disraeli sketched. Although import duties had been cut, increased consumption meant that total tax revenues had increased. Derby was irritated with Disraeli for 'making out a triumphant case for the Free Trade policy which is the mainstay of our opponents'. What about the interests of the British producer? Disraeli had never been concerned about the conflict of producer versus consumer interests in the tariff question and as a politician, attached more weight to the fact that there were more votes in pleasing consumers than producers. As he commented privately in 1852: 'We ought now to be for as complete Free Trade as we can obtain and let the English farmer and the English landlord too, buy the best and cheapest silks for their wives and daughters.' He was certainly determined that the 1852 election should *not* be seen as a referendum on the Corn Laws. Far from repeal bringing ruin upon agriculture, as the protectionists had warned, the years after 1846 saw a period of general trade expansion, in which agriculture shared. Disraeli believed that a party backing a return to protection and increased food prices would have no electoral future and he had not entered politics to sacrifice his career to a lost cause. As early as 1849 he had remarked in a letter that 'Protection is not only dead but damned,' while in 1852, he referred to protection as 'that infernal question'. Of course, the rapidity with which he abandoned the very principle upon which he had helped break up the old Conservative party raises the question of how far he ever actually believed in the Corn Laws. Derby, for one, 'did not think Mr. Disraeli had ever a strong feeling, one way or the other, about Protection or Free Trade…' Though it might be countered that Disraeli's chief argument against Peel was not repeal itself but the fact it was contrary to party policy, the Conservatives in 1852 were far more closely associated with protection than in 1841 and yet, Disraeli showed little compunction in dropping the policy.

Derby, though confessing in private that the reintroduction of any corn duty was politically impossible, was not ready to abandon publicly the protectionist cause. As a consequence, the Whigs were able to claim that the 1852 election was a test of support for free trade and the result did indeed end agricultural protection as a political issue for the rest of the century. For, although the Conservatives were the largest single party, with around 300 MPs, they had no overall majority and could be outvoted by the 270 Whigs and Liberals, 40 Peelites and 40 Irishmen. Nevertheless the Conservatives remained in government and Disraeli drew up his first full scale budget.

Disraeli's December 1852 Budget

Disraeli was determined to use this budget to disassociate the Conservatives from any idea of a return to agricultural protection. The 1852 election had proven that the 'genius of the age was in favour of free exchange' and it was 'vain to struggle against it'. For assistance farmers should look to reduced costs of production and especially a reduced tax burden on agriculture.[8] This was how Disraeli proposed to assist the landed interest. In broader terms, the budget represented an attempt by Disraeli to achieve success in that most complex and strategic area of Victorian politics – the reconciliation of the conflicting interests in society by means of fiscal policy. His goal was to seize for the Conservatives the ascendancy in this vital territory, removing 'many well-founded causes of discontent among the people of this country' and laying the foundations of a system 'which should enlist in its favour the sympathies of all classes'.[9] The outcome would do much to shape the future of Victorian politics and 'his expectations of success' were reportedly 'unbounded'.[10]

The demise of protection gave Disraeli more scope for innovation. But he was subject to three constraints:

1. *He had to grant concessions to the Conservatives' core agrarian supporters*, but in such a way as not to reinforce the image of the Conservatives as a narrow class-based party.
2. *Derby insisted that defence spending, which took up one-third of total government spending, be maintained.* In 1852, Louis Napoleon declared himself Emperor of France and there were fears of a return to an expansionist French Empire. The Admiralty and War Office pressed for increased spending, as did the Court. This was a blow for Disraeli, who had anticipated reductions in military spending. With interest payments on the national debt accounting for half of government spending, Disraeli had little scope for expenditure reductions.
3. *According to the treasury figures, government finances were in a weak condition.* However, these were estimates, because the budget was not being presented in the normal spring period and were, in fact, a mistake. The revenues were stronger than initially thought and if Disraeli had presented the same budget in the spring of 1853, he could have covered his proposed measures with ease.

Disraeli's main measures were as follows:

1. *To assist the rural interest*, he proposed to:

    a. Halve the tax on malt (barley cultivated for the brewing industry) and on hops. This was presented as a free trade measure, reducing the price of beer a 'prime necessity of the poor'. Yet as Disraeli acknowledged privately to John Bright, he 'was forced to try something for the farmers and to venture on malt'.[11]
    b. Estimate farmers' profits for income tax purposes as being one-third, instead of one-half, the amount they paid in rents – the effect of which was to reduce by one-half the income tax they would pay.

2. *As a populist measure* he planned to more than halve the duty on tea – 'the principle solace of every cottage in the kingdom' – over a period of six years.
3. *To appeal to Liberal and Radical support* he proposed to distinguish, for the first time in the levying of income tax, between income that was earned through business or employment ('precarious incomes') and income that derived from more predictable sources like property and investments ('permanent income'). The former was to pay tax at the reduced rate of 5.25 pence in the pound compared to the standard rate of 7 pence. This differentiation of income tax was at odds with Peelite belief in a flat rate tax. It reflected, argues Ghosh, the fact that, whereas the Peelites still regarded income tax as a transitory necessity, Disraeli and sections of Whig-Liberal opinion recognized its likely permanence – in which case it ought to be reformed in its application.[12]

To cover these tax reductions (around £4 million), he proposed to increase and extend direct taxation:

1. The tax on houses and shops was to be doubled and extended from houses rated above £20 per annum to those rated above £10. This would generate an extra million pounds, but would have a big impact on owners of urban property. In 1834, an earlier house tax had been abandoned because of householder opposition in London.
2. The exemption limit for the payment of income tax was to be lowered from £150 to £100 per annum – so taking in the whole of the middle class.
3. Income tax was to be extended to Ireland.

Initially considered ingenious, as the debate proceeded over the following days, three basic flaws in the budget were exposed:

1. The proposed increases to income and house tax removed any benefits which the urban middle class derived from the differentiation of income tax. The urban property owner, it seemed, had to pay more tax to benefit farmers and landowners. Similarly, the extension of income tax to Ireland was not a good move when the Conservatives needed Irish support. Strangely for Disraeli, it was the politics of the budget which were its greatest weakness.
2. Disraeli's financial inexperience meant that he failed to realize that the income tax schedules did not allow any easy division between earned and unearned income since each income tax schedule contained *both* types of income. As a result, the proposal came under fierce attack from the Whigs and Peelites, led by Gladstone, who denounced it as unorthodox and reflective of Disraeli's financial ignorance.

3. Owing to last minute increases in naval expenditure – those 'damned defences' as Disraeli called them – the budget did not quite add up – or rather, it did only because Disraeli proposed to wind up the Public Works Loan Board and credit its funds, which arose through borrowing, to the income side of his accounts. This move, which treated borrowed money as income, was denounced as wholly inappropriate by the opposition.

By 15 December 1852, Disraeli realized his budget was facing defeat and late that evening he asked the Radical politician and former leader of the Anti-Corn Law League, John Bright, to call on him. He pleaded with the Radicals to abstain on the budget vote, promising that, if the budget were passed, he would drop the proposed increase in the House Tax. He would then proceed with a series of reformist measures, 'get rid of the old stagers', and looked forward to a day when he and the Radicals would sit in the same Cabinet. The Tory party had stood much from him and 'would stand a good deal more if necessary'.[13] Bright heard him out but was unable to take seriously any such deal with the Radical's erstwhile enemy – adding, in his Diary: 'he seems unable to comprehend the morality of our political course.'

Disraeli resolved to go down fighting and on 16 December 1852 made his closing speech. It was a powerful performance, though stronger on personal invective and sarcasm than financial reasoning, delivered against the backdrop of a thunderstorm and it was 1.00am when he sat down. The peroration was described by a contemporary:

> 'Yes!', he cried, 'I know what I have to face. I have to face a Coalition!' There was tremendous cheering as the orator looked significantly at the two benches opposite, the one above the gangway tenanted by the Whig leaders and the one below the gangway by the Peelite chiefs. 'The combination may be successful. A Coalition has before this been successful.' Then, raising his voice and lifting his right hand, he proceeded: 'But Coalitions, although successful, have always found this, that their triumph has been brief.' And, after a pause for an assenting cheer, he brought his right hand down on the table of the House: 'This too, I know, that England does not love Coalitions.'[14]

At this point, amid rowdiness and jeers, Gladstone rose in response. At first he could barely be heard, but gradually he won the attention of the House with a speech which was both a technical critique of Disraeli's proposals and a moral protest at what he regarded as the Chancellor's attempt to disguise the fact that what he proposed was, in fact, a deficit budget. What made Gladstone's attack so potent was the fact that he was still seen as a

Conservative and in concluding his speech he appealed to general Conservative principles:

> It is my firm conviction that the Budget is one of ...the most subversive in its tendencies and ultimate effects which I have ever known submitted to this House... If I vote against the Government I vote in support of those Conservative principles which I thank God are common in a great degree to all parties in the British House of Commons, but of which I thought it was the peculiar pride and glory of the Conservative party to be the champions and the leaders.

Gladstone's speech was of considerable importance. By intervening to ensure the destruction of the Government, Gladstone had burnt his boats. More than any other single event, it made reconciliation between the Peelites and Conservatives impossible. The personal duel between Gladstone and Disraeli, that was to be such an important theme of the next 28 years, had begun.

The budget was rejected by 305 votes to 286. Disraeli had secured no allies – the Radicals, Peelites and Irish all voted against it. Derby resigned, the government being replaced by a coalition government of Whigs and Peelites, led by the Peelite, Lord Aberdeen. Gladstone became Chancellor of the Exchequer.

Assessment

Disraeli's 1852 budget represented, says Ghosh, a considered attempt to reward the Tory's core supporters whilst simultaneously appealing to the middle class and wider population. Yet the arithmetic of the Commons was against him. He felt bound to do something for his own supporters and this meant antagonising the wider interests whose votes he required if the budget were to pass – the urban middle class and the Irish. The propertied classes welcomed the steady reduction in indirect taxes but were not yet ready to accept the increase in *direct* taxes that this made necessary. Gladstone would try to square the circle by cutting expenditure, with only indifferent success. Of course he was, as Vincent notes, also unlucky – the national finances were healthier than he thought and he could have afforded his malt tax reduction without increasing the unpopular house tax. Nevertheless, comments Blake, Disraeli 'courted unnecessary trouble' in his budget, which remained a 'bundle of expedients'.[15] Ironically, it was Gladstone who got the benefit of this surplus and Disraeli was unfortunate to come up against, in Gladstone, a politician determined to preserve to himself the posthumous reputation of Peel's fiscal orthodoxy.

The Budgets of 1858 and 1867

Unlike the budget of 1852, neither of these budgets was controversial and they left little mark. In 1858, Disraeli again had ill-luck. In addition to the impact of a financial crisis, Britain was still emerging from the financial strain of the Crimean War and was engaged in suppressing the Indian Mutiny, so defence spending remained high. Moreover technological advances in shipbuilding meant the navy had to pay for ironclad and steam powered ships. As a result, he faced a deficit of £4 million. The simplest way to cover this shortfall was to raise income tax, but Disraeli, conscious of the tax's unpopularity, remained committed to Gladstone's plan to phase it out by 1860. To balance the budget, it was instead decided to postpone repayment on the national debt, to raise, to English levels, the tax on spirits in Ireland, and introduce a tax on bankers' cheques. Gladstone approved of the measures, but Disraeli was, argue Monypenny and Buckle, being essentially reactive in his thinking. In 1852, he had recognized that income tax was an inevitable counterpart to the reduction in indirect taxes and had tried to refine its operation by distinguishing between types of income. With government spending on a generally upward course this was still more true by 1858 – yet Disraeli allowed himself to be bound by Gladstone's unrealistic objective of abolishing income tax. He thus diminished his already limited room for manoeuvre still further.

In 1867, Disraeli was subject to pressure for greater military spending at a time of economic difficulty. He was in no mood to yield, writing to Derby:

> Leave the Canadians to defend themselves; recall the African squadron; give up the settlements on the west coast of Africa; and we shall make a saving which will, at the same time, enable us to build ships and have a good budget.

By applying principles of 'inexorable economy' to military departments Disraeli was able to generate a surplus of £1.2 million. This money he used not, as his backbenchers would have liked, to cut the malt tax, but to pay-off part of the national debt.

Disraeli's Record as Chancellor

Disraeli staked no claim to be considered a great Chancellor of the Exchequer. He had little occasion to; he was Chancellor for only brief periods of minority government when the House of Commons would have been quick to punish any deviation from fiscal orthodoxy. In each case he had little room for manoeuvre and produced mainly uncontroversial budgets. The one exception was 1852, when he both increased and extended direct taxes in order to allow a reduced tax burden on agriculture. This may have been necessary politically, but it alienated more people than it pleased and guaranteed the budget's rejection. Disraeli simply lacked the political or financial leeway for such a move and did not endeavour to repeat it. Henceforward he was, in financial matters, impeccably orthodox – a point well made by Peter Ghosh. While Disraeli's political consistency has been questioned, says Ghosh, his *financial* consistency has been overlooked. Disraeli was a liberal financier, favouring reductions in government spending (especially military spending) and the lowest possible rate of taxation – if only because he realized that 'high or increasing taxation was politically vulnerable'.[16]

Monypenny and Buckle had earlier criticized Disraeli for being excessively conformist in his fiscal policy, remaining wedded to Gladstone's flawed forecasts and policy of abolishing income tax. Disraeli, they argue, should have stated in his later budgets, as he had done in 1852, that the public's insistence upon reduced *indirect* taxes required counter-balancing with increases in *direct* taxes and this would have given him the scope for a more imaginative budgetary policy. Blake makes a similar point that his budgets after 1852 were 'mere imitations of Gladstone's' and by seeking to 'out-Gladstone Gladstone' he displayed in 1858 and 1867 'a surprising streak of Little-Englander hostility to armaments'.[17] However, the weight of mid-Victorian public opinion was such that any attempt to raise the burden of direct taxation would have been politically suicidal. Besides, as Ghosh argues, Disraeli shared in the economic consensus for low spending and minimum taxation. Financial policy was one area where he was consistent throughout his career – consistently orthodox.

Disraeli's Opposition Strategy 1846–1865

Let us now step back and review, for the period 1846–1865 as a whole, the measures taken by Disraeli in an effort to form a stable Conservative dominated government.

1. Gaining the support of key groups within parliament

As we have noted, a constellation of interest groups, parties and connections peopled the benches of the House of Commons and Disraeli made a number of attempts to form an alliance that could bring down the Liberals. This was especially true in the 1850s and Hawkins has characterized Disraeli's conduct in this period as one of 'tactical promiscuity'.

(a) Irish Catholics

Disraeli believed that Irish Catholics could be persuaded to support a Conservative government, remarking to Stanley in 1861 that 'the union of the Roman Catholics with the Conservative party has been his object for twenty years'. 'Ireland,' he remarked, 'is agricultural, aristocratic and religious: therefore Ireland ought to be Tory.'[18] It was certainly the case that on the continent the Catholic Church was a bulwark against liberalism and 'progress'.[19] However, in Ireland, land, class and religion were all interconnected and shot through with conflict. Even so, there were more grounds for Disraeli's optimism than we would now credit. In 1845–1846, the Irish Home Rulers worked with the Protectionists in attacking and finally bringing down Peel. Irish Catholics naturally disliked the anti-Papal traditions of the Whigs and Irish Conservatism was a significant parliamentary force – by 1859, half of Ireland's MPs were Tory. The group Disraeli wished to target was the Irish tenant right party, known as the Irish Brigade. This was a group of mainly Catholic MPs, numbering about 40 in 1852, who wished to see a reform of landlord-tenant law and measures to stimulate the Irish economy. Disraeli was prepared to consider this and, in his *Life of Bentinck*, perceptively identified the land issue as lying at the heart of the Irish problem. In 1847, he supported Bentinck's wide-ranging proposal for Irish reform, which included endowment of the Catholic Church, compensation for agricultural improvements, and state loans to encourage railway construction. But only 118 voted for Bentinck's proposals. Five years later, Disraeli, seeking Irish support for his budget, pressed for Bills to be drawn up giving Irish tenants compensation for land improvements and opposed moves to reopen the question of the Maynooth grant, thereby, notes Machin, abandoning another of the causes that had formed the pretext for his 'oratorical onslaughts' on Peel.[20] After the 1852 government had fallen, he continued to negotiate with Irish leaders, who promised him the support of around 30 men. The 1858–1859 Conservative government introduced a series of reforms designed to cultivate Catholic support, including granting Catholic army chaplains permanent rank and salary, facilitating the access of Catholic priests to prisons, and considering again the issue of Irish land reform.[21] In 1859, Disraeli contemplated taking up the cause of the Pope, who was losing his temporal power as the process of Italian unification proceeded – a development welcomed by the Liberals. In the election of that year, the Tories gained eight seats in Ireland, taking their representation to a 19th century high point of 57 – compared to a Liberal 48.[22]

Unfortunately, anti-Catholic feeling within the Conservative party was simply too strong to allow Disraeli to pursue seriously measures to 'pacify Ireland'. The Conservatives were the party of the Church of England and Ireland and there was similar resistance (in a party of the landed interest) to the idea of interfering with property rights in Ireland in the interests of the tenant. Derby was opposed to both land reform and the suggestion of a pro-Papal policy, was sympathetic to the cause of Italian unification and remained unpopular amongst Irish nationalists who remembered his period as Whig Secretary of State for Ireland. For most of the period, the Irish remained part of the Liberal's majority coalition.

(b) Radicals

Radicals were left-wing Liberals who wished to see more thorough political reform (including extension of the franchise) and were critical of the exclusivity and patronising assumptions of the aristocratic Whig elite which dominated the upper levels of the Liberal grouping. Representing about 6 per cent of MPs in 1852, the position they occupied was not dissimilar to Disraeli's. Like him, they wished to break the hold of the Whig elite over government, although their solution, a furtherance of democratic reform, had more in common with the Disraeli of the 1830s than the 1850s. Still, their semi-detached position gave Disraeli hope that they might support a Conservative government conducted along liberal lines. He commented in 1850 that 'the radicals would be glad to have us in…since they would then be relieved from their present irksome position, as involuntary and unthanked supporters of a [Whig] ministry which they disliked.' Indeed, in 1852, some 55 Radical MPs regularly voted against the Whigs and, as Hawkins observes, 'when, in January 1855, March 1857 and February 1858, non-Conservative governments suffered major defeats, it was as a result of *Radical*, not *Conservative* Commons motions'.[23] Here, perhaps, was the basis of a Radical-Conservative anti-Whig alliance. Disraeli had no problem with such an idea. He flattered the old Radical Joseph Hume and had a personal regard for John Bright. More generally, he respected the rising industrial civilization of the north and saw that Conservatives could not afford to be at odds with the expanding commercial middle class. With protectionism abandoned, the biggest obstacle to such a coalition was removed. There was also much to unite the two groups. The Radicals represented the propertied middle class and might support a party standing for the interests of property in general. A point of common concern was local taxation, which placed the burden of expenditure on poor relief, highway maintenance and local justice on real property, urban as well as rural. Here was an issue which could unite the propertied classes.

Disraeli's major attempt to achieve this alliance was the 1852 budget and, as we have seen, he had a conversation with Bright to this end. Yet, the attempt failed for two reasons:

1. The budget did not do enough for middle class property. Proposed increases in house and income tax hit the urban middle class for a purpose they could not support – the reduction in the malt tax. At the same time, no reduction was made in the local government burden on property. Disraeli could not afford to ride both horses.
2. Ultimately, the prospects of such an alliance floundered on mutual mistrust. The worldview of the country landowners and the rising urban middle class was as yet too different. Conservative backbenchers disliked and distrusted

the Radicals who, after all, made no secret of their disapproval of the landed elite and had been the driving force behind the Corn Law repeal.

Radicals like Cobden and Bright considered that their agenda was more likely to be furthered by working with the Liberals, while Derby was unhappy with the idea of the Conservatives cooperating with their ideological opponents. When, in 1853, Disraeli resumed contacts with Radical politicians, he was forced to do so secretly. These negotiations continued through the 1850s but nothing, ultimately, came of the alliance plan.

(c) The Peelites

These were the obvious group to win back to the Tory fold, providing both votes and political ability. After the death of Peel, this seemed a real possibility and throughout the 1850s attempts were made by Derby and Disraeli to persuade the Peelites to return. On the day following the announcement of Peel's death, Disraeli was telling Edward Stanley that Gladstone and Graham might be recovered by 'definitely abandoning a protective duty.'[24] Minor Peelites *did* return (notably Peel's brother, Captain Peel), but not the leading figures. The Duke of Newcastle refused to sit in the same Cabinet as Disraeli. Gladstone was repeatedly approached, for the final time directly by Disraeli in 1858, who wrote that 'I think it of...paramount importance to the public interests that you should assume at this time a commanding position in the administration of the state.'[25] But he did not take the bait. He realized that the Conservatives were unlikely to provide a long-term political home and his dislike of Disraeli remained strong. Where Palmerston was 25 years his senior, Disraeli was only five years older and, says Blake, 'the truth was that he could never cooperate with Disraeli'. In any case, Gladstone was intensely unpopular with rank and file Tories, who disliked his High Church religion and his introduction, when Chancellor of the Exchequer, of inheritance taxes, and both Derby and Disraeli knew that if the Peelites returned, their dominance of the Party would end.[26]

(d) The Whigs

Another group to be cultivated were the more moderate Whigs who might be induced to join the Conservatives as the forces of radicalism and liberalism within the Liberal party strengthened. So as early as 1846 Disraeli was writing of the need for an alliance between the Conservatives and the 'real Whigs' in defence of the territorial constitution.[27] In 1853, Stanley found Disraeli 'full of a project of alliance with Lord Grey and the discontented Whigs',[28] and indeed in 1858, Grey observed that he had more in common with Derby than with the Radicals. Disraeli kept up his communications with several of the Whig leaders but again drew a blank. The problem was that the Whigs were not yet prepared to sever their historic connections: 'they would use us,' Derby observed, 'until their quarrels amongst themselves are made up and then turn us out.'[29]

A key figure here was Palmerston, a former Tory who commanded a significant personal parliamentary following. Disraeli admired Palmerston and the two had a close but somewhat unclear relationship in the 1850s – Disraeli boasting in 1851 that he could arrange for Palmerston to join a Conservative administration within 24 hours if permitted.[30] He and Derby made several attempts to win him back to the Conservative party. Again, however, they were unsuccessful as Palmerston was too senior a figure to accept second place in a Tory administration and remained content to pursue his agenda from within the ranks of the Liberals. In 1852, he declined an offer to join the Conservative government despite Disraeli's preparedness to relinquish the leadership of the Commons in his favour and a further request in 1855 came to nothing. A final effort to win over Palmerston was made by Disraeli in 1859, who suggested, without consulting Derby, that if Palmerston helped the Conservatives achieve a stable majority, Derby might be prepared to quit the scene. Palmerston politely declined the offer. This failure to secure Palmerston had serious consequences for the Conservatives as the veteran politician's unique personal appeal, founded upon a well-judged combination of conservatism in domestic policy and nationalist bombast in foreign diplomacy, effectively blocked Disraeli's ambitions until his death in 1865.

Thus, Disraeli's attempts to construct a parliamentary alliance that would sustain a Conservative-led government ended in failure before 1867. Why was this?

- Since the Liberals were politically ascendant and had such a strong grip on office, and since the Liberals were themselves a coalition of differing political beliefs, there was a strong incentive for individuals and groups to remain within the party to pursue their interests rather than opt for a possible political wilderness of Conservative opposition.
- In several cases, ideological differences were simply too great to be bridged – for example, the Catholic Irish and Manchester Radicals.
- Disraeli's personality was itself an obstacle to coalition building. Widely considered a Jew, an opportunist, and something less than a gentleman, he was distrusted and disliked by many MPs, including those within his own party. The 'hatred and distrust of Disraeli', observed Grenville in 1860, 'is greater than ever in the Conservative ranks.'[31] Indeed his very flexibility in seeking allies only made people less willing to join with him. In the case of the former Peelites like Gladstone, dislike turned to hatred; they simply would not enter a government with the destroyer of their hero.
- Neither Disraeli nor Derby wished to risk their personal ascendancy over any future government – something that would inevitably have occurred if Gladstone, Palmerston, or the Whigs had joined a Conservative coalition government. Derby was particularly adamant on this point, telling his son that he would be first in any Cabinet and would lead none but a 'distinctly and avowedly Conservative government'.[32]

2. Cultivating key groups outside parliament

(a) The Church of England

In religion, Disraeli presented the Conservatives as the Church of England party, in contrast to the 'secularist' and 'dissenting' Liberals. The Church needed such support. Though occupying a unique position in the state, during the mid-Victorian period, it was being challenged on several fronts and its privileges were under threat. Nonconformists and Catholics had been allowed to hold office and enter Parliament; the collection of tithes and church rates was becoming unenforceable in certain areas; the Church was struggling to keep pace with shifting population, as people left villages for towns; its educational privileges were under attack, especially in Oxford and Cambridge; and the Church itself was riven by factions such as Evangelical, Middle, High, Tractarian and so forth. The Oxford Movement engendered tremendous controversy within the Church and the decision of its leading figure, J.H. Newman, to become a Catholic in 1846 was a shattering blow.

The discomfiture of the Church of England was of fundamental importance to the Conservative party, which regarded itself as the custodian of the special relationship between Church and State. It was not merely that the bulk of Churchmen were Conservatives and the vast majority of Nonconformists, Liberals. The Church, they believed, was essential to the moral justification of the constitutional and social order.

Disraeli, though in Stanley's words 'personally incapable of religious belief', was a staunch supporter of the Church of England and held that 'a nation which has lost its faith in religion is in a state of decadence'.[33] He recognized its importance as a pillar of the state and social order and did not underestimate the power of religion over men's hearts and minds. Accordingly he had no problem with adopting a pro-Church policy and advocated the cause of the established Church in a series of speeches in the early 1860s. 'Can anyone,' he asked in a speech at Aylesbury in 1861, 'now pretend that the union between Church and State in this country is not assailed and endangered?' The Church, he continued, was a 'majestic corporation' that was 'deeply planted in the land...and one of the main guarantees of our local government and therefore one of the prime securities of our common liberties'.[34] He strongly supported and voted in parliament for the continuation of the Church's power to levy rates for the maintenance of its buildings and services and called upon the clergy to unite to resist the sustained Nonconformist assault on the privileges of the Church. In November 1864, Disraeli made a celebrated visit to Oxford, the centre of Anglicanism and addressed members of the University in a wide-ranging lecture on religion. Intense controversy was then in progress over the implications of Darwin's book, *The Origin of Species*, which had appeared in 1859. Disraeli's contribution to the debate showed few signs of doubt, although it is interesting to observe that his reasoning was ethical rather than scientific:

> The question is this – Is man an ape or an angel? My Lord, I am on the side of the angels. I repudiate with indignation and abhorrence the contrary view, which I believe foreign to the conscience of humanity... What does the Church teach us? That man is made in the image of his Maker. Between the two contending interpretations of the nature of man and their consequences, society will have to decide. The rivalry is at the bottom of all human affairs.

The Church of England was a useful bloc-vote, representing, potentially, about half the country's churchgoers.[35] But it was only in the 1870s that Disraeli's championship of the Church yielded electoral dividends and even then, it was the actions of Gladstone, the high-minded Churchman, that pushed the clergy and their congregations towards Conservatism with such measures as the disestablishment of the Church of England in Ireland and educational reform.

(b) The Court

Another key institution Disraeli tried to cultivate was the Court. Disraeli's vision of the constitution involved the preservation and even enhancement of the power and prestige of the monarch, which, he argued, had seen its political powers eroded by the dominant Whig families over the previous two centuries. Though Disraeli had no intention of *increasing* the actual power of the monarch, he did believe that the prestige and symbolism of monarchy was a force for social integration that ought to be exploited by government. This was one element of Young England thinking which he never abandoned. In addition, the more prosaic fact remained that the monarchy still possessed significant influence and there were real benefits from having the monarch on his and the Conservative party's side. The Queen's power to obstruct was considerable. In 1839, she had blocked Peel's attempt to form a Conservative government. In 1852, she excluded Palmerston from the Foreign Office. And she still had significant discretion when it came to choosing who to appoint as Prime Minister.

The monarch, then, had real power. But could that power ever shine benevolently upon Disraeli? The omens were inauspicious. During the 1830s, the Court had been Whig, while from the 1840s it became a 'Peelite salon'.[36] Prince Albert was impressed by Peel's dedication to public duty and commitment to modernising reform. Victoria and Albert supported Peel's attempt to abolish the Corn Laws and, not surprisingly, they had no time for Disraeli and hated him for his attacks on Peel – Victoria referring in 1846 to 'that detestable Mr D' Israeli'. Albert particularly distrusted

Disraeli, who he saw as an unstable, affected personality with 'not one parti-cle of a gentleman in his composition'. Viewed through Albert's earnest German eyes, Disraeli's mocking and ironic character assumed more sinister overtones. In 1852, he expressed to Derby his suspicion that Disraeli was, at heart, a democrat who was not committed to the established order 'and if that is the case, he may become one of the most dangerous men in Europe'.[37]

As ever, therefore, Disraeli had to begin from a highly disadvantaged posi-tion if he were to win the Court for the Conservatives. Yet, this was one area where he was to be strikingly successful. During the 1850s, Disraeli sought to cultivate his personal relationship with both the Queen and Albert. Victoria enjoyed reading the racy accounts of House of Commons business he supplied in his capacity as Leader of the House and in the 1860s, her suspicions evaporated. In 1861, the Disraelis stayed at Windsor Castle and Disraeli had a long conversation with Albert, for whom he had a genuine regard – stating in private correspondence that he had one of the 'most richly cultivated minds I ever met'. When Albert died later in the year, Disraeli strongly praised his virtues and supported various schemes to commemorate his memory. To Queen Victoria he wrote that 'the Prince is the only person who Mr Disraeli has ever known who realized the Ideal…the name of Albert will be accepted as the master-type of a generation of profounder feeling and vaster range than that which he formed and guided with his benignant power.' (Readers may recall Disraeli's remark to Matthew Arnold: 'You have heard me described as a flatterer and it is true. Everyone likes flattery; and when you come to Royalty you should lay it on with a trowel.') In 1863, the Disraelis were singled out above most aristocrats to receive an invitation to the wed-ding of the Prince of Wales as a reward for his support for Edward's generous financial settlement.

Disraeli's developing relationship with Victoria had consequences. In particular, when Derby retired as Prime Minister in 1868, Victoria had no hesitation in summoning Disraeli to succeed him, although aristocratic alternatives were available and she could have called upon them. Even so, Court favour by itself could do little to overcome the Conservatives' political weakness in the 1850s and 1860s – especially as the Queen was not yet as alienated from the Liberals as she was later to become during the period of Gladstone's ascendancy.

3. Liberal Reformism

In his quest for power, Disraeli naturally sought to associate the Conservative party with more popular policies – which meant, in practice, policies likely to appeal to the middle class electorate. The problem here was that he had little room for manoeuvre as the middle decades of the

19th century were ones, ideologically, of Liberal ascendancy. In economic and social matters, free trade liberalism ruled supreme. It had produced unparalleled prosperity and was, notes Vincent, accepted by Tories as much as by Liberals. From the 1850s, the Tories supported the capitalist market economy from profound belief, not out of a tactical concession to modernity. This was true of Disraeli. Although he did not worship the free market economy, he accepted it as the fundamental means of economic organization and had no wish to challenge the Victorian economic consensus – he was not a 'manor-house pink'.[38]

In this context, Disraeli had little alternative but to seek to outflank the Liberals in the advocacy of economic orthodoxy. The demand for cheap, economical and efficient government was an important theme of Disraeli's Conservatism in the 1850s – though this tends to be forgotten precisely because it was not particularly distinctive. If the Conservatives were to appeal to the propertied classes outside the rural sector, they needed to recover the reputation for safe but progressive government which Peel had built up and which Disraeli himself had helped to destroy in 1846. Disraeli's argument was that it was the Conservatives who were the truly practical, moderate, party, not the exclusive and dogmatic Whigs. As he told Stanley:

> the old Whig monopoly of liberalism is obsolete...our position is this: we represent progress, which is essentially practical, against mere Liberal opinions, which are fruitless. We are prepared to do all which the requirements of the State and the thought and feeling of the country will sanction: anything beyond that is mere doctrinaire gossip, which we should studiously avoid.

Ironically, this represented a return to the Conservatism of the Tamworth Manifesto. Like Peel, Disraeli was seeking to show that liberalism and conservatism were complements, not opposites.

Disraeli's claim that it was the Liberals who failed on the test of cheap and efficient government had some plausibility whilst Palmerston was Prime Minister. Palmerston's aggressive and 'turbulent' foreign policy produced 'excessive expenditure, heavy taxation and the stoppage of all social improvement'. He noted to Derby in 1858 that 'A good management of the finances is the only thing which really will get the country with us and make us independent of Court and Parliament.' In 1862, criticizing the high government spending necessitated by the defence estimates, he enunciated his dictum that 'expenditure depends on policy' – government spending was high because of the government's extravagant foreign policy. As Chancellor of the Exchequer, he did all he could to keep defence spending as low as possible.

Institutional and legal reform was another area in which the Conservatives of the 1850s sought to establish their progressive credentials. This was most apparent during the 1858–1859 minority-Conservative administration. This government

1. Settled the question of the future government of India in the wake of the Mutiny. The India Act brought the rule of the East India Company to an end and replaced it with direct rule by the British government, represented in India through the person of the Viceroy. This Act established the basic structure of the Raj for more than half a century.
2. Established the Newcastle Commission to inquire into the 'present state of Popular Education' and on the measures needed to extend 'sound and cheap elementary education'.[39]
3. Accepted a change in the law to allow practising Jews to enter the Commons.
4. Acquiesced in a Radical Bill to abolish the property qualification for MPs, thus realising one of the Chartist demands of the 1830s.
5. Most important, the government brought forward a measure for parliamentary reform.

The 1859 Reform Bill

'Of all Derby's and Disraeli's studied breaches of Liberal copyright,' says Smith, 'this was the most daring and the most necessary.'[40] The Whig leader, Lord John Russell, had re-activated demands for reform of the electoral system in 1852 and the issue had been periodically raised since then. Although there was no popular pressure for change and most MPs were sceptical or opposed, senior political figures realized that further reform had to come; it was a question of when and how much.

What was Disraeli's attitude? Disraeli was not a democrat by principle and had no wish to create an electoral system dominated by a popular majority – which would, he believed, be driven by short-term emotion into expensive wars, taxes on property and restrictions on liberty. In the early 1850s, he had asked: 'Is the possession of the franchise to be a privilege, the privilege of industry and public virtue, or is it to be the right of everyone, however degraded, however indolent, however unworthy?' Yet neither was Disraeli a rigid opponent of reform. His object was the good of the Conservative party and the maintenance of the aristocratic structure of British government. If these ends could be better realized through limited electoral reform, he was prepared to countenance it. The political 'rights' of those without the vote were not an issue. The question was whether the enfranchisement of sections of the working class would represent a threat to social stability. Disraeli thought not. In 1851, he declared that he thought the skilled working class would support the Monarchy and Empire and in his 1852 election manifesto he had raised the possibility of parliamentary reform 'in the spirit of our popular, though not democratic, institutions'. Approaching the issue from the perspective of political expediency, he and Derby were persuaded, by 1859, of the desirability of the Conservatives presenting their own reform bill for three reasons:

1. They had no interest in the existing settlement which had been forced through by the Whigs in 1832 and had since given the Conservatives only one election victory.
2. They did not wish the Liberals to have a monopoly of reform and saw that, in its absence, Russell and the Liberals could bring up the issue whenever it suited them.
3. If franchise reform were to come, then it was better that the Conservatives oversaw it, so that they could shape it in their own interests.

The result of these deliberations was the 1859 Reform Bill, which contained the following provisions:

1. The qualification to vote in the Counties was to be reduced from occupancy of property worth £50 per annum in rent to one worth £10 per annum – the figure existing in the boroughs. It was believed that these extra county voters (about 200,000) would vote Conservative. There was to be no reduction in the borough property qualification.
2. Under the so-called 'fancy franchises', votes were to be given in boroughs to such 'respectable' figures as university graduates, doctors, lawyers, ministers of religion and some school masters, as well as those with £60 in savings or receiving £10 per annum from investments in government funds. The total borough electorate would increase by about 200,000, the expectation being that these new voters would increase the Tory presence in traditional Liberal strongholds.
3. Under a redistribution clause, 70 small boroughs (which tended to vote Liberal) were to lose seats to large boroughs and counties, the latter being predominantly Tory.

The modesty of these proposals, comments Jenkins, demonstrates 'the limitations of the Conservatives as a serious party of "liberal" govern-ment...the government's opponents quickly perceived that the measure was essentially an exercise in electoral gerrymandering...'[41] They did little more than bring the county franchise into line with that of the boroughs and increase the number of potentially Tory seats. No member of the working class would gain the vote. The Radicals were unimpressed and the Liberals, whose support was necessary if it were to pass, had no wish to see the Conservatives trespass upon their territory for such partisan ends. Not surprisingly, the Bill was defeated on its second reading by 330 votes to 291. Faced with this rebuff, the government decided to dissolve parliament and call a general election. However, the issue of parliamentary reform generated little enthusiasm and the result of the 1859 election was:

Conservatives 297
Liberals and Others 357

The Conservatives gained about 30 seats – a good result, but not good enough. Desperate to keep the Tories in, Disraeli sought to win Radical support by promising a more radical reform bill. But they would not be bought and in June 1859, the Conservative government fell, to be replaced by a Liberal government led by Lord Palmerston.

Assessing the Liberal Reformist Strategy
In the 1850s and early 1860s, Disraeli sought to portray the Conservatives as the party of reasonable liberal reform, to return, in effect, to the Conservatism of Peel's Tamworth Manifesto. Given the social dynamics of mid-Victorian Britain, with its expanding middle class, economic prosperity, and desire for cheap and efficient government, such a political stance was almost a condition of electoral success. Even so, there were two conspicuous problems with this strategy:

1. It was Disraeli who had, in the 1840s, so publicly and effectively denounced Peel's new Conservatism of 'Tory men and Whig measures' and called for the Conservative party to remain true to its historic principles and defend established institutions, not reform them according to utilitarian tests. The idea of Disraeli as the pragmatic reforming minister was simply too hard to swallow.
2. The Liberals had no intention of allowing the Conservatives to encroach upon their domain. As Disraeli recognized: 'The more Liberal our measures, the less inclined they will be to accept them. They will never permit us to poach on their manor and we must postpone our Liberal battle until we have a Conservative majority.' Moreover, by the 1860s, the Liberals had, in Gladstone, the embodiment of Victorian fiscal orthodoxy whose performance as Chancellor of the Exchequer meant that the cause of economical government could never be a winning one for the Conservatives.

In short, Disraeli the literary Jew, the adventurer, the Young Englander, the destroyer of Peel, lacked credibility in his pose as the liberal man of business. If the Victorian electorate wanted those virtues they were unlikely to turn to Disraeli for them.

4. *Parliamentary tactics – harassing the government*

According to Blake, Disraeli was 'the first statesman to systematically uphold the doctrine that it was the duty of the Opposition to oppose'.[42] Here he differed from Derby, whose relaxed attitude to parliamentary opposition was more in keeping with the traditions of the first half of the 19th century. Hawkins describes his opposition strategy as one of 'vigilant inactivity', supporting the government when it behaved with moderation and assisting it in resisting pressure from backbench Radicals. He was, consequently, opposed to Disraeli's attempts to court support in unlikely sources, such as the Radicals, criticizing Disraeli's attempts to secure Radical support for his 1852 budget: 'If we are to be a government we must be so by our friends…and not by purchasing a short-lived existence upon the forbearance of the Radical party.' When the 1852 government fell, his son, Lord Stanley, reported to Disraeli that 'the Captain does not care for office but wishes to keep things as they are and impede "progress"'. Derby's motives were mixed. He was reluctant to incur the humiliation of short-lived minority governments; he saw the role of the Conservatives as resisting the advance of liberal and democratic ideas; and he also believed that, when confronted by coalition governments, it was better to let them fall out amongst themselves rather than to push them to unite in response to Conservative attacks initiated by such a disliked figure as Disraeli.

Disraeli had no time for such passive subtleties. Political power was the vehicle of his ambition and this would not be realized on the opposition benches. He harried governments with flexibility and tactical skill, occupying rival political positions, exploiting party divisions and continually looking to build alliances with alienated groups. 'The actual merits of government policies,' writes Machin, 'were of minor importance when compared to the overriding desire to give perennially active opposition.'[43] When a section of the government's usual supporters was discontented with some aspect of policy, Disraeli was quick to back them with opposition votes, hoping to inflict surprise defeats on the government. For example, in March 1853, he sought to swing Conservative votes behind a Radical motion to abolish certain protectionist tariffs. Unfortunately, his followers were less tactically nimble and the motion was lost.[44] In April 1853, he voted for a Radical resolution for the abolition of duties on newspaper advertisements. It was a move he had himself contemplated as Chancellor and would hopefully appeal to the press. The government was defeated by 41 votes, though many Tories did not like to see the party associated with a Radical pro-press policy. Foreign policy was another area where he sought to attack. In reaction to Palmerston's nationalist populism, Disraeli advocated a cool and reasoned, even 'little Englander', approach. He joined with the likes of Peel and Gladstone in attacking Palmerston's aggressive handling of the Don Pacifico issue and counselled a moderate and conciliatory approach to the Indian Mutiny of 1857.

Foreign affairs indeed possessed the capacity to bring down governments. During the Crimean War, in December 1854, he delivered a scathing indictment of the vacillation that had characterized the Aberdeen government's drift into war with Russia and the inefficiency with which it had prosecuted the resulting conflict. The 'Cabinet of Coalitionists' had indulged in false hopes that it would 'not be called upon to act' and, as a result, they stumbled into war without a true appreciation of what this implied.

> You have invaded the Crimea; you have attacked Sebastapol; but you have chosen to do so at the very worst period. You have commenced a winter campaign in a country which most of all others should be avoided. You have commenced such a campaign – a great blunder – without providing for it – the next great blunder. The huts will arrive in January and the furs will meet the sun of May. These are your preparations![45]

When, in January 1855, Aberdeen's discredited government resigned, the Queen sent for Derby. The following days were probably the most critical of Disraeli's career. The Conservatives had a great opportunity. By forming a determined war government, to public acclaim, and prosecuting the conflict to a successful outcome, they could easily have established themselves as the dominant party of the mid-19th century. Yet this was not to be. Derby told Victoria that he would undertake to form a government in which the popular figure of Palmerston was Leader of the House of Commons. But Palmerston was no longer prepared to occupy a subordinate position and declined to serve under Derby – as did Gladstone, who seems to have been angling for a wider invitation to the main body of the Peelites. Derby gave up his attempt as a result. Reluctantly, for the Court deeply disapproved of Palmerston, the Queen called on the former Foreign Secretary, who became Prime Minister for the first time at the age of 70 and saw the war through to a successful conclusion. Disraeli was reportedly 'in a state of disgust beyond all control' at Derby's failure of nerve and 'spoke his mind to Lord Derby and told him some very disagreeable truths'. To Stanley, he complained 'bitterly that we had lost our opportunity – he saw no prospects for the future: this failure was final.'[46] He expressed his frustration in a letter to Lady Londonderry:

> I was so annoyed and worn out yesterday that I could not send you two lines to say that our chief has again bolted! This is the third time that, in the course of six years, during which I have had the led the Opposition in the House of Commons, I have stormed the Treasury

Benches: twice, fruitlessly, the third time with a tin kettle to my tail
[i.e. agricultural protection] which rendered the race almost hope-
less…What is most annoying is that, this time we had actually the
Court with us…our rivals were Johnny [Russell] in disgrace and
Palmerston, ever detested.[47]

Disraeli was somewhat unfair here. Prior to Derby's meeting with the Queen,
he had agreed that the Conservatives could not form a Cabinet if Palmerston
held aloof. The point was that Disraeli misread the situation. He was convinced that Palmerston was physically played out and that he would, consequently, look for a chance to serve as Leader of the Commons under Derby,
knowing that he was not up to the job of Prime Minister. This same physical
infirmity would mean that the real power in the Commons would lie with
Disraeli. Disraeli's assessment was seriously flawed. Palmerston did not consider himself incapable of being Prime Minister and not only did he see the
Crimean War through to a successful conclusion, but he remained Prime
Minister for most of the remaining ten years until his death in 1865. This was
ominous for Disraeli, since Palmerston's dominating presence in mid-Victorian
politics acted as an insuperable obstacle to the advance of the Conservatives.
For, although Palmerston was the head of Liberal governments, he retained
many features of his earlier Toryism, notably scepticism towards
Parliamentary reform. With his bluff and hearty manner and simple patriotism,
he was, for many, the embodiment of the John Bull spirit and this enabled
him to appeal to both Liberal and Tory voters. With such a popular and essentially conservative figure in power, it was hard for the Conservative party to
mount a credible opposition. Indeed, in 1860, Derby unofficially agreed with
Palmerston not to oppose him, viewing the Prime Minister as a bulwark
against the more radical forces within the Liberal party. Disraeli acquiesced
in Derby's decision – in 1863 he voted in only eight out of 188 Commons
divisions; in 1864, 17 out of 156.[48] Put simply, the Conservative party could
not grow in the shade created by Palmerston's mighty branches.

Even so, Disraeli did help to inflict two major defeats on Palmerston's
administrations. In 1857, he voted with Radicals and Peelites to bring down
Palmerston's government over its war with China, though the resulting
general election only reaffirmed the Prime Minister's electoral popularity. The
following year he played a decisive part in another defeat for Palmerston, this
time over his proposed Conspiracy to Murder Bill. The pretext for this measure
was an assassination attempt on Napoleon III of France by the Italian nationalist, Orsini. Orsini's plot was hatched in England using a bomb manufactured
in Birmingham. Responding to French complaints, Palmerston proposed to
make it a criminal offence to plan murders abroad on British soil. Disraeli
agreed in principle with Palmerston's measure and the Conservatives

supported the Bill on its first reading. Unlike most Englishmen, Disraeli had no sympathy with nationalist movements and a positive dread of 'secret societies' and revolutionary conspirators like Orsini. Similarly, he generally favoured a pro-French foreign policy, declaring, later in the year, that 'the alliance between England and France rests upon a principle wholly independent of forms of government and even of the personal characters of rulers'. However, the fact that a British Prime Minister was restricting British 'liberties' at the behest of France provoked much resentment, especially amongst Liberals who disliked Napoleon's regime, and during the second reading the Radical Milner Gibson moved an amendment censuring the government. Listening to the debate, Disraeli recognized the hostility towards the government and saw the chance to bring it down. Accordingly, in a purely cynical manoeuvre, he led the majority of Conservatives into the division lobbies against the government and the Bill fell and with it, Palmerston. For the second time, Derby and Disraeli formed a Conservative administration. Unfortunately, it was again a minority government which lasted only until 1859, another reminder that tactical victories in opposition, however skilfully won, were unlikely to yield fundamental strength in government.

5. Publicity

Another of the problems that the Conservatives faced was the anti-Conservative bias of the national daily press. Their only reliable supporters were the Morning Post and Standard, both of which had small circulations. Most Conservatives, admitted Stanley, 'regarded all journalists as hacks' and 'seemed to regard the newspaper interest as their natural enemy and any attempt to turn it into a friend as mere waste of time'.[49] Derby shared this view and disliked dealing with journalists, an attitude that had little to recommend it in an age which had witnessed, says Bentley, 'a spectacular rise in the power of the printed word in general and of newspapers in particular'.[50] Disraeli's attitude was very different. He once described himself as a 'man of the press' and was determined to do something about the party's ineptitude in the cultivation of public opinion. In 1849, he entered separate negotiations to buy both the Morning Post and the Peelite Morning Chronicle. However, these schemes came to anything and the Post later switched its allegiance to Palmerston.

By far the most influential paper of the day was The Times and in 1858, Disraeli sent its editor, Delane, a personal note giving him advance notice of the formation of the Cabinet. He was not rewarded with any better coverage. At this stage the Times was pro-Palmerston and was not to be won for the Conservatives. What Disraeli wanted, writes Blake, was 'an organ for progressive Toryism' and, coming to the conclusion that 'nothing could be done with existing journals', decided to found one himself. In 1853, he made an appeal for funds:

> The state of the press as regards our party has become so intolerable that we think of making a great effort to terminate a condition of affairs which exercises a very bad influence on our prospects. It seems that the whole ability of the country is arrayed against us and the rising generation is half ashamed of a cause which would seem to have neither wit nor reason to sustain and adorn it.

The whole scheme energized Disraeli – for a while. He spoke of a circulation of 10–15,000, of driving its rivals from the field, and even of shaking the power of *The Times*: 'I have never seen him so much excited on any subject' noted Stanley in his diary. The journal, a weekly named *The Press*, appeared in May 1853 under the editorship of Sammuel Lucas. Disraeli (and Stanley) contributed extensively to the paper in the early years, writing ten of the first eleven editorials. He also contributed £2,500 of his own money he could ill afford.

Unfortunately, the paper was never a success, political or financial, and by itself made little difference to the public debate. Its circulation struggled to exceed 2,000. Derby was opposed to the whole scheme, believing that the Conservative leadership would be compromised by whatever appeared in the paper and expressing his distrust of all the individuals engaged in the scheme – 'not entirely excepting Disraeli.'[51] Derby's opposition caused potential Tory benefactors to withdraw and Disraeli's participation did him more harm than good. Journalism was not yet a wholly respectable trade and his half-concealed association became another count against him within the Conservative party, especially as the paper pushed a liberal-reformist agenda. In 1858, Disraeli sold his interest and the paper finally closed in 1866. The press situation for the Tories thus remained bleak – as Prince Albert rather insensitively reminded Disraeli in 1861: 'the country is governed by newspapers and you have not a newspaper.'

6. *Party organization*

Disraeli also moved to strengthen the central organization of the Conservative party. There were two motives for this. First, the party organization had been in disarray since the split with the Peelites. The Chief Whip, the elections manager, and the party funds, all left with Peel. Disraeli and his allies had effectively to begin from scratch. It was important that they do so since revived party organization was necessary if the Conservatives were to remain a political force and maximize their vote. Second, the Tory rank and file were notoriously difficult to control as most owed their seats to local connections and not to the party leadership. As Peel had discovered, they could be unmanageable and unreliable. By tightening organization, Disraeli hoped to increase his authority within the party. In the early 1850s, Disraeli took two measures to this end:

1. He appointed Sir William Jolliffe as Chief Conservative Whip in 1852 in place of William Beresford. Beresford, who remembered his career as a backbench rebel, had a low opinion of Disraeli, on one occasion writing to Derby that he 'would not trust D'Israeli any more than I would a committed felon'.[52] By contrast, Disraeli established a good working relationship with Jolliffe over many years.
2. He placed the national organization of the party under the direction of his own solicitor, Philip Rose. Rose re-established the party's central organization and paid a member of his firm, Markham Spofforth, to oversee the conduct of elections. They gave advice to candidates and recreated the network of local agents which had existed under Peel. Spofforth succeeded as head of the party organization in 1859.

With members of parliament still men of independent means, commanding personal support within their constituencies and paying the bulk of their own election expenses, there was little these reforms could do to secure either party discipline or influence the outcome of a general election. Still, they laid the basis for a system of party organization that would, in 1874, play a part in the Conservative victory.

Assessment of Disraeli as Opposition Leader

How successful was Disraeli's Opposition Strategy?

Successes

1. *Representation*
In terms of seats won in elections the Conservatives achieved a limited success. Table 1 gives the number of seats won by the Conservatives.

From a low point in 1847, the party quickly recovered in 1852 to secure the backing of more than 300 MPs. Thereafter, there was a fallback followed by stagnation. Though no striking success, these figures do represent something of an achievement. After the shock of the Corn Law crisis, the Conservatives were thrown back onto their traditional rural support. Devoid of political talent and party organization, it was not certain they would remain a major national party. But this they did. Indeed, for most of the time, the Conservatives were the largest single party. The problem was that the

Table 1: Number of
Conservative MPs, 1847–1868

Election Year	Number of Conservative MPs
1847	226
1852	310
1857	264
1859	297
1865	288
1868	271

anti-Conservative coalition of Whigs, Liberals, Radicals, Peelites, and Irish was too large to be overcome, except when its elements fell out amongst themselves.

2. Targeting key institutions

Disraeli was relatively successful in his attempts to cultivate influential institutions. He consolidated Conservative support within the Church of England, though the electoral dividends from this were limited until after 1868, when Gladstone played into Disraeli's hands with his Irish and education reforms. He also managed to win over the Queen, who had been successively Whig and Peelite and initially hostile to Disraeli.

3. Rebuilding Party organization

These years saw a rebuilding of national party organization, a process which Disraeli facilitated, even if he did not closely shape it. The Conservatives also became the richest party. In effect, observes Blake, starting afresh in 1846, a 'new party came into being', which had a better claim to represent the true founding of the modern Conservative party than Peel's foundation of 1832–1834.[53]

4. Parliamentary opposition

Disraeli made a career out of opposing the government, spending long hours on the Commons benches watching for a chance to exploit government divisions or attack an unpopular policy. He played an important part in bringing down governments in 1852, 1855, 1857, 1858 and 1866.

Failures

1. Failure to secure a majority

Judged by results, the basic failure of Disraeli's leadership was the inability of the Conservatives to win an overall majority in any general election in the entire period 1847–1868, over which Disraeli and Derby lost six general elections. Parliamentary manoeuvring brought periods in office, but it could not bring power.

2. Failure to build alliances
Disraeli tried hard to attract the support of other politicians to the Conservatives, including the Peelites, moderate Whigs (notably Palmerston) and even Radicals. All these attempts failed. The Conservatives made no long-term allies. Disraeli himself was a powerful factor operating against successful coalitions. As Tory backbenchers were want to remark: 'Jews make no converts.'[54] Only after his death did members of the Liberal party move across to the Conservatives in significant numbers.

3. Failure to develop a consistent and innovative theme of opposition
There was a lack of coherence and imagination in Disraeli's leadership, which saw an emphasis on tactics over strategy. Essentially, the Conservatives allied themselves to the prevailing liberal orthodoxy, in short, returning to Peelism. Unfortunately, it was Disraeli who had initially helped to destroy Peelism and, in any case, this was overcrowded territory already occupied by Peelites and Liberals.

Another potential theme for the Conservatives was to play the patriotic card. But here again, scope was limited. The British, by their resistance to high taxation, had decided against being a great military power and this meant that an aggressive foreign policy was not an option. More important, just as Gladstone had a monopoly of fiscal probity, Palmerston had a monopoly of simple English patriotism. He would always be a more convincing advocate of the English instincts than a Jewish-Italian outsider.

Thus, concludes Vincent:

> For all the agility of Disraeli's parliamentary tactics, his opposition leadership lacked a theme. Mid-Victorian Toryism became a pale echo of dominant liberalism... Conservative progress...curiously resembled Liberal progress. Where policy was concerned, Disraelian Conservatism before 1874 was open to the charges of latitudinarianism that Disraeli had made against Peel. The neo-feudalism of Young England had virtually vanished: the clock was not to be put back.[55]

There was little of that imaginative leadership, reaching out and inspiring the nation, that Disraeli had called for during the 1840s. Disraeli ceased to wage the battle of ideas and went to sleep. Raymond draws the contrast: 'In 1844 he had only a tiny following, but he was an intellectual force.' After 1847, he was the leader of the largest single party in the Commons, but to do this successfully he had to represent and confirm the wishes of his followers. 'Except as regards his career...Disraeli from now onwards must be regarded as a disappointed man.'[56]

4. *Failure to cultivate the working class*

Disraeli did not fear the working class, thinking them a conservative force within society. But he did little to explicitly cultivate them and there was no attempt to construct an alliance between the Conservative party and the working class. Similarly, he did little to forward the agenda of social reform he had called for in the 1840s – an area which the Liberals consistently failed to take seriously. Disraeli's neglect here was understandable, given that workers possessed few votes. Yet they had no more votes when *Sybil* was published and foresight would have suggested that sections of the working class would soon have greater electoral power. It was a lost opportunity.

These are serious criticisms of Disraeli's performance as opposition leader. True, the Conservatives did finally win in 1874, but this reflected more the failures of Gladstone than the successes of Disraeli. Paradoxically, Gladstone was the Conservatives' greatest asset. According to Lord Salisbury, a High-Tory critic, Disraeli's achievement was a purely negative one. 'To crush the Whigs by combining with the Radicals was the first and last maxim of Mr Disraeli's tactics.' His methods 'were so various, so flexible, so shameless' that he managed to persuade 'proud old Tories' and 'foaming Radicals' to enter the same lobby. It was, however, a purely negative talent. Disraeli had never led the Conservatives to victory; what he had done was make 'any Government while he was in opposition next to an impossibility'.[57]

Explaining Disraeli's Failures

1. The basic fact was that the economic and social trends continued to run against the Tories. They were the defenders of rural interests in an ever more urban society. They were the defenders of the Church of England in a society increasingly nonconformist and secular. And the Whig-Liberal governments of the age presided over a phase of growing prosperity.

2. In the mid-Victorian period, intellectual ideas also went against the Conservatives. It was the golden age of liberal orthodoxy and, says Blake, 'it was hard for the party as a whole to escape the charge of being "the stupid party"'. Only from the early 1870s did the intellectual tide begin to turn in ways that challenged Liberal assumptions with, for example, the shift towards a more interventionist and 'collectivist' state identified by Dicey and the role of empire in an age of great power diplomacy.[58]

3. The Conservatives continued to lack parliamentary talent. At times of great crisis, like the 1852 budget debate, Disraeli had to shoulder the burden of defending the measure. They were without the men who could counter the likes of Gladstone, Cobden, and Graham. Paradoxically,

Disraeli occupied a leading position within the parliamentary Conservative party precisely because that party was so short of political strength.

4. There was the fact of Disraeli's personality itself. 'Able as he is,' wrote Stanley in 1858, 'this man will never command public confidence.'[59] As such he was a potent obstacle to an effective anti-Liberal alliance. Many, especially Peelites, positively hated him. His own party leader described him as 'the most powerful *repellent* we could offer to any repentant or hesitating Peelites'.[60] Even within the Conservatives, he was mistrusted and not greatly liked. The very flexibility he displayed in the search for allies only fuelled the suspicions of men like Lord Malmesbury that 'to get office he would do anything and act with anyone'. This lack of loyalty had consequences. In 1861, for instance, when Gladstone made a second attempt to abolish the paper duties, Disraeli led a fierce attack that reduced the government's majority to only 15. Coming so close to defeating the budget, and probably bringing down Gladstone, Disraeli was accordingly bitter that 20 Tory MPs failed to turn up and vote.[61] There were periodic attempts to remove him from the leadership and, comments Vincent, from 1849 to 1881, 'Disraeli held his position only on sufferance... Before 1868 he was expected to retire with Derby; after 1868 he was tolerated...because he was not expected to last long anyway'.[62] Ironically, despite the importance he attached to 'party', Disraeli was never properly integrated into his own.

5. The attitudes of the Conservative backbenchers and the political character of his party limited his capacity to do deals with other groups, such as Catholics.

6. Disraeli was not the leader of the Party; Derby was. During the 1850s, Derby's ascendancy over the Conservative party was unquestioned. Disraeli was his House of Commons manager. 'Disraeli proposed; Derby decided.'[63] Though Derby was flexible and prepared to push a liberal agenda within the party, he adopted a more passive approach to the conduct of opposition. 'It does not seem,' observed Stanley of his father in 1855, 'that Lord Derby contemplates, or even desires, a return to office: nor has he any definite policy. He is content to watch events, keeping under his command as large a body of Conservative Peers and MPs as will remain satisfied with inaction. But Disraeli is not among these...'[64] Derby was cool or hostile towards many of Disraeli's schemes to build the party's strength – he opposed attempts to ally with the Radicals or Irish and was critical of plans to launch a newspaper. Naturally, Disraeli resented this and occasionally gave vent to his frustrations. He complained in 1854:

As for our Chief we never see him. His House is always closed, he subscribes to nothing tho' his fortune is very large; and expects nevertheless everything to be done. I have never yet been fairly backed in my life. All the great persons I have known…have been unequal to the grand game. This has been my fate and I never felt it more keenly than at the present moment… There cannot be too much vigilance, too much thought, too much daring – all seem wanting.

Yet, notes Hawkins, Disraeli realized that his 'position remained wholly dependent on the grace of Derby's endorsement'.[65]

Thus, although Disraeli was partly responsible for Conservative failures, when assessing his performance as opposition leader, it is essential to emphasize the circumstances and constraints within which he operated. From the commencement of his political career, the odds were against him. He had endeavoured to overcome them with a combination of tenacity, imagination, and opportunism. Yet the greatest single step he took, the destruction of Peel, not only shattered the prospect of Conservative hegemony in the mid-19th century, but fatally compromised his own personal reputation. He laboured long and hard to restore the fortunes of his party. It was, however, an uphill struggle against the liberal forces of his time and one in which his own personality, the character of the Conservatives themselves, and his subordination to the looming political and social presence of Lord Derby acted as powerful encumbrances. 'In an intrinsically liberal world,' says Vincent, 'all that could be done was to slowly create a counterculture to the liberal monopoly of wisdom.' Only in the 1870s, when Derby and Palmerston had quit the scene and Gladstone had himself begun to fracture the Liberal coalition, was Disraeli able to shift the parameters of debate in favour of the Conservatives and establish an independent claim on power.

Historians' Debate: How effective an opposition leader was Disraeli?

Disraeli spent around 25 years as leader of the opposition in the Commons. How successful was he? Historians disagree markedly on this question. Some writers contend that Disraeli was an effective opposition leader.

Walton

[After becoming Tory leader in 1849, Disraeli] had to prevent the doubt, distrust and dejection into which the Tory Party were plunged from sinking into absolute despair and ending in practical dissolution. He had to keep up their spirits by any and every means that presented itself; and the tactics for which he has occasionally been blamed frequently had their origin in this necessity, compelling him at times to fight battles without profit and to take office without power, solely for the sake of stimulating the energies and reviving the confidence of his followers.[66]

Jenkins
Disraeli was really the only Conservative in the Lower House capable of competing with speakers of this calibre and, for all the carping that went on in the benches behind him, it could hardly be denied that he was an invaluable asset to his party.[67]

Smith
Disraeli was a wonderful House of Commons performer, not least in the interminable years of opposition, whose sinuousness and dexterity of argument, fertility of invention, vivacity of wit, force of sarcasm and power of endurance beneath the famous frozen imperturbability with which his features masked his feelings never ceased to enthral, fascinate and infuriate supporters and opponents alike.[68]

Yet for other's Disraeli's tactics were counterproductive and he was, in fact, a liability for his party.

Bagehot
On all the minor parliamentary questions, Mr Disraeli has simply no conscience at all. He regards them as a game – as an old special pleader regarded litigation – to be played as to show your skill and so as to win, but without any regard for the consequences.[69]

Vincent
He was not good at prediction. He was not good at handling public opinion. He was sometimes outstandingly good in parliament and Cabinet, but at other times, capable of great insensitivity. He spent much of his life scheming, but hardly any of his schemes materialized. He always searched restlessly for allies outside his own party, but never secured them. He spoke frequently outside parliament, but built up no great oratorical reputation.[70]

Feuchtwanger
But the endless manoeuvring and angling for partners was keeping distrust and distaste running high… Many of his followers remained suspicious that he would, as on previous occasions, not scruple to seek an alliance with Radicals like Bright…if it would secure his own return to office.[71]

In the years up to Palmerston's death (1865), his leadership of the opposition had been conducted in the spirit of defensive conservatism. His claim was that on key domestic issues, such as parliamentary reform and the defence of the established Church, it was he who had held Palmerston to a Conservative position and protected him from Radical pressure. This did not accord with the notion of Conservative progress that he had often preached and practised in the past…[72]

Other writers argue that Disraeli's failure to build a governing majority reflected, not weaknesses in his own leadership, but the adverse conditions within which he had to operate.

Kebbel
[During the 1850s and 1860s, Britain was] governed on Conservative principles and in the most vigorous sallies of the Opposition, there always seemed to be a flavour of unreality. The country was willing to take its Conservatism from Lord Palmerston and a considerable section of the Opposition preferred it to their own.[73]

Feuchtwanger
In finding a solution to his party's policy and strategy dilemmas, Disraeli was sorely handicapped by the fact that he was not in untrammelled command. Derby was unequivocally 'the Chief'.[74]

III

THE 1867 REFORM ACT

Although many had considered the 1832 Reform Act an almost revolutionary measure, the passing years only exposed its limitations and anomalies. Indeed, these became more pronounced as the disenfranchised working population grew and the economic centre of gravity continued to shift towards the under-represented north and midlands. By 1866, the electorate in the United Kingdom was 1.3 million out of a total population of 31 million. Hence the issue of electoral reform never entirely went away. From 1851, Lord Russell, a key figure behind the 1832 Act, brought forward proposals to lower the property qualification for voting. The Liberal Cabinet declined to take up the idea and in the 1850s, Russell's further attempts to introduce reform failed. In 1859, the Conservatives introduced a reform bill, but this too failed to find favour with the Commons.

There was, in fact, little pressure for reform in the 1850s. The economy was prosperous, easing the social tensions of the 1830s and 1840s. Most MPs, beneficiaries of a political system which concentrated power in the landed elite, saw no reason to change it, especially as it was held to work so well. Lord Palmerston, the dominant politician of the period, exemplified this attitude and did all he could to stifle demands for reform from within the Liberal party.

Yet from the early 1860s, the cause of electoral reform began to exhibit signs of life. In 1864, Gladstone, impressed by the greater social harmony of recent years and the sobriety of upper sections of working class (the so-called Labour Aristocracy), declared that 'every man who is not presumably incapacitated by some consideration of personal unfitness or of political danger, is morally entitled to come within the pale of the constitution'. It was a section of these Labour Aristocrats who formed, in 1865, the Reform League to campaign for adult male suffrage. Middle class Radicals also returned to the issue of electoral reform. Manchester saw the formation of the National Reform Union in 1864, with a programme which included the secret ballot; redistribution of seats according to population and property; triennial parliaments; and the franchise for all male persons paying rates.

Thus pressure for reform was steadily, if quietly, growing. The chief obstacle remained the formidable presence of Lord Palmerston, who in July 1865 fought his last general election and did not mention reform in his nomination address. Most of the Liberal MPs elected in his majority that year similarly made no reference to reform. Palmerston's death in October 1865 opened up the Liberal leadership and with it, the issue of electoral reform. The 73-year-old Russell was at last able to return as Prime Minister and anticipated ending his career with a new Reform Bill.

The 1866 Reform Bill

While Russell was set on the idea of electoral reform, this was less true of the Liberals so recently returned to power under Palmerston's leadership. Though the Radicals, led by Bright, pressed for a comprehensive measure of reform, moderate Whigs in the Cabinet sought to stave off a new bill, while sections of mainstream Liberal opinion were sceptical of the benefits of extending the right to vote to the less well-educated. Russell nevertheless secured Cabinet backing for the principle of a Reform Bill in December 1865. To understand what followed, it is essential to note that the work of formulating the details of this bill fell to Gladstone, who presented its terms to the Commons on 12 March 1866. The controversies of the next two years were as much about Gladstone's leadership of the Liberal party as about the issue of reform as such.

The 1866 Bill was a moderate measure designed to build upon the terms of the 1832 Reform Act. The government rejected the calls of Radicals for household suffrage, which would give the vote to all men within the boroughs who occupied a house. They proposed instead to maintain a property qualification for the right to vote, the purpose being to extend the vote to the upper working class 'Labour Aristocracy'. These were workers who had skilled, stable, jobs, were often literate, were members of respectable trade unions and who were more likely to attend church. By extending the vote only to this group, the unstable, feckless and immoral sections of the working class would be excluded and the working class would not be in a position to swamp all the other classes in the electorate. As Gladstone argued in the Commons, 'I believe that those persons whom we ask you to enfranchise ought rather to be welcomed as you would recruits to your army or children to your family.' They represented no 'Trojan horse approaching the walls of the sacred city and filled with armed men, bent upon ruin, plunder and conflagration'.

The Bill proposed:

1. **In the boroughs,** to give the vote to all those occupying property worth £7 per annum in rent. This replaced the existing property qualification of £10 per annum.
2. **In the Counties,** to give the vote to those occupying property with an annual rental value of £14, instead of the existing £50 rateable value.
3. To give the vote to anyone possessing savings with a bank worth more than £50 for two years in a row.

In all, the electorate would increase by about 40 per cent – or around 400,000.[1] There would be no redistribution of seats because the Bill was not assured of a majority and the government did not want to alienate those who would lose their seats with a measure of redistribution. This was therefore to be brought forward once the principle of reform was accepted.

Notwithstanding the Bill's moderation, it exposed serious divisions within the Liberal party. For Radicals, it did not go far enough; for Liberal opponents of reform, it went too far. Even under the existing franchise, over 25 per cent of the borough electorate was already working class. With the proposed extension, the working class would be in a clear majority in most boroughs. Liberal opposition to reform coalesced around Robert Lowe and the former Peelite, Lord Elcho. This group, which numbered between 12 and 40, was known as the Adullamites – a Biblical reference by Bright to the Book of Samuel, where David took refuge from Saul in the Cave of Adullam and gathered malcontents around him. Lowe was no aristocratic backwoodsman. He was in fact a believer in efficient and enlightened government and attacked the Bill on utilitarian grounds. The test of a government, he said, was how well it worked. The existing system of government worked well. It represented the diverse range of class interests in the country and ensured that most of the electors were educated men of property. A mass working class franchise would place power in the hands of the least intelligent and educated section of society whose voting decisions would be swayed by popular prejudice and low demagoguery. Lowe's powerful speeches against reform had a dual effect. On the one hand, they spurred Gladstone into making the case for reform more forcefully, in the process alienating more moderate supporters. On the other hand, they offended the working class and helped supply impetus to the reform campaign outside parliament.

Forty opposition Liberals could not have defeated the Bill if the Conservatives had acquiesced in a moderate reform. Yet there was no reason why they should do so. In general terms, writes Cowling, 'the 1866 Bill was likely in every way to have been disastrous to the Conservative party'.[2] By extending the franchise to the Liberal-supporting Labour Aristocracy and shifting seats to urban centres, it would, Derby remarked, threaten 'the extinction of the Conservative party and...of the real Whigs'. More specifically, Derby, despite ill-health, retained an appetite for power, while Disraeli, in a career of thirty years, had enjoyed barely a taste of office and his position within the Conservative party remained weak. With the death of Palmerston, Disraeli's political interest reawakened. Might there not be a chance of detaching moderate Whigs, uncomfortably positioned amongst reformers, radicals and Irish?[3] If so, then there was a chance to defeat the Bill, bring down the government and terminate Gladstone's leadership ambitions. Consequently, the Conservatives adopted a position of outright opposition to the Bill and cooperated with the Adullamites.

Gladstone was now under pressure and his response only worsened the government's plight. He was an inexperienced Leader of the Commons, and with Russell taking little active part in politics, the burden of running the party's affairs also fell on Gladstone, who became tired and irritable. Additionally, his position within the Liberal party was not yet secure. Many Liberals resented his rapid rise to a commanding position within their party, while others did not trust him, believing he had tendencies to Radicalism. He therefore lacked respect and goodwill. But instead of trying to mollify the opposition, Gladstone's basic Peelite attitude came to the fore; he refused to listen to criticism, expecting the party to fall into line. 'Rather than lead the Commons', comments Angus Hawkins, 'Gladstone seemed determined to drive it.'[4]

Gladstone worsened his position by an ill-judged appeal to the 'people' for support in getting his Reform Bill passed. Under pressure in the Commons, he used two speeches in his Liverpool constituency in April 1866 to call upon the people to put Parliament straight. In strong language, he criticized two notable members of the aristocracy (Stanley and Grosvenor) as 'selfish aristocrats' for setting up impediments to the popular will, with possibly damaging effects for the aristocratic order. The workers had 'in a moral sense a right' to vote: 'It is not in our power to secure the passing of the measure: that rests with you.' This, writes Shannon, was later to become Gladstone's basic method of political operation, namely 'the imposition of his will as "leader of the nation" over the will of his parliamentary party in particular and of Parliament in general'. But for a senior politician to direct such an appeal over the heads of parliamentarians to the wider population was almost unprecedented. Not only was it ungentlemanly, it was positively dangerous. Gladstone seemed to be trying to intimidate MPs, hinting at class conflict if they failed to bend to the popular will.

On 27 April 1866, the government's Reform Bill was subject to a great test when a hostile amendment was moved calling for the planned Redistribution Bill to be made public before the Franchise Bill was passed. Disraeli, in his speech, reminded Gladstone of his strong opposition to the 1832 Reform Bill. Gladstone, in response, made one of his great parliamentary speeches in defence of the principle of reform. The working classes, he argued, were not adequately represented 'in proportion to their intelligence, their virtue, or their loyalty...I believe...that the increased representation of the working classes would supply us more largely with the description of Members whom we want, who would not look to the interest of classes, but to the "public interest"'. 'You cannot fight against the future,' Gladstone concluded, 'time is on our side.' It was a great performance and it was all the more disturbing that the government's majority, which after the 1865 election had been around seventy, fell to only five; 36 Liberals voted for the hostile amendment.

The Cabinet responded to the challenge by bringing forward a Redistribution Bill. Yet this only exacerbated opposition as those who saw their seats disappearing voted against the reform measures. Disraeli and the Conservatives recognized there was now a real possibility of defeating the government. In June 1866, a meeting of Conservative leaders and Liberal dissidents agreed to put forward a 'wrecking' amendment proposing that the borough franchise qualification be based on payment of rates rather than on rental value. The amendment would have the effect of significantly reducing the number of extra voters. The government opposed the amendment, but was defeated on 18 June 1866 by 315 votes to 304; 51 Liberals voted against their own government.

The Cabinet again faced the question of how to respond to this setback. Gladstone advocated dissolving parliament and calling a general election. He had been radicalized by his involvement with the Bill and an election, he argued, was the only way to 'keep faith with the people'. Russell agreed, but the majority of the Cabinet did not. The Liberals were seriously divided and an election that was centred on such a controversial issue as reform might well have proven fatal to party unity. In any case, a financial crisis was underway, with interest rates standing at 10 per cent and a costly election so soon after that of 1865 was considered unacceptable. As a result, the Liberal government resigned and 'the wreckage of yet another Reform Bill now littered the political landscape'.[5]

The Conservative Government and Reform

Following the resignation of the Russell-Gladstone administration, it appeared that a coalition of Conservatives and moderate Liberals was quite likely, blocking further reform and knocking the increasingly mistrusted Gladstone into the political long grass. That this did not happen primarily reflected the fact that the Adullamites pitched their demands unacceptably high. They wanted to form a centrist coalition and certainly did not want to merely serve within a Tory government headed by Derby and Disraeli. Consequently, they proposed that a moderate Whig, like Lord Clarendon, become Prime Minister in the Lords, whilst Derby's son, Lord Stanley, would lead the government in the Commons. Now Derby and Disraeli were not prepared to commit political euthanasia for the sake of an anti-reform coalition. Disraeli recognized that the accession of moderate Whigs could have seen him shunted to the sidelines and he urged Derby to stand firm: 'The question is not Adullamite; it is national. You *must* take the government: the honour of your house and the necessity of the country alike require it.' Derby needed little prompting. He was determined to become Prime Minister once again and, with the support of the majority of leading Conservatives, rejected the coalition proposals and formed a minority Conservative government – postponing, for twenty years, a union between the Conservatives and the moderate Liberals.

The new government faced the immediate problem of what to do about reform. However tempting the option of doing nothing, the case for taking up the reform question was more compelling. Two factors were relevant here.

1. Popular Agitation

With the failure of the Reform Bill, the extra-parliamentary reform movement briefly took centre stage. A large public demonstration planned by the Reform League for London's Hyde Park on 23 July 1866 turned to violence when police tried to bar the way, leaving one constable dead, many injured, and 1,400 yards of railings pushed to the ground. The Hyde Park riots caused some alarm and anger. Though the League leaders had no wish to court violence, the riots raised the profile of the reform issue. The veteran Radical, John Bright, saw the demonstrations as evidence of working class demand for reform and embarked on a reform crusade, addressing mass meetings in Birmingham, Manchester, Leeds, Glasgow, Dublin and London, in which he called for a union of the working and middle classes against the entrenched aristocracy.

In response to this widespread popular agitation there was a feeling amongst the propertied classes that the reform question ought to be dealt with. This was the view of Queen Victoria, who told Derby that she would like to see a moderate Reform Bill passed with the agreement of the parties, and Derby remarked to Disraeli that 'I am coming reluctantly to the conclusion that we shall have to deal with the question of Reform'.

2. Party Advantage

As in 1859, Derby and Disraeli saw that it would be to the advantage of the Conservatives if they brought forward their own Reform Bill. If they did so, they could cut the ground from under Gladstone, gain the credit for extending the franchise, and shape a Bill in their own interests – in particular, with respect to the redistribution of seats. If they did not, it was likely that the Liberals would regroup, turf out the Conservatives, and bring in their own Bill. So Derby and Disraeli decided to proceed and this decision created a momentum that was to carry the Conservatives further than they anticipated.

Formulating a Conservative Reform Bill

The basic question was – who should be enfranchised by a new Bill? The answer Derby and Disraeli formulated was a surprising one, namely to give the vote to all men who were resident in boroughs and who personally paid rates (rated residential suffrage). This was a democratic measure that would enfranchise more members of the working class than Gladstone's unsuccessful 1866 Bill. Motivating this curious proposal were a series of potential benefits. First, by trumping Gladstone's more limited position, it was hoped to attract the votes of pro-reform Liberals – necessary if the measure was to have any chance of being passed. Second, the Labour Aristocrats, beloved of Gladstone, were assumed to be solidly Liberal and there was no reason not to press through to the potentially more Conservative average working man. Certainly, it was expected that Whig control over the borough electorate would be weakened. Third, a rated franchise offered 'finality' on the franchise question in a way that simply lowering the property qualification would not. If the rateable qualification were reduced from, say, £10 to £7, pressure would soon revive to reduce it still further. The payment of rates was a fixed principle which most people would consider a sound qualification to vote and one which yet avoided full manhood suffrage, thus excluding the poorest section of the working class. In addition, the Conservatives proposed various 'fancy franchises' (such as plural voting for property owners) to increase the weight of the middle and upper classes.

However, when Derby and Disraeli presented these proposals to the Cabinet in February 1867, they encountered opposition from General Peel (Secretary of State for War), Lord Cranborne (Secretary of State for India) and Lord Carnarvon (Colonial Secretary). Cranborne was an articulate opponent of democracy. He was also suspicious of Disraeli, remarking on one occasion that he would sooner predict the direction of a weather vane than Disraeli's opinion on a given issue. At a Cabinet meeting on 23 February 1867, Disraeli sought to allay fears by presenting statistics drawn up by Dudley Baxter showing the relatively moderate effects on the electorate of household suffrage. Yet, when Cranborne reflected on the figures over the weekend, he became concerned at the position in small boroughs, like his own at Stamford, where he thought Baxter had underestimated the effect on electorate. When Cranborne and Carnarvon threatened to resign during an emergency Cabinet meeting on 25

February 1867, Derby and Disraeli were forced to withdraw their proposed Bill. With Disraeli being due to address the House later that day, a new Bill was hurriedly put together – known accordingly as the *10-minute Bill* – which proposed giving the vote to those rated at £6 in the boroughs and £20 in the counties.

This new Bill differed little from the failed Liberal measure and pleased no one. It seemed that Gladstone, who had been steering a moderate course to build trust amongst Whigs and moderates in the Liberal party, would be able to defeat the government and proceed with a more thorough measure tailored to Liberal needs, especially in the matter of redistribution. The only way out for the government was to revert to the previous Bill and face the resignations of Cranbourne, Carnarvon and Peel – calculating that the majority of Conservatives would prefer a Conservative household suffrage bill to a triumph for Gladstone. Indeed, a meeting of backbench Conservatives at the Carlton Club on 28 February 1867 made clear its preparedness to support a household rate-paying suffrage in the boroughs (diluted by safeguards such as plural voting for those with university degrees) as a defence against Gladstone and manhood suffrage. Derby, similarly, was determined to retain power and was prepared to make whatever concessions were necessary. Both he and Disraeli believed that the Conservatives could live with whatever franchise emerged and were keen that the Conservatives take a firm and distinctive line and not merely seek to appease Adullamites and moderate Whigs.[6] Hence, on 2 March 1867, the Cabinet reverted to the earlier scheme of household suffrage based on personal payment of rates, counter-balanced with safeguards such as the Commons would accept. True to their word, Cranborne, Carnarvon and Peel resigned.

How would the Liberals respond to this more radical measure? Crucially, Gladstone decided that the Liberals should oppose it. Why?

1. Gladstone saw no reason to depart from the principle of his own more-moderate Bill. He had always wanted to distinguish *between* the members of the working class according to the extent of their wealth, which he considered an indicator of their moral worth. By simply giving the vote to *all* who paid rates, this distinction was lost and too many of the feckless 'residuum' would be enfranchised. Gladstone, therefore, wished to retain a rating qualification and decided to set this at the payment of at least £5 in rates per annum.

2. Gladstone believed that the proposal to exclude the vote from compounders (tenants who did not pay rates directly, but indirectly via a sum added to their rent) would be unsustainable for this would eventuate in a situation where someone who paid compounded rates to the value of £10 would *not* get the vote, whereas someone who personally paid rates of only £3 *would* get the vote. But if all the compounders were given the vote, on

the grounds that they did in fact pay rates (if only indirectly), then the number of people enfranchised would be much larger and the result would effectively be *household suffrage* – i.e. a situation where anyone who owned or rented any property would have the right to vote. This was an advanced Radical proposal and was beyond anything which either the Liberal or Conservative parties had been prepared to countenance.

Gladstone's proposal was, therefore, to give the vote to everyone who paid £5 or more in rates. Whatever the merits of Gladstone's decision, tactically it was a mistake. First of all, Gladstone failed to consult his party. In a classic example of Peelite executive arrogance, he called a meeting of the Liberal party on 5 April 1867 and simply told it that it should vote for his proposal for a fixed rating qualification. Unfortunately, many Liberals objected to being told what to do and did not understand how they could be seen to be voting in favour of a less liberal measure than that proposed by the Conservatives. Accordingly, three days later a meeting of 50 centre-left Liberals in the Tea Room of the Commons agreed that they could not accept Gladstone's instructions and he was forced to withdraw them.

Second, the fact was that a majority of MPs were actually prepared to vote for the Conservative proposals. The crucial point was that, although some Conservatives opposed the radicalism of Disraeli's measure, the great majority (as well as some Adullamites like Lord Elcho) were attracted by the idea of finally settling the issue in a way that avoided the more democratic implications of manhood suffrage and, as a result, supported the Conservative leadership. In addition, many Liberals were also prepared to support the proposals. Together, this was enough to produce a majority. In effect, Disraeli was appealing over the head of Gladstone to the House of Commons as a whole.

Gladstone, however, was still not prepared to concede victory to the Conservatives. He still wanted either to bring the government down, or introduce his proposed scheme of reform. Accordingly, on 9 April 1867, he moved an amendment proposing, in effect, to bring in the £5 rateable qualification he had only the previous day promised the Liberals he would drop. In the Commons, Disraeli attacked the move as a 'declaration of war' by a 'candidate for power' who had 'had his innings'. The House was now tired of Gladstone's fine distinctions and resolved to have finality. Forty-five Liberals failed to vote for Gladstone's amendment; some were Radicals hoping to get household suffrage from the Conservatives; eighteen were Adullamites hostile to Gladstone; and some simply wanted to avoid dissolution and an election. The government therefore won by 21 votes. It was a decisive moment and a great victory for Disraeli, who was cheered at the Carlton Club and upon returning home was greeted by his wife with champagne and a Fortnum and Mason pie, prompting his remark: 'Why, my dear, you are more like a mistress than a wife.' Gladstone called it a 'smash perhaps without example'.

The Liberals were now in disarray and Disraeli dextrously exploited the opportunity. Yet the final form of the Bill was not established and he was not truly in control of the situation. The Conservatives remained in a minority and the threat from Gladstone had not entirely disappeared. Having seen his attempt to maintain a moderate line rejected, Gladstone now moved to a more Radical position, 'partly,' writes Feuchtwanger, 'because he was convinced that popular demands would have to be appeased and partly because it seemed increasingly likely that the Liberal Party he might come to lead would have to be more democratic and less Whiggish'.[7] In a speech to a large meeting of the Reform Union on 11 May 1867, he pledged himself to household suffrage. He again took to cautioning the Commons of the consequences of failing to meet the legitimate aspirations of the working class. Following another mass pro-reform demonstration in Hyde Park he warned his fellow MPs of 'the probable recommencement and continuance of a most resolute opposition out of doors of a character which I cannot pronounce to be illegitimate.'

Gladstone now took up the cause of the compounders – those who paid their rates *via* their rent. Disraeli saw the danger, but his determination to avoid any amendment from Gladstone remained as strong as ever. He found an escape from this prospect in the form of an amendment moved by G. Hodgkinson, who proposed to solve the compounding problem by abolishing it – in future, the compounding of rates and rents was to be made illegal, so all tenants would pay rates directly and thus qualify for the vote. This proposal would effectively bring about household suffrage and add another 500,000 to the electorate. Gladstone could not believe that Disraeli would accept such a radical proposal and left for dinner. But he had again misread the situation as Disraeli announced that he *was* prepared to accept the amendment – as well as another allowing for a £10 lodger franchise. The fact was that Disraeli's prime concern was to keep on winning and outmanoeuvring Gladstone, hoping to open still wider the division between moderate and radical Liberals. As he wrote shortly afterwards: 'I felt that the critical moment had arrived when…we might take a step which would destroy the present agitation and extinguish Gladstone and Co.' Gladstone was indeed taken completely by surprise by Disraeli's decision. He later remarked:

Even as a dog loves and follows his master drunk not less than his master sober, so the 250 Conservative gentlemen, who had hailed the measure in its narrow and reactionary form, continued to support it with equal fidelity when it had assumed its present wide and, as some would say, democratic proportions.

With this action, the controversy over the Reform Bill was effectively over and Disraeli's measure completed its passage through Parliament. Household suffrage had arrived; a result which hardly anyone had foreseen or favoured in 1866, certainly not Gladstone, Disraeli, the Adullamites, or even the leader of the Radicals, John Bright.

The Terms of the Act

Under the 1867 Act, the vote was extended to:

1. All householders in boroughs (owner-occupiers or tenants) who had been resident for one year and who paid rates.
2. Lodgers in boroughs paying an annual rent of £10.
3. People in the counties who paid rates annually to the value of £12.
4. Free and lease holders in counties with land valued at £5 a year.
5. The franchise in Scotland was brought into line with England and 7 seats transferred from England to Scotland.
6. In Irish boroughs, the vote was given to £4 rate payers.

These measures increased the size of the electorate by 80 per cent, from 1.36 million to 2.46 million. In the English boroughs, the increase was 670,000 or 134 per cent. There was a five-fold increase in the number of working class voters and there was, in the boroughs, something approaching democracy. Where one in five adult males in England and Wales had possessed the vote before 1867, one in three now did so.

[Meanwhile, a Redistribution Bill was proceeding through Parliament and here Disraeli had notable success in shaping the measure in the Tory interest.] Boroughs with a population under 10,000 lost one MP. This released 45 seats for redistribution. Of these, 25 were given to the (mainly Tory voting) Counties, 15 to boroughs which had not previously had an MP, one was given to the University of London, while the great urban centres of Liverpool, Manchester, Leeds and Birmingham, where most of the new voters lived, gained only a third member each. This was the smallest transfer of seats of any of the 19th century Reform Acts.[8] Equally important, the commission appointed to oversee the drawing of the new constituency boundaries was instructed by the government to separate, as far as possible, urban and rural electorates. Consequently, it recommended removing the growing suburbs of the towns from the Counties and including them in the Borough constituencies. Though the Conservatives hoped that this would prevent urban voters upsetting the party's position in the Counties, the main effect was, unexpectedly, to strengthen Conservatism in the

Boroughs as the wealthy members of the middle class who resided in the suburbs increasingly shifted their support from the Liberals to the Conservatives. Even in 1868, the Conservatives did best in those constituencies where a significant redrawing of boundaries occurred,[9] it being estimated that the Liberals incurred a net loss of 25 seats as a result.[10]

Explaining the 1867 Reform Act

The year 1867 thus saw the first extension of the franchise since 1832 and, moreover, saw the vote given to men much further down the social and educational scale. It was, said Derby at the time, a 'leap in the dark'. So why had it been taken; and why, moreover, was it taken by a Conservative party which had shortly before successfully blocked a more moderate measure?

Popular Agitation

According to one perspective, the radical agitation of artisans and respectable working men, echoing the popular protests of 1831–1832, overcame the resistance of a hostile Conservative party. If, wrote Murray in 1927, the Conservative party was 'inclined to shirk' the issue of reform, 'events showed that it dare not do so.'[11] Blake cites the mass agitation around the issue of reform as one reason why Derby took up the idea and why the Conservatives were prepared to acquiesce in an Act significantly more radical than that originally envisaged.[12] Democracy was clearly going to arrive and to stand in its way would foolishly risk revolution. Organizations such as the Reform League and the London Working Men's Association and individuals like Bright thus played a pivotal part in bringing about the Bill. As Trevelyan remarked, even Disraeli would not have ventured to enfranchise the working class 'but for the agitation in the country over which Bright presided in the autumn of 1866'.[13]

This view was specifically rejected by Cowling in his important 1967 study:

> The passage of the Reform Act of 1867 was effected in the context of public agitation: it cannot be explained as a simple consequence. Parliament in the sixties was not *afraid* of public agitation: nor was its action *determined* by it.[14]

For Bentley, 'the masses...served not as players but as spectators in a match between overheated politicians...'[15] The case against a significant role for public agitation is indeed persuasive:

1. Many leading politicians did not take the agitation as a serious expression of working class feeling. Lord Stanley, for instance, a moderate

Conservative, thought the large crowds were mainly drawn by curiosity and the riots chiefly a desire for mischief and larking.

2. There was a six-month gap between the disturbances and the introduction of the Conservative Bill, which hardly suggests a panicked reaction to unrest.

3. Moderate Liberals and Conservatives felt their hands strengthened by the unrest and violence, promoting a feeling for order and discipline.

The basic effect of the agitation was to keep reform in the public eye and to persuade politicians and even the Queen that it was better to diffuse the issue by granting a measure of moderate reform.

Conservatives Motives

It was the Conservative party that took up and carried through the Reform Act. Hence to answer why it was passed, we must ultimately consider the motives of Derby and Disraeli, who brought the Reform forward and the motives of the backbench Tories who supported them.

The most important figure was Derby. He was the leader of the party and controlled the Cabinet. Moreover it was he who, in the autumn of 1866, decided to proceed with reform despite the initial reluctance of Disraeli — who wished only to appoint a Royal Commission to inquire into the reform issue.[16] It was Derby who first suggested the idea of household suffrage: 'of all possible hares to start,' he wrote to Disraeli, 'I do not know a better...'[17] Derby was the real father of the 1867 Reform Act. What were Derby's motives? His basic aim was to secure and maintain power for the Conservatives. They had been in opposition for most of the previous 20 years. He wanted to end this by showing that the Conservatives were capable of effective and moderate government. As his son wrote in his journal, Derby is 'bent on remaining in power at whatever cost and ready to make the largest concessions with that object'.[18] As he explained in the Lords in July 1867:

> I did not intend for a third time to be made a mere stop gap until it would suit the convenience of the Liberal party to forget their dissensions and bring forward a measure which would oust us from office and replace them there: and I determined that I would take such a course as would convert, if possible, an existing minority into a practical majority.

Reform had split the Liberals in 1866; continuing with reform in 1867 would keep them divided.

A secondary consideration was a desire to undermine Gladstone's position within the Liberal party. As a former Conservative, Gladstone was widely disliked on the Conservative benches and his leftward move caused him to be distrusted. Derby realized that reform was inevitable. If the Conservatives failed to introduce a reform measure, Gladstone and the Liberals would do so. This would consolidate their position as the 1832 Act had done and enable them to shape its terms – especially over redistribution – to their own advantage. By proceeding with reform themselves, the Tories could shape the details in their own interest. This was most obviously the case in the areas of redistribution, where the Conservatives engineered in 1867 a settlement highly favourable to themselves.

Having taken the decision to proceed with reform, Derby fixed on household suffrage as a suitable bottom line for the franchise. This would provide a logical cut-off point which would attract general support and settle the franchise question for the foreseeable future. If defeated, he could take the proposal to the country. As initially proposed, urban household suffrage had the merit of showing trust in the respectability of 'the people', thereby pleasing reformers like the Reform League, while pleasing moderates by ruling out the more alarming prospect of manhood suffrage.

Derby was the initiating force behind the Reform Bill. However, his ill health and presence in the Lords meant that from January 1867 onwards it was Disraeli in the Commons who was chiefly responsible for determining the final shape of the Bill. The basic feature of the period from March was the way in which Disraeli accepted various amendments to the Bill which had the effect of removing most of the safeguards which initially surrounded it. On several occasions, he accepted radical amendments which removed limitations to the household suffrage principle – plural voting was abandoned; the residential qualification reduced from two years to one; a Radical amendment reducing the county franchise from a £15 to a £12 annual rental was accepted, as was Hodgkinson's amendment abolishing the compounding of rates. The net effect of these amendments was to treble the number the Bill was expected to enfranchise.

Why, then, did Disraeli accept these amendments which made the Reform Bill more liberal than originally envisaged? Two explanations have been advanced.

Tory Democracy

A traditional idea is that Disraeli was motivated by an underlying vision of *Tory Democracy*. This view had its origins in later 19th century Conservative accounts of Disraeli's conduct, according to which the 1867 Reform Act demonstrated Disraeli's faith in the inherent conservatism of the working man. Disraeli saw that beneath the Liberal middle class and respectable artisans lay the mass of the working class, which was much more Conservative in its politics. Hence he was prepared to go beyond many in the Liberal party to give the vote to the bulk of householders, trusting them to vote Conservative. Disraeli went on to build on this during the early 1870s by attracting working class support through the themes of social reform, Empire and preservation of the constitution. In the process, the Conservative party became a truly national party. Vindication for this view appeared to come in 1874 when the Conservatives achieved their first Commons majority since 1841. Moreover, between 1885 and 1918, the Conservatives never had less than 48 per cent of the popular vote, holding office almost continuously from 1885 to 1905.

However, since Blake's 1966 biography, the idea that Disraeli was motivated by a belief in 'Tory Democracy' has been widely rejected. Though, says Blake, he subsequently spoke of 'educating' his party, 'this was a piece of retrospective boasting'. He 'was never a Tory democrat' and did not expect the urban working class to vote Conservative. Why else, asks Blake, did Disraeli devote 'so much care to neutralizing the effect of household suffrage by redrawing the county and borough franchises'?[19]

Disraeli the Opportunist

It is now generally recognized that Disraeli's conduct was, in Cowling's words, one of 'consistent opportunism'.[20] His goal was to retain power by destroying Gladstone's leadership of the Liberal party and strengthening his own position in the Conservative party. He wanted, in short, to keep on winning even if this meant appealing to Radical MPs. He was, says Shannon, 'willing to accept almost any amendment provided it was not from Gladstone'.[21] In the short run, he achieved a personal triumph, defeating his rival and consolidating his claim to the leadership of the Conservative party when Derby retired.

But why did the bulk of the Conservative backbenchers accept this unorthodox strategy rather than follow Cranborne and Peel and their own anti-reform instincts? Basically, because they were tired – tired of being in opposition, of being defeated by the Liberals and of the periodic resurgence of the reform issue. At last, the Conservatives were winning and offering a solution to the reform question that was 'bold, decisive and final'.[22] Disraeli had humbled Gladstone and apparently disposed of the reform issue for a generation, and in a way that contained important Conservative elements. 'Why,' joked Conservatives, 'is Gladstone like a telescope? Because Disraeli draws him out, sees through him and shuts him up.'

Summary

Reform was not a popular or widely supported cause in the House of Commons. The reason that it was nonetheless taken up and passed was because it suited the objectives of the leading political figures in both main parties. Gladstone and Russell on the one side, and Derby and Disraeli on the other, were convinced that reform was in their strategic political interest. Of course, the Liberals had a longstanding ideological commitment to reform which was not true of the Conservatives. Derby and Disraeli were not committed to reform. But neither were they committed to the existing Whig-made electoral system which had brought them no benefits. They had tried to change it in 1859 and now, as then, they thought that they would gain more than they lost by taking the lead on reform. To this strategic consideration must be added Disraeli's short term tactical goal of carrying the measure and defeating the Liberals. He was determined to go on winning and beating Gladstone and this produced an Act that was more radical than any of the leading figures had initially intended. Ironically, Gladstone determined, almost by repulsion, the eventual shape of the reform bill. To the question of why the parliament of 1867 did not resist such a democratic reform, Cowling answers as follows:

> The fact is that many of its members thought it had resisted it, had taken the wind out of the democratic movement...and had delayed, for at least a generation...the democratizing of the British political system.[23]

The Consequences of the 1867 Reform Act

Some contemporaries were fearful of the effects of allowing the vote to those with little education or property. In a famous article, 'Shooting Niagara: And After' (1867), Thomas Carlyle saw the Reform Act as another decisive step in a process which had begun earlier in the 19th century of removing the restraints on the lawless and ignorant forces which lay within society. The Reform Act 'pushes us at once into the Niagara Rapids: irresistibly propelled, with ever increasing velocity, we shall now arrive; who knows how soon!'

However, the effects of the Reform Act were not so drastic as some feared. As with the 1832 Reform Act, it was a more conservative measure than many realized.

1. Voting continued to take place in public, with the result that workers could still come under pressure from employers and landowners.
2. In the counties, the electorate increased by only 40% and the voting qualification of £12 was sufficiently high to deny the vote to agricultural labourers and industrial workers in rural areas, such as coal miners. Democracy was therefore not extended to the counties which became, especially after the redrawing of the constituency boundaries to exclude the suburbs, ever more solidly Conservative. In 1865, the Conservatives won 99 English county seats; in 1868, they won 127 and in 1874, they

won 145. During the same period, the Liberal county representation fell from 48 to 45 to 27.

3. The distribution of seats still failed to reflect the pattern of population, with the industrial urban centres of the north under-represented compared to the more sparsely populated south and east. Wiltshire and Dorset, for example, had 25 MPs for a population of 450,000, yet the West Riding of Yorkshire had only 22 MPs for a population of 2 million. Many small boroughs also remained. More than 70 had fewer than 10,000 voters and in these small boroughs, corruption and bribery continued. Tiverton, with a population of 100,000, had 2 MPs, as did Glasgow, with a population of 500,000. Consequently, Liberal votes tended to pile up in the great centres of population, while the Conservative vote was more evenly spread throughout the country.

Rather than inaugurate the rule of the masses, the most important result of the Reform Act is generally seen to be the impetus it gave to the development of the organized party system. It was not enough for people to be entitled to vote, they also had to be on the electoral register. With over a million new potential voters to be registered, this was a substantial job. It has been estimated that in 1868, of the 300,000 lodgers in London boroughs entitled to vote, only 14,000 were registered. Parties now began to organize more professionally at the local level to see that it was done. Electoral organization could no longer be left to the part time work of solicitors. Clubs and associations were formed and full time agents appointed. Further, since the electorate had expanded significantly in size and included new sections of the population, traditional methods of securing votes such as bribery, social influence, patronage and the provision of food and drink were no longer sufficient. Politicians needed to get their message across to the voters and persuade them to vote for them. This required a more organized approach to campaigning, with rallies, propagandist literature, posters etc. All of this again necessitated party organizations with the resources and members to undertake this extensive campaigning.

The Reform Act therefore promoted the growth of party organization. Palmerston had already, in 1860, encouraged the formation of a Liberal Registration Association in an attempt to stop the growth of unofficial Liberal organizations which were often radical in their politics. This Registration Association developed into a more broadly based Liberal Association, which in turn absorbed other organizations of working men such as the Reform League, which, with its 65,000 members, merged into the Liberal party after the passing of the Reform Act. However, on the Liberal side, the most important development was the formation of the Birmingham Liberal Association in 1865. Under the leadership of the local businessman Joseph Chamberlain, the Association brought together the votes of Birmingham's working and middle classes to ensure the Liberals retained a strong grip on the politics of the town. In the elections of 1868, 1874 and 1880, all three of Birmingham's MPs were Liberal.

The Conservative party also began to organize more comprehensively. In 1867, the National Union of Conservative Associations was formed and in 1870, Disraeli appointed J.A. Gorst as the head of a new Conservative Central Office. In 1871, Gorst also became Secretary of the National Union and this became, in effect, the national propaganda arm of the Central Office. By 1873, Gorst had founded 69 Conservative Associations, bringing the total in the country to 400. Gorst's particular aim was to improve Conservative organization in the large urban boroughs.

In summary, the Reform Act's most important effect was to change the nature of the relationship between politicians and the electorate. Nominally, power shifted from the Westminster Parliament to the electorate. In reality, this meant a shift away from Parliament to the national party organizations which campaigned and secured the votes necessary for the formation of governments. As a result, the Reform Act began the decline of traditional parliamentary government. Westminster politics was no longer a closed world in which MPs governed independently of the people. They were increasingly subordinated to the disciplines of the party organizations, with their resources and members, which were hence able to define the national political agenda.

Disraeli as Prime Minister, 1868

The bulk of the Conservative party had been impressed by Disraeli's skill in steering the reform measure through the Commons, outwitting the Liberal leadership and giving the party an unfamiliar taste of victory. He had confirmed his position as the heir to Derby and one of the great parliamentarians of his day. With his confidence enhanced, he took advantage of a Conservative banquet in Edinburgh to articulate his vision of the Conservatives as the truly national party.

> I have always considered that the Tory party was the national party of England. It is not formed of a combination of oligarchs and philosophers who practise on the sectarian prejudices of a portion of the people. It is formed of all classes from the highest to the most homely and it upholds a series of institutions that are in theory and ought to be in practice, an embodiment of the national requirements and the security of the national rights. Whenever the Tory party degenerates into an oligarchy it becomes unpopular; whenever the national institutions do not fulfil their original intention, the Tory party becomes odious; but when the people are led by their natural leaders and when, by their united influence, the national institutions fulfil their original

intention, the Tory party is triumphant and then under Providence will secure the prosperity and the power of the country.

Disraeli's reward soon followed. Derby was afflicted by ever more painful bouts of gout and, in February 1868, he asked Disraeli if he was ready to assume the leadership. Disraeli said he was and on 27 February 1868, the Queen formally appointed Disraeli as Prime Minister. Victoria recorded the event to her daughter:

> Mr Disraeli is Prime Minister! A proud thing for a Man 'risen from the people' to have obtained! And I must say really most loyally; and it is his real talent, his good temper and the way in which he managed the Reform Bill last year – which have brought this about.

Disraeli acknowledged to his friends: 'Yes, I have climbed to the top of the greasy pole.' Unfortunately, the pole was as slippery in its upper reaches as in its lower. Despite success over reform, the Conservatives remained a minority government and had retained power chiefly because of Liberal divisions. Ominously for Disraeli, he was soon to face a resurgent Gladstone at the head of a revitalized Liberal majority.

Gladstone's Leadership

Gladstone's position in the wake of his defeats over the 1866 and 1867 Reform Bills was far from secure. Where the events of those years had highlighted Disraeli's flexibility, as he applied the skills of bringing together coalitions and maximizing potential support learnt in opposition, they had only exposed Gladstone's deficiencies as a party politician:

1. *Inflexibility*. Having perceived the need to lower, but not end, the property qualification for voting, he would not budge from it despite the adverse response of important sections of his own party and the likelihood of defeat in the Commons.
2. *Executive arrogance*. Where Disraeli behaved in government as if he were in opposition, Gladstone behaved in opposition as if he were still in government. Despite having his own Bill rejected in 1866 and despite being out of office, Gladstone still assumed that he could set the agenda and get his own preferred Reform Bill passed. He had failed to do so in 1866 despite the weight of executive authority; in 1867 he failed again.
3. *Instrumental approach to Party*. Gladstone made little effort to win over his party to his strategy. Aloof and superior, he merely announced his view and elaborated upon it in long speeches. He made little attempt to show that he was prepared to consider alternative viewpoints and effectively ignored the backbenchers. His 'man management' skills were utterly

defective and stood in sharp contrast with those of Disraeli, who, writes Hawkins, 'energetically devoted himself to organizing the opposition; flattering and coaxing Conservatives while befriending Liberal malcontents'.[24]

4. *Uneasy relationship with the Liberal party.* The events of 1866–7 demonstrated how far the Liberal party was a mixed coalition. It contained vehement critics of democratic reform as well as its warmest supporters. Gladstone had failed to bring these disparate groups together. Although this was probably inevitable, Gladstone's own equivocal relationship with the party was also highlighted. Many established Liberals, especially from among the old Whigs, resented his rise to dominance and were wary of his Radical and unstable tendencies. They were not at all unhappy to see him come to grief.

5. *Willingness to appeal beyond parliament to the people.* It was during the Reform Bill crises that Gladstone's technique of appealing over the heads of parliamentarians to the 'people' was first clearly established. By doing so, he sought to bolster his position by effectively warning those who resisted his proposals that by so doing they were placing social and political stability in danger. 'This style of argument,' writes Shannon, 'would become Gladstone's grand leitmotiv.'[25] But in 1866–1867, it backfired as those whom Gladstone was seeking to warn resented the implied blackmail of his position. They thought it was Gladstone who was creating a threat to public order by his provocative speeches outside the Commons.

Gladstone Resurgent: The Issue of Ireland

It was a measure of Gladstone's greatness that he responded to this crisis of his career with skill and vision. He quickly succeeded in turning the tables on Disraeli and laid the basis for a considerable electoral victory. Gladstone saw that he needed to do two things – reunite the Liberal party and find an issue around which he could mobilize the new mass electorate and direct its reforming energy. The answer he came up with was *Ireland*.

Gladstone realised that there were several aspects to the Irish problem. The main ones he focused on were those of religion and land. Both were highly controversial and, in the case of the established church, he had previously said that a solution would not be possible for a further five or ten years. But in 1867, he revised his estimate and decided to take up the issue. Why?

1. *Events*

In 1867, Irish grievances were brought forcibly before the English people. In September 1867, two members of the Irish revolutionary group, *The Fenians* (formed in 1858), were freed from prison in Manchester, a police officer being killed in the process, while in December 1867, a bomb exploded against the wall of Clerkenwell prison in London, killing

12 people. Although Gladstone advocated a firm response to these attacks, he also urged that the time had come to undertake a broad based approach to tackling the main Irish grievances of land, church and education. The one to which Gladstone had given the greatest consideration was that of the church and he now argued that the solution to this problem was the radical one of *disestablishment and disendowment*, i.e. he believed that the Anglican Irish Church should lose not only its official position as the established Church of Ireland, but relinquish its large holdings of property as well.

2. *Political opportunity*

The Irish issue had important advantages for Gladstone in terms of domestic politics. The Irish Church question united the Liberal party – Radicals, nonconformists, Adullamites and Whigs. It was classic Whig territory, with the idea of concurrent endowment having been raised by the Whigs as early as the 1830s. Indeed, Russell smoothed the way for Gladstone by writing a pamphlet on the Irish Church Question in late December 1867 calling for concurrent endowment of the Church of Ireland, the Roman Catholic Church, and the Presbyterian Church. Even more important, Russell told Gladstone privately in late December 1867, that he intended to retire from active politics. 'The leadership of the Liberals,' writes Feuchtwanger, 'was open to Gladstone more than ever, but he still needed a way of reasserting himself.' Ireland offered him that issue.

It was clear to Gladstone that the time had come for him to seize the political initiative and, on 16 March 1868, he announced to the Commons his scheme for tackling the problems of Ireland. The Conservative government had 'failed to realize in any degree the solemn fact that we have reached a crisis in the affairs and in the state of Ireland'. The land and education questions both needed attention. But the most urgent was the Church and here, Gladstone proposed simultaneous disestablishment and disendowment.

Disraeli was taken completely by surprise. His own government had been planning to appease Irish feeling by establishing a Catholic university, but now found itself trumped by Gladstone's proposals. The Parliamentary session was drawing to a close and a new election on the basis of the 1867 Reform Act was anticipated. It had not occurred to him that such a wide-ranging and controversial plan for reform would be introduced at this late stage. Gladstone pressed home his advantage. On 23 March 1868, he gave notice of his intention to move three resolutions on the Irish Church, the essence of which was that 'the Established Church of Ireland should cease to exist as an establishment' and that the property of the Church should be acquired by Parliament. When the Government proposed that discussion of the proposals should be deferred until after the election, it was defeated by 330 votes to 270. This vote was a triumph for Gladstone and helped to offset the memories of Disraeli's successes of the year before. Gladstone pushed on and, on 30 April 1868, his first resolution on the principle of disestablishing the Church passed by 330 votes to 265.

Disraeli was now in a humiliating position. Although nominally Prime Minister, it was Gladstone who was in the driving seat. The situation was unsustainable. One solution was for the government to resign. But Disraeli did not want to simply allow Gladstone to go ahead with such sweeping reforms and argued that the newly enlarged electorate should be given the right to vote on the matter. He therefore asked the Queen to dissolve parliament and call fresh elections – which were in fact delayed until November 1868, to allow the new electoral registers to be in place.

Disraeli appears to have been optimistic concerning Tory prospects. The 1866–1868 government had achieved much, considering its short-lived and minority status. Besides reform, there was an early foray in 'imperialism' with a successful expedition to free British prisoners held in Abyssinia by King Theodore, and some pioneering social reform, including a Public Health Act and an extension of factory legislation. Even so, Disraeli was destined for disappointment as November 1868 yielded yet another electoral defeat for the Conservatives, who lost 20 seats to the Liberals:

Conservatives 274
Liberals 384

Rather than try to form an administration and allow the previously disparate Liberals to unite against him, Disraeli resigned straightaway. Thus, after nine months, Disraeli's first period as Prime Minister had ended. The Queen offered him a peerage. But Disraeli, who wished to remain in the Commons, declined. Instead he asked for a peerage for his 76 year-old wife, Mary Anne. Victoria reluctantly agreed and Mary Anne, to her immense satisfaction, became Viscountess Beaconsfield.

Historians' Debate: What motivated Disraeli's role in the 1867 Reform Act: short term expediency or long-term Tory Democratic vision?

Early writers – Liberal as well as Tory – argued that Disraeli saw electoral reform as a means to bring into politics an instinctively Conservative urban working class.

Kebbel
[Disraeli saw that] the Toryism of the future must be popular Toryism or nothing... When the people were entrusted with power, it was absurd to suppose they would not use it; and the only way by which our ancient order could be maintained was by making the people themselves its guardians

and custodians. Hence, the Conservative working man. It might or might not be possible to create or discover such an entity; but unless it was, Conservatism was manifestly impotent...before he died [Disraeli] had the satisfaction of knowing that his countrymen had done justice to his motives... His Radicalism had consisted in trying to make the working class Conservative.[26]

Democratic Tory
Mr Disraeli...held that the settlement of 1832 was a Whig settlement; that it had swept away the popular franchises; and that the old alliance between the country party and the people should if possible be restored.[27]

Earl of Cromer
[Disraeli] saw [in the 1830s] that the tide of democracy was rising and that both the aristocracies [Whigs and Tories] were wholly out of sympathy with democratic ideas. He rightly judged that they could not or would not combine... The remedy that at once suggested itself to his powerful and subtle brain was that the aristocracy with which he was connected should outbid its rivals in the democratic market... Hence the genesis of Tory Democracy... Disraeli's general conception of democratising the Tory Party eventually led to the enactment of the Reform Act of 1867...which was his own handiwork...[28]

Bagehot
Mr Disraeli all along wished to go down very low, to beat the Whigs – if possible, the Radicals too – by basing the support of the Conservative party upon a lower class than those which they could influence.[29]

However, the majority of recent commentators have emphasized the tactical imperatives driving Disraeli and discount the role of Tory Democracy.

Feuchtwanger
His course was entirely dictated by the exigencies of parliamentary tactics and it was only after the event that he justified it as the logical consequence of views he had always held... Disraeli...did not really put his faith in some grand design of undercutting the Liberal bourgeoisie by allying with the Conservative working classes. His contemporaries, Napoleon III and Bismarck, might be thinking in such terms, but their labouring classes were mainly peasants... He could not resist, however, linking what he had done pragmatically and by sleight of hand with his own earlier views of his Young England days... Now he propagated the myth that the events of 1867 were the logical outcome of his deeply held and long-proclaimed...

Jenkins
But in reality, the Reform Act was not the product of a preconceived plan on Disraeli's (or anyone else's) part, inspired by a belief in the conservatism of

the masses; it can properly be understood only as an improvized measure, the details of which were largely dependent on the tactical situation facing Disraeli in the House of Commons.[30]

Disraeli did not mind giving way to demands made by the Radicals, but he had no intention of letting Gladstone dictate the terms of the Bill. By exploiting divisions within the Liberal ranks and thus thwarting Gladstone's attempts to create difficulties for the government, Disraeli succeeded in carrying the Reform Bill, even though its provisions were transformed in the process.[31]

Walton

Disraeli's vision of Tory democracy did not involve most people and certainly not the lower classes, being entitled to *vote* – their needs were supposed to be met by the responsible behaviour of the propertied members of the political nation, who were expected to recognize the duties as well as the rights of property and to rule in the interests of the *nation*, not just their own class.[32]

The important point is that the aspects of the Second Reform Act which protected the political influence of the aristocracy and gentry in the county seats were more fundamentally Disraelian in their philosophy than were the self-consciously daring concessions to urban democracy. Perhaps the crucial effect of the whole measure…was that it gave an additional lease of life and legitimacy to the aristocratic constitution whose defence gave shape and focus to Disraeli's whole political career.[33]

Murray

Undoubtedly, by thus handing over the government of the country to democracy, Disraeli had betrayed all those ideas of the balance of 'Estates' and the proportionate representation of different interests which had for years been the burden of his Toryism… He had capitulated to numbers… His defence…must lie in the plea of necessity… If it be granted that the alternative was the concession of a democratic franchise or a continuance of unrest ending in revolution, then there is justification for Disraeli's policy of generous surrender and for his view that the Tories had as good a right as the Whigs to open the doors and earn whatever gratitude the people might show.[34]

Historians today often argue that Disraeli's reputation as a Tory Democrat was constructed after his death by a Conservative party looking for a popular icon.

Parry

Disraeli always looked backwards more than forwards. Arguably he did not understand or seriously court the emerging urban democracy. Yet the circumstances have given him a different posthumous image. To suit the interests of the Conservative party after 1881, he was reinvented as a populist, a social reformer and an imperialist.[35]

IV

DISRAELI'S POLITICAL IDEOLOGY

The question of what, precisely, Disraeli believed is a difficult one to answer – but not as difficult as it has been made to appear, by Disraeli himself and by subsequent commentators. Disraeli reflected upon the principles of political action more than almost any leading politician of his or subsequent generations. Unfortunately, much of his political thinking was expounded in fictional form. This meant, naturally, that characters expressed ideas that were not necessarily Disraeli's, or were ones which he was prepared to contemplate or have fun with, rather than explicitly endorse. Further, Disraeli delighted in articulating ideas in paradoxical forms, seeking to startle the reader and disturb his complacent Whiggish opinions. Clarity was subordinated to cleverness and he frequently spoke cryptically and obscurely, indeed, in ways that are simply too affected to be taken seriously. There were reasons for this, not all of them to do with the fact that Disraeli considered himself an artist with the capacity to see through the humdrum vanities of established interests. Yet, it was also the case that rhetoric and romantic phraseology was intrinsic to the very political programme that Disraeli advocated. Like Enoch Powell, he believed that the life of nations is lived in the imagination. 'You can,' he once remarked, 'only act upon the opinion of Eastern nations through their imagination,' and the Asiatic Mystery had apparently held the East in thrall for centuries. The Disraelian Aristocratic or Territorial Mystery was to do the same for England; neither profited from being dragged too readily into the light.

Since Disraeli's time, two red herrings have distorted our understanding of Disraeli's political thought. The first is the idea that he had no consistent beliefs, or alternatively, that he had beliefs but failed to act upon them, his political conduct being essentially opportunistic. This view was expressed by Taylor in characteristically forthright terms:

Nothing connected him with the Tory party of the early nineteenth century – nothing, that is, except his calculation that its leadership would be easier to attain than that of the Whigs. He owned no land; he was not English in blood; he was lucky to be even a nominal member of the Anglican Church. In temperament he was even less conservative than in origin. He had a flighty mind which drifted from smart triviality to adolescent daydreaming and back again. He held nothing sacred except perhaps some Hebrew phrases vaguely remembered.[1]

This perspective has a long pedigree. As early as 1849, Gladstone was complaining in his diary that it was 'a very unsatisfactory state of things to have to deal with a man whose objects appear to be those of personal ambition and is not thought to have any strong convictions of any kind upon public matters'.[2] In the 1850s, Disraeli's close friend, Lord Stanley, was commenting in his diary that 'it cannot be pretended that he is attached to any political principles as such...'[3] Bagehot observed in 1859 that 'He has never had a political faith... No man has invented so many political theories'.[4] Yet it is misplaced. Disraeli definitely had principles in the sense that he had some kind of coherent political system and articulated it for a period of almost fifty years. He was passionate about ideas and these ideas remained, from their first developed exposition in his *Vindication* of 1835, surprisingly consistent over his long political life.[5] Disraeli clearly passes the belief test. The second proposition may or may not be true, but is it relevant? In one sense, clearly not – we can distinguish between beliefs and actions and the former are what we are concerned with in this chapter. But in one sense, it is relevant. We cannot know the actual content of Disraeli's mind. What we can know are his recorded utterances – his speeches, letters, books and pamphlets. In other words, it is Disraeli's articulated ideology that concerns us and this *was* a part of the political process, and if indeed he was truly opportunistic and said and did whatever would advance his career at any given moment, then we could legitimately say that he had no coherent political system that *we* can discern. However, this is not the case. Disraeli did advocate a broadly consistent approach to political issues during his career. Yes, he changed his views or shifted his position on some issues. But this is true of most thinkers and necessarily true of politicians. He himself distinguished between *principles*, such as a belief in the importance of the landed interest to a healthy state, and *measures*, such as the Corn Laws, and made it clear that he would not pin his political fate to the latter.[6] Gladstone shifted his political position far more than Disraeli in the course of his career; Disraeli remained in the same party – Gladstone did not.

In recent years, a new distorting factor has intruded – race. Disraeli undoubtedly made some striking remarks about race. 'All is race; there is no other truth.' But it is an exaggeration to categorize him, as Vincent does, as 'a racial thinker' for whom 'race...transcended everything: it explained religion; it explained politics'.[7] Disraeli's references to the importance of race had more to do with his personal insecurities and need to position himself within society than to explain political processes. 'What Disraeli is trying to do,' reflects Blake, 'is to vindicate his own Jewish descent and proclaim that the Hebrews, far from deserving contempt, ought to be favoured above all other nations.'[8] It would be better to label him a Semitic thinker, for race was indeed the key to the history of the Jewish peoples – their religion, their survival, their role in European civilization. Here, race was indeed all. But the case of the Jews was unique, for the Jews were a race without a nation state. The English, by contrast, were a nation state made up of diverse races. Race was certainly a factor in determining the 'genius' of the English people. As in other historic nations, it both helped to form and was in turn subsumed into the broader entity of a national character, but this English character owed more to the country's island position, its climate and geography, the experienced history of centuries, and the impact of great men, than to some compound of racial types – Angles, Saxons, Normans and Celts and what not. 'There is,' he said, 'a great difference between nationality and race. Nationality is the miracle of political independence. Race is the principle of physical analogy.'[9] Disraeli was clever enough to have fun with his racial speculations but too clever to make them a serious part of his political analysis. As Vincent admits, he said 'as little as was decently possible about the merits of the Anglo-Saxon race; his heart was clearly not in it. His object was to celebrate the Semitic races...'[10] The great political problems Disraeli confronted, namely the centralizing tendency of an oligarchical elite and the need to sustain social cohesion, were hardly amenable to a racial analysis.

The 18th Century Heritage

Disraeli, then, had ideas and these are worth considering as a coherent ideology. But where did they come from? Like most 19th century thinkers, he was a product of the 18th century. The two writers who did most to shape Disraeli's political thinking were Bolingbroke and Burke. Of the two, the latter was more important. Disraeli spoke more explicitly of his debt to Bolingbroke, but this reflected his political requirements; where Burke was the 'trumpeter' of the Whig oligarchy Disraeli was determined to destroy, Bolingbroke stood for a submerged Tory tradition of which he considered himself the inheritor. Nevertheless, Disraelian Conservatism was Burkian in its essentials, although it was certainly spiced up with Bolingbroke and Disraeli's understanding of his own oriental heritage.

Bolingbroke

'Who reads Bolingbroke now?' asked Burke. Well, Disraeli did and he made much of the fact in the 1830s.[11] Succeeding writers have struggled to explain

Bolingbroke's hold upon Disraeli and have tended to dismiss it as a pose that did little more than influence Disraeli's handling of Queen Victoria.[12] Now the key step to understanding Bolingbroke, and therefore his influence on the young Disraeli, is to strike the word 'king' from the title of his most famous work *The Idea of a Patriot King* and substitute the word 'leader' or 'government'. Failure to do so has caused commentators to discard the work as impractical, a throwback to a lost Tudor age, written to flatter the Prince of Wales. Of course, it flattered the Prince, just as it flattered his son, George III. But, though Bolingbroke refers throughout to a 'king', he does not mean what we might assume by the word. He expressly denies that a king rules by divine right. He is just like any other man and certainly the monarch of his ideal is a constitutional one, ruling in conjunction with a parliament and respecting the liberties of his people. He rejects, too, the idea that heredity has any relevance to a claim to be king: 'Royal blood can give no right, nor length of succession any prescription, against the constitution…'[13] His power, authority, and duties owe nothing to his status as king *per se*; they owe everything to his discharging specific constitutional duties with the backing of the people. Kingship is a function, not a state, and anyone fulfilling that function is a king – whether so named or not.

What Bolingbroke provided was a political manual upon the subject of how a patriotic government should be established and conducted in the first half of the 18th century, a period in which, for Bolingbroke, the dominant problem was the stranglehold on government obtained by the corrupt Whig elite. Bolingbroke's chief motive for writing was to overturn Walpole's Whig government and resecure his own entry into government. But in arguing his case, he set out certain themes that are of more lasting interest. His argument was that the function of government was to secure the well-being of the nation; that the well-being of a nation rested chiefly in its liberty; that liberty was best secured by a balance of powers in the constitution, with a correct equilibrium between the different classes and assemblies of men – the orders of society.[14] And that this balance was being undermined by a Whig elite which dominated parliament, ruled by corruption, and marginalized the King – eroding the historic liberties of the people in the process. What was the solution to this state of affairs? It was not enough, said Bolingbroke, to oppose *one* party with another, for parties can never represent the nation and always descend into faction. He looked, instead, to the accession of a patriotic monarch determined to break the hold of the ruling elite, appoint men with the good of the nation at heart, and rally the national majority against the corrupt few. 'Instead of putting himself at the head of *one party* in order to govern *his people*, he will put himself at the head of *his people* in order to govern, or more properly subdue, *all parties*.'[15] It was by his actions that he would be judged: kings have 'a divine right to govern well and conformably to the constitution at the head of which they are placed.'[16]

The logic here was clear enough – the practicalities more troublesome. George III indeed sought to implement aspects of this programme – though Bute turned out to lack the resolution for such a proceeding and the reign of party proved too powerful. But the real problem, as Bolingbroke candidly acknowledged, is that a Patriot King is a 'miracle' and for a notorious religious sceptic, that is tantamount to inconceivable. So, Bolingbroke poses a problem and provides a solution which, on his own reasoning, is implausible. It is easy to see why his political thinking is so often dismissed as 'worthless'.[17]

But this is not quite the end of the matter. Remember that for Bolingbroke Kingship is a function. A patriotic King may be a miracle, but patriotic men observably exist; was not Bolingbroke himself one? In other words, a patriotic ruler, however he secured power, might well purge a government of corruption and embark on a patriotic administration. A model here might be Napoleon III of France. Thus, Bolingbroke's pamphlet was a defence, not of monarchical government, but of strong and uncorrupted rule by a patriotic regime in the national interest. Now this, too, may well be chimerical. But it was clearly not an outmoded idea in 1738. The real weakness of Bolingbroke's work was his failure to specify a mechanism by which men of good will devoted to the national interest could break free of faction and secure a sustained hold on government. It was this problem Disraeli tried to solve.

Disraeli borrowed selectively from Bolingbroke and reinterpreted his ideas in the light of 19th century conditions. Still, he was an important constituent of Disraeli's conservative identity. First, there was the inspiration he derived from the career of someone who was, in Disraeli's own words, gifted with 'fiery imagination', 'the ablest writer and orator of his age...blending with that intuitive knowledge of his race...all the wisdom which can be derived from literature and a comprehensive experience of human affairs,' and yet who found himself implacably opposed to the 'Whig oligarchy'.[18] Bolingbroke had sought to block the rise of the Whigs; had been driven into exile by them; and maintained to the end of his days a continuous contest with them. More even than Disraeli was he the originator of the idea that it is the job of oppositions to oppose. Too many, he argued, looked on opposition as an adventure, to be pursued only as it suited, where it was, in fact, a duty. 'Every administration is a system of conduct: opposition, therefore, should be a system of conduct likewise.'[19] This oppositional model struck a chord with Disraeli – as did the techniques Bolingbroke employed. Barred from taking his seat in the House of Lords, Bolingbroke assailed the government through his writings, founding his own newspaper and conducting political journalism on an intensity not previously seen. He also devoted much effort to building an anti-Walpole opposition, compounded out of a disparate set of groups united only in their alienation from the established government – Jacobites, Hanoverian Tories and dissident Whigs. Disraeli was to employ similar tactics with, ironically, as little success.

Second, Disraeli was impressed by Bolingbroke's willingness to purge Toryism of its outdated and unpopular associations, which in the context of the 1730s meant its support for the exiled Stuarts and the doctrine of the divine right of kings. He 'eradicated from Toryism,' wrote Disraeli:

> all those absurd and odious doctrines which Toryism had adventitiously adopted, clearly developed its essential and permanent character, discarded *jure divino*, demolished passive obedience, threw to the winds the doctrine of non-resistance, placed the abolition of James and the accession of George on their right basis and in the complete reorganization of the public mind laid the foundation for the future accession of the Tory party to power and to that popular and triumphant career which must ever await the policy of an administration inspired by the spirit of our free and ancient institutions.[20]

In like manner, Disraeli saw himself as the man to dissociate the Tories from the unthinking and inflexible Toryism of the early 19th century – the 'pseudo-Toryism' of Eldon, Croker and the 'arch-mediocrity' Liverpool, which 'made exclusion the principle of their political constitution and restriction the genius of their commercial code' and show themselves open to popular demands for reform. Indeed, his very allusions to the Toryism of Bolingbroke, Wyndham, Shelburne and the Younger Pitt was a conscious attempt to reconstruct an authentic Tory heritage which was popular and reformist and which had been submerged by the authoritarian rigidity of the Napoleonic and post-Napoleonic war years. He was creating his own Tory pedigree and Bolingbroke was central in defining its type.

Third, Disraeli found in Bolingbroke the idea of a national interest as distinct from the sectional interest of the ruling party – or, to be more specific, the Whigs. Beyond the clash of faction was the body of the people who remained free from the selfish objects of party. A genuinely patriotic government would represent this national interest and seek to advance the unity of the whole nation. In this context, narrow party distinctions were irrelevant and Bolingbroke's language concerning the need for a national party bears obvious similarities with Disraeli's in his pre-Tory period.

For both Bolingbroke and Disraeli, a strong and public-spirited monarch played an important role as the unifying focus of a nation of orders. This image was a recurring one in Disraeli's thinking, especially in his Young England period and was prominently expressed in his novels, *Coningsby* and *Sybil*. 'The only power that has no class sympathy is the sovereign,' declared Sidonia in *Coningsby*. 'The House of Commons is the house of a few; the Sovereign is the sovereign of many.' Even so, neither author can be taken literally in their respective remarks exalting the role of kingly power. For both, the *goal* was a benevolent and popular government at the head of a united nation. The monarch was not intrinsic to this result. Certainly Disraeli did nothing to increase the powers or authority of the monarch in practice, though he did seek to cultivate and exploit its symbolic importance.

Fourth, Disraeli appealed to Bolingbroke's attempted commercial treaty with France to vindicate his claim that the Tories were the true originators of the doctrine of free trade. Disraeli was never a protectionist in principle and high tariffs were for him just the kind of policy that the Tories ought not to be associated with. Accordingly, he was a strong supporter of Peel's free trade budgets. Similarly, Disraeli cited Bolingbroke's relatively lenient Treaty of Utrecht with France as a model for his own basic foreign policy precept, namely that, by working together, England and France could always maintain the peace of Europe.[21] As he later remarked: 'With respect to our alliance with France generally, my opinions are upon record...even so late as 1853. I inherited them from Lord Bolingbroke and the changes in the world, subsequent to his time, only confirm his prescience.'[22]

One area of apparent divergence between Bolingbroke and Disraeli was over the issue of party. Bolingbroke had been a vehement party man. In his days of active power, he had been motivated almost entirely by party and personal advantage. Indeed, it was the crudity with which he sought these ends that permanently tainted his reputation. However, his later experience of being confronted by a powerful governing connection caused him to revise his opinions. He regretted that he had 'paid more than I owed to party' and his *Patriot King* was a sustained critique of party as such. Parties, he argued, were inevitably sectional, consisting of 'numbers of men associated together for certain purposes and certain interests, which are not...those of the community...'[23] 'Party is a political evil; and faction is the worst of all parties.' Hence, of course, the need for a patriot king who could see beyond party loyalties to national interests.

Now Disraeli was at least as much a party man as Bolingbroke. He owed his social as well as his political position to party and famously appealed to the principle of party allegiance to justify his assault on Peel – who had all the hallmarks of a Patriot King. Yet here Disraeli rather contradicted himself. The Whigs, he never tired of repeating, were a narrow oligarchy, at odds with the nation. But was this not, as Bolingbroke had come to see, inherent in the very concept of party? Would the Tories not become a corrupt faction if fortunate enough to secure a grip on power – as they had done in the first two decades of the 19th century? Yet Disraeli's reliance upon party was too strong for him to reject the idea *in toto*. His solution to this dilemma was to advance the idea of the landed elite as representative of the nation. A Whig party was inherently oligarchical; a Tory party founded upon the landed interest was inherently national. By this means, Disraeli slipped from the trap he had set for himself, though his escape owed, perhaps, more to dextrous reasoning than realism. In essence, Disraeli, like most great political leaders – Gladstone, Peel, Lloyd George, Churchill, Blair – *used* party, though his suppleness of mind meant that he avoided breaking with his – rather, he broke his party *against* Peel.

There were other important areas of difference between Disraeli and Bolingbroke. Bolingbroke, for instance, held a contractual theory of the state derived from Locke, something which found no place in Disraeli's more historicist thinking. Yet here, too, Bolingbroke was feeling his way towards an organic theory of the state – prefiguring, again, Disraelian one-nation Conservatism:

> The true image of a free people, governed by a Patriot King, is that of a patriarchal family, where the head and all the members are united by one common interest and animated by a common spirit.[24]

Burke

It was 'the supreme genius' Burke who provided the texture of Disraeli's Toryism, often, indeed, his very words.[25] This was notably true of the *Vindication of the English Constitution*, Disraeli's most sustained piece of political writing. The following passage gives a flavour of its Burkian qualities:

> This respect for precedent, this clinging to prescription, this reverence for antiquity, which are so often ridiculed by conceited and superficial minds and move the especial contempt of the gentlemen who admire abstract principles, appear to me to have their origin in a profound knowledge of human nature and in a fine observation of public affairs and satisfactorily account for the permanent character of our liberties. Those great men who have periodically risen to guide the helm of government in times of tumultuous and stormy exigency, knew that a state is a complicated creation of refined art…knew that if once they admitted the abstract rights of subjects, they must inevitably advance to the abstract rights of men and then the very foundations of their civil polity would sink beneath them.[26]

To enumerate all that Disraeli took from Burke would fill many pages. Let us consider the essentials.

1. The rejection of abstract reasoning as a guide to political problems. The character and function of institutions, argued Burke, could only be understood in relation to their history and evolution. Thus considered, it would be seen that society itself is an organic entity constantly in flux though remaining stable, as elements within it variously rise, fall and decay. As such, it is a permanent and binding contract between men and between the generations.

Society is indeed a contract... It is a partnership in all science; a partnership in all art; a partnership in every virtue and in all perfection. As the ends of such a partnership cannot be obtained in many generations, it becomes a partnership not only between those who are living, but between those who are living, those who are dead and those who are to be born.[27]

2. The idea that a healthy society, promoting the freedom and well-being of all its members, is an organized hierarchy compounded out of countless sub-communities. It was in their local community or workplace or recreational society that individuals found their sense of place and governed themselves and enjoyed protection.

To be attached to the sub-division, to love the little platoon we belong to in society, is the first principle (the germ, as it were) of public affections. It is the first link in the series by which we proceed towards a love of our country and to mankind.

These sub-divisions train us in the duties of citizenship, preparing us for our contribution to the life of the kingdom. As such, they are the basis of true liberty and equality.

3. Burke believed that government was a complex art and that only the landed aristocracy had the traditions of service, the long view, and education to perform it properly, though assisted by men of talent from the middle classes – such as Burke himself.

4. Constitutions and states need to change. 'A state without the means of some change is without the means of its conservation.'[28] But change must be gradual and occur within the context of established institutions. The correct principles were correction and conservation. Deficient parts of the constitution should be regenerated through the operation of parts that were not impaired. The alternative was general dissolution, which would destroy the stability essential to society's well-being and destroy, too, many institutions and customs which serve the social good.

A good patriot and a true politician, always considers how he shall make the most of the existing materials of his country. A disposition to preserve and an ability to improve, taken together, must be my standard of a statesman.[29]

These four propositions represent the essence of Burke's thinking. They represent the essence of Disraeli's too, which is a measure of the debt he owed to the 'arch-Whig trumpeter.'

Yet there were aspects of Disraeli's situation that had little troubled Burke. Most importantly, Disraeli, unlike Burke, was placed in a situation of opposition to a ruling Whig elite. It was here that Bolingbroke came in. For from *The Idea of a Patriot King*, Disraeli took over the concept of a national interest at variance with the sectional interest of the ruling party. By associating this national interest with the *landed* interest, Disraeli in effect grafted Bolingbroke onto Burke, the landed interest became not merely the class best fitted to rule but the patriot kings – the upholders of the structured self-governing communities of England and the guardians of the national interest.

Outline of Disraeli's Conservatism

The core narrative of Disraelian Conservatism was the need to unify the English nation and restore the ancient balance of its constitution, thereby ensuring that the essential character of the nation was maintained amidst the disruptive forces of the 19th century. He believed, writes Vincent, 'that conservatism and modernity could be happily reconciled.'[30] This basic assumption placed him in the 'reformist' Conservative tradition – that change was inevitable but that, correctly handled, could be used to strengthen the existing political and social structure. By the 1830s, the period of Disraeli's active entry into politics, the unity and balance of society was, he believed, under severe threat and with it, the traditional virtues of England. While the rapid economic changes of the industrial revolution had shattered old communities and ties of loyalty, producing Two Nations 'between whom there is no intercourse and no sympathy... THE RICH AND THE POOR', the 1832 Reform Act had subverted the balance of the constitution by entrusting excessive power into the hands of the industrial and commercial middle class. How were these forces of disintegration and division to be resisted? That was the question which preoccupied Disraeli throughout his career.

According to the solution at which he arrived in the 1830s and 1840s (with obvious affinities to Burke), unifying the nation did not mean standardizing it, subjecting it to a strong central government, or, in the manner of Peel, granting piecemeal reform to retain the allegiance of various interest groups. What it entailed was ensuring the correct and just balance between the different interest groups or 'estates' of England, such as the Church, the industrial middle class, the aristocracy and the working class. These vested interest groups were not to be deprecated, as in varieties of liberalism, but celebrated – they were integral to the richness of English life and the chief guarantee of freedom from oppressive government. Yet, if they were to fulfil this positive function, they had to be held in balance since no one estate could completely represent the nation. According to Disraeli, this balance had been fatally compromised by the 1832 Reform Act:

> The most striking mistake in the settlement of 1832 is that it took property as the only qualification for the exercise of political rights… There was no educational suffrage, no industrial suffrage, no attempt to increase or vary the elements of suffrage, but property alone as its basis.

The result, he observed in 1846, was a growing hegemony of the commercial middle class which, by working with sections of the Whig aristocracy, was able to dominate the other estates of the realm. Having been told that all social evils were the result of class interests, it was mortifying to discover 'that we are to be rescued from the alleged power of one class only to sink under the avowed dominion of another'.

This was bad in itself. But what made it especially so was that the Whig-capitalist elite had adopted a crude abstract philosophy through which they clothed their selfish rule. They appealed to the concepts of liberalism and Benthamism to *justify* their attacks on the historic privileges of the other estates and the 'manners and customs of the people of this country', thereby undermining the fabric of existing institutions, threatening liberty and opening the way to the domination of the country in their selfish interests. This is what Disraeli presented himself as wishing to stop. He wanted to assert the interests of the Church, defend the rights of the poor, rally to the side of the beleaguered monarch, and preserve the power and social position of the aristocracy and the House of Lords – 'the most eminent existing example of representation without election.'

So, Disraeli wanted to restore equilibrium between the estates, thereby sustaining, too, the institutions and historic liberties of England and ensuring the well-being of the whole nation, for all, including the middle class, would suffer if the fabric of English national life were eroded. There were two aspects to this restoration of an equitable and harmonious society. One was to defend the rights and privileges of the existing estates and interests. In his *Vindication of the English Constitution*, Disraeli defended (on behalf of his then mentor, Lord Lyndhurst) the constitutional position of the House of Lords against attacks upon its non-elective character by Benthamite-Whigs. In *Coningsby* and *Sybil*, he called for a restoration of monarchical authority from the subservient position it had occupied since the Whigs had brought George I from Hanover, while in those same novels he drew attention to the just claims of the poor.

The second approach was to provide an integrative ideology that would unite Englishmen and make them proud to be part of an historic nation. One way to do this was to celebrate England's glorious past of progress and liberty. Another, which increasingly came to the fore in the later stages of Disraeli's career, was to unite the country behind a sense of collective achievement in the form of the Empire. A third was to reinvigorate religion and emphasize the Christian unity of all men. The religious principle, said Disraeli, was the most powerful principle governing men. 'Man is a being born to believe,' he told a receptive audience of Dons in Oxford in 1864. It was, he continued, the equality of each man before God that was the ultimate guarantee of the moral equality and hence humanity of all men. It was this message of theocratic equality through brotherhood that was vouchsafed to Tancred by the Angel of Arabia upon Mount Sinai.[31] This will to believe, Disraeli argued, needed to be directed if it were not to give birth to 'a flitting scene of spiritual phantasmagoria', where there would be no tenets, however extravagant and no practices, however objectionable, that would not find a hearing. Hence the importance of the Divine interpretation provided for Englishmen by the Church of England. As an institution, the Church of England was of capital importance to Disraeli, whatever were his private opinions on the content of its doctrines. 'There were few great things left in England,' he recalled in 1870, 'and the Church was one of them.' It was, more than any other single institution, the skeleton that sustained the English body politic and always enjoyed his fervent support. The following remarks from a speech in Aylesbury in 1861 convey Disraeli's respect for the institution:

> By the side of the state in England there has gradually arisen a majestic corporation – wealthy, powerful, independent – with the sanctity of a long tradition, yet sympathising with authority and full of concilia-tion, even deference, to the civil power. Broadly and deeply planted in the land, mixed up with all our manners and customs, one of the main guarantees of our local government and therefore one of the prime securities of our common liberties, the Church of England is part of our history, part of our life, part of England itself.[32]

Admittedly, this speech comes from a period when Disraeli was angling for Church support. Still, the substance and language of his text was consistent with his established attitudes towards religion and social organization.

To summarize, what Disraeli stood for was a balanced, organic, society in which each component group recognized its allotted place and did not seek to exceed it and thereby encroach upon the privileges and interests of other groups. By this means, social harmony would be preserved, national would prevail over sectional interests, and the historic liberties of England, founded on self-government, would be preserved. This, for Disraeli, was the Conservative cause:

> By the Conservative cause I mean the splendour of the Crown, the lustre of the Peerage, the privileges of the Commons, the rights of the

poor. I mean that harmonious union, that magnificent concord of all interests, of all classes, on which our greatness depends.[33]

The Elements of Disraeli's Conservatism

Let us now consider the essential propositions of Disraeli's Conservatism in more detail.

1. Social complexity precludes government according to abstract principle.
For Disraeli, as for Burke, society was a complex organic entity, a 'great body corporate…a vast assemblage of human beings knit together by laws and arts and customs, by the necessities of the present and the memory of the past'.[34] Such an entity could not be understood or re-engineered on the basis of theoretical calculation. It could be comprehended only historically, in terms of its evolution and with this came an appreciation that the institutions, practices and traditions of England were ideally suited to the country's character and needs. They were the product of a long process of development, adapting to suit the practical requirements of real men, often in ways that were not immediately apparent to any given observer or generation. Where Burke had done battle with the idea of abstract rights of men, Disraeli directed his fire on the idea of the rational pursuit of social happiness. 'Nations have characters as well as individuals' and what had to be realized was that there was an English national character and the nation's institutions reflected and sustained this and they ought therefore, to be maintained unless there were strong reasons to the contrary.[35] Utilitarianism, which sought to apply a theoretic formula to government and make and remake institutions according to some 'greatest happiness' principle, failed to understand this and was guilty of an intellectual conceit. 'It would appear that this scheme originated in the fallacy of supposing that theories produce circumstances, whereas the very converse of the proposition is correct and circumstances indeed produce theories.'[36] The motives of individual men were too complex to be modelled according to some happiness-through-consumption approach and this was still truer of societies, whose conceptions of national well being had changed radically over time. To fall back upon the argument that 'when a man acts he acts from self-interest is only to announce that when a man does act, he acts… Utility, pain, power, pleasure, happiness, self-interest are all phrases to which any man may annex any meaning he pleases…'[37] Utilitarianism was thus a false guide to action which would do more harm than good, for even if the goal of societies was to maximize happiness, no individual or set of individuals would possess sufficient knowledge of the complexities of the social organism to know how to bring such a result about. The 'wisdom of our

ancestors' counted for more than the knowledge of 'our great utilitarian schoolmen...'[38]

'In a progressive country' Disraeli reflected in an important speech in Edinburgh shortly after his Reform Act triumph of 1867, 'change is constant':

> but the point is whether that change shall be caused only in deference to the manners, the customs, the laws, the traditions of the people, or whether it shall be carried in deference to abstract principles and arbitrary and general doctrines... The national system, although it may occasionally represent the prejudices of a nation, never injures the national character, while the philosophic system, though it may occasionally improve...the condition of the country...may occasion revolution and destroy states.[39]

The true statesman would build on the wisdom of the ages, not knock it over.

2. Centralization of the enemy of liberty

For Disraeli, the English were 'the freest people in Europe' and the essence of English liberty was self-government.[40] It was in local communities that men learned to govern themselves, enjoyed status and exercised their rights and duties. It was the quality and character of these communities that determined the quality and character of the people and hence of nations. A thriving and well-ordered community was based on the principle of pluralism – with power decentralized to a multiplicity of points, each sustained by venerable institutions. 'The rights and liberties of a nation,' Disraeli argued, 'can only be preserved by institutions,' and it was:

> on the maintenance of those institutions the liberties of the nation depended: that if the Crown, the Church, the House of Lords, the corporations, the magistracy, the poor laws were successfully attacked, we should fall, as once before we nearly fell, under a grinding oligarchy and inevitably be governed by a metropolis.[41]

It was this decentralized England that was under threat from the centralising Whig-middle class elite. This 'small knot of great families' had 'no object but their own aggrandizement'. They had broken the power of the king, a process beginning during the Civil War. They had sought to control the Church, a process beginning with the destruction of the monasteries. They had robbed the poor of their rights, a process symbolized by the removal of a working class electorate in the 1832 Reform Act and the subsequent introduction of the New Poor Law. They were now building a bureaucratic state which appealed to the principles of Bentham to disguise its sectional character and to the 'Divine Right of People' to justify its autocratic pretensions. Where English liberties had previously been threatened by the absolutist ambitions of monarchs, in the 19th century it was the domineering claims of the House of Commons that were the danger. As Disraeli argued in his *A Vindication of the English Constitution*, the utilitarians were 'indefatigable in promulgating the creed that the branch of our legislature hitherto styled the House of Commons is, in fact, the House of the People,' and that since *vox populi vox Dei*, then 'it is also the House of God; it is omniscient and omnipotent'. 'In such a belief I, for one, see no security for our cherished liberties; and still less a guarantee for our boasted civilization; in such a belief it seems to me the prolific seeds are deeply sown of tyranny and barbarism…'[42] It was, in fact, a mistake to say that the House of Commons was the 'voice of the people'; it was an estate of the realm representing a section of the population. As such it was important; indeed 'it may be the most important estate'. Yet, it was still only a 'privileged class' representing 'in comparison with the whole nation…only an insignificant fraction of the mass…' Like the cuckoo, the House of Commons was hungrily grasping at power, trampling upon the other estates of the realm and threatening to turf out of the nest the liberties of England.

Disraeli considered these tendencies disastrous, for they were undermining the communities that were the key to England's character and greatness. 'It is not,' warned Sidonia in *Coningsby*, 'in the increased feebleness of its institutions that I see the peril of England; it is in the decline of its character as a community'. Sometimes Disraeli spoke as if the principle of community had disappeared entirely from England – that there remained only the principle of 'aggregation'. But such a bleak diagnosis was not his natural motif. He was, by disposition, an optimist and his words and political beliefs generally implied that there remained, yet, life in the communities and institutions of England. It was, certainly, the Tory principle to oppose 'everything like central government and favouring in every way the distribution of power'.[43]

Disraeli often expressed this point in another way, in terms of a conflict between national and sectional interests. The Whig-middle class elite dominated politics and public opinion and claimed to represent democratic principles. But this did not change the fact that they were a minority advocating alien ideas. The majority of English people were opposed to their project. This national consciousness needed to be asserted. It was this that Bolingbroke had tried to do. Disraeli believed that it was the role of the Conservative party to represent the nation and interests against the Whig elite.

3. The peculiar virtues of a landed aristocracy
Bolingbroke looked to a 'Patriot King' to uphold the national interest. Disraeli often talked in such terms, but mainly for rhetorical affect. A revival of monarchical power, writes Blake, was 'quite unrealistic' and 'bore no relation

to practical politics in the 1840s'.[44] Disraeli's solution was to appeal to another force which, he believed, was co-terminate with the real English nation – the landed interest. He was quite unambiguous about the importance he attached to the constitutional role of the landed elite. 'What I wish to secure,' he told his constituents in Shrewsbury in 1843, '...is the preponderance of the landed interest.' 'I believe,' he continued, 'the landed interest should be the basis of our political and social system.' In defending this proposition, Disraeli elaborated upon and gave new meaning to Burke's contention that the landed interest had the leisure, long views and education to rule. He asked his readers to consider whether the qualities of a legislator would not:

> necessarily be found among individuals of average intelligence and high education; and whether an order of men who, from their vast possessions, have not only a great, a palpable and immediate interest in the welfare of a country, but by ease and leisure and freedom from anxiety are encouraged in the humanizing pursuits of learning and liberal love of arts; an order of men who are born honoured and taught to respect themselves by the good fame and glory of their ancestors...the question is, whether an order of men thus set apart...does not afford the choicest elements in a senate...[45]

But more than this, said Disraeli, Britain's historic constitution was a 'territorial constitution'. By this phrase he meant that the pluralism and decentralization which he considered characteristic of Britain's system of government was founded on land. It was land revenue that supported the Church and parish clergy, that funded the ancient universities and public schools, and which supported the poor through the poor rate. It was, above all, land revenue that allowed the aristocracy and gentry to devote themselves to public service as MPs, magistrates, courtiers, officers, ministers and ambassadors. Land, in other words, was the basis of the English system of government – and hence of English liberty, as Disraeli explained in 1860.

> I look round upon Europe at the present moment and I see no country of any importance in which political liberty can be said to exist. I attribute the creation and maintenance of our liberties to the influence of the land and to our tenure of land. In England there are large properties round which men can rally and that in my mind forms the only security in an old European country against that centralized form of government which has prevailed and must prevail, in every European country where there is no such counterpoise. It is our tenure of land to which we are indebted for our public liberties, because it is the tenure of land which makes local government a fact in England and which allows the great body of Englishmen to be ruled by

traditionary influence and habit, instead of being governed, as in other countries, by mere police.[46]

Thus, the landed interest needed to be sustained in its historic position as it was the foundation of the entire political fabric.

4. Solicitude for the poor

Disraeli had genuine sympathy for the common people. He knew how they suffered in the process of industrialization and urbanization. In *Sybil* he described the desperate lot of the handloom weavers, driven from their country towns into cramped urban cellars, breathing squalid air and unable to afford even the necessaries of existence, while the capitalists, with their new machines, amassed immense wealth and preached 'that the interests of Capital and Labour are identical'. He depicted, too, the 'savage rudeness' of the lives of the Midlands miners, where men, women and infants 'wet with toil and black as children of the tropics' entered the daylight at the end of hours of toil. He spoke of the metal working town of Wodgate, the 'ugliest spot in England, to which neither Nature nor Art had contributed a single charm; where a tree could not be seen, a flower was unknown; where there was neither belfry nor steeple, nor a single sight or sound that could soften the heart or humanize the mind'.[47] These deplorable circumstances to which the working people of England had been reduced were a standing indictment of governments since, as he acknowledged in his 1872 Manchester and Crystal Palace speeches, 'the health of the people was the most important subject for statesmen' as the fate of nations and empires 'will ultimately depend upon the strength and health of the population'.

Yet, more was implied by the 'condition of England' question than the hardships of the poor. For it was essential for the balance of the constitution that the interests of the poor be represented. If property had its duties as well as its rights, then 'Labour has its rights as well as its duties,' he declared in 1843. This again brought Disraeli back to the importance of institutions. 'The rich and the powerful,' he told an audience of working men in 1867, 'will not find much difficulty under any circumstance in maintaining their rights, but the privileges of the people can only be defended and secured by popular institutions.'[48] Under the plea of liberalism, the Whig elite, he argued in 1870, had 'suppressed and weakened' the institutions that were the bulwarks of the multitude and nothing had been substituted for them. 'The people were without education and, relatively to the advance of science and the comfort of the superior classes, their condition had deteriorated.'[49] The 1832 Reform Act, for instance, had withdrawn the vote from the working class in the popular boroughs and since that date there had been 'an invasion of the civil rights of the English people', most notably in the form of the New Poor Law, which replaced the right to social support administered at local level with a system of charity dictated by the central government. To this infringement of the historic rights of the poor in the cause of cheap and centralized government he attributed the Chartist movement. The poor, then, were an historic estate which had been overridden by the newly dominant commercial middle class – new men with little conception of the social duties that were the true condition for the tenure of property. The estate of the poor needed its claims to be considered and if the Conservative party and the landed aristocracy were to truly represent the national interest, they had to represent, too, the working class.[50]

What did this imply? First, Disraeli trusted the working class. He believed they were loyal and revered the traditional social order. 'I have always looked on the interests of the labouring classes,' he told a working class audience in 1867, 'as essentially the most conservative interests in the country.'[51] They were not theoretic utilitarians or atomistic liberals. They respected the monarch and looked up to the aristocracy and gentry. They were essentially deferential. They had also demonstrated, through their trades unions, friendly societies and cooperative stores, that capacity for self-organization that for Disraeli was the ultimate source of civic virtue. Since 1815, he remarked in 1860, the working classes 'have shown a remarkable talent for organization and a power of discipline and combination inferior to none'. It followed from this that Disraeli did not object, in principle, to extending the franchise to the 'people'. Indeed, he often spoke of raising the working people to the franchise to counterbalance the middle class elite. If, he reflected in the Commons in 1846, a new force were needed to maintain the ancient constitution of England, then rather than fall under the 'thraldom of capital – under those who, while they boast of their intelligence, are more proud of their wealth' – he would 'hope that we may find that power in the invigorating energies of an educated and enfranchised people'.

Yet, if Disraeli would have enfranchised sections of the working class to restore *balance* to the constitution, he had no wish to see the working class predominate within the constitution. Entrusting power to classes was no way to end the evil of class legislation. This is an important point and needs emphasis in terms of the wider context of Disraeli's political thinking. Disraeli saw the role of the House of Commons as that of representing the *nation*, of mirroring 'the mind as well as the material interests of England' and since a nation is a complex whole made up of different interest groups, these, accordingly, should find reflection in the Commons. The Commons did not represent 'the people', for this was a vague, abstract, concept which, if implemented in the form of a universal franchise, would lead the Commons to represent merely the numerically largest *section* of the nation. Hence Disraeli's lifelong advocacy of 'fancy franchises', which sought to recognize the distinctive contributions of different sets of Englishmen when allocating the right to vote. This idea of a calibrated franchise, with educational and other tests for voting, found little favour amongst politicians of the day but was, interestingly, advocated also by the Liberal philosopher John Stuart Mill, who shared Disraeli's distrust of the consequences of a mass working class franchise and belief in the virtues of a pluralistic self-governing society. Disraeli's search for a forum representative of the mind as well as material interests of the nation caused him, also, to look favourably upon the press, for in its pages the diverse interests and opinions of the entire nation found reflection, not merely the common opinions of the multitude.

Neither did Disraeli forget the limitations of the working class. They were a 'neglected democracy' who had received no education. Many, indeed, lived their lives outside the sphere of Christian civilization. Of the residents of his fictionalized town of Wodgate, he wrote that 'the people are not immoral, for immorality implies some forethought; or ignorant, for ignorance is relative; but they are animals; unconscious; their minds a blank; and their actions only the impulse of a gross or savage instinct'.[52] Disraeli did not, therefore, seek to actively advance a working class suffrage and would – if he could – have excluded the least educated sections of the poor from the vote. As a warning, he drew in 1853 a parallel with the fate of Athenian democracy after the admission to voting rights of the poor inhabitants of the port of Piraeus:

> Hence from that moment there arose the dictator and the demagogue…the flatterer and the tyrant of mobs; hence, the rapid fluctuations, greedy enterprises, the dominion of the have nots, the ruin of the fleet, the loss of the colonies…license – corruption – servitude – dissolution. Give the popular assembly of Great Britain up to the *controlling* influence of the *lowest* voters in large towns and you have brought again a Piraeus to destroy your Athens.

Pure democracy, in other words, would lead straight to the tyranny of one class – 'and that one the least enlightened'.

What, then, of that much vaunted phrase 'Tory Democracy'? Disraeli's preferred social model was one in which the landed interest took a paternalistic concern for the wellbeing of the poor. This would entail not only the traditional assistance given to the poor at local level by the rural elite, but also state intervention in the operation of the free market to restrict working hours, regulate air and water quality, improve housing, monitor food quality and so forth. These measures, resisted by doctrinaire Liberals, would bring more benefit to the working class than any measure of electoral reform and it was for the landed elite and the Tories to seize this agenda. By this means they would vindicate their moral claim to national leadership. 'The aristocracy are the natural leaders of the people,' he told the Commons in 1840, 'for they and the labouring classes form the nation.' Disraeli's popular politics, comments Smith, 'relied on trading paternalism for deference, not pledges for votes'.[53] Yet there was always a tension at the heart of such a Tory Democracy. Whilst aristocratic concern for the well-being of the local poor was an unequivocal good, this was not true of the kind of state intervention necessitated by the problems of an industrial society. For, as we have seen, Disraeli was a principled opponent of an interfering centralized state as the enemy of the institutionalized pluralism that was his core belief.[54] This tempered his social reformism in practice and meant that Disraeli never advocated an interventionist anti-*laissez faire* strategy. He was as much opposed to a big state as any classical liberal; he was never, as Vincent aptly observes, a 'manor house pink'. One solution to this dilemma was to look to local government as the engine of social reform. Another was to reach out to the minds rather than the stomachs of the poor.

5. Empire and the politics of the imagination

To harness national unity, governments needed to evoke national sentiment, to generate a sense of what has since been called an 'imagined community'. 'Imagination in the government of nations,' Disraeli reflected in 1870, 'is a quality not less important than reason.' Exalting England's great national traditions and the gorgeous symbolism of monarchy was one way to do this, though not an especially imaginative one. Disraeli made a real contribution when, in his 1872 Crystal Palace speech, he introduced into Conservatism an idea around which the nation could coalesce – the Empire.

Empire came to play a dual role in Disraeli's Conservatism. First, it reflected and underpinned British power. This was important as Disraeli's emphasis upon the distinctiveness of British national character and the attendant opposition to the introduction into domestic politics of continental ideas such as the rights of man, seemed to render him a Little Englander. Yet Disraeli, the descendent of Italian Jews, the man who had travelled in the East and imbibed the Asiatic Mystery, the man who had a continental mind, could never be entirely comfortable in the mantle of the parochial Tory squire. Empire allowed him to embrace a world politics for patriotic reasons. The England of woodlands, green fields and beamed cottages clustering around Gothic churches, was also 'the metropolis of a Colonial Empire' with interests stretching through the middle east, into Egypt, Persia, South Africa, India and beyond – the seats of once great empires that fired Disraeli's imagination. The idea of Britain as an Asiatic and world power was seductive to Disraeli and seemed to offer an escape from the inherent smallness of Britain, its cramped and marginal position. 'Our colonial empire,' he stated in 1863, 'which is the national estate that assures to every subject...as it were, a freehold and which gives to the energies and ambitions of Englishmen an inexhaustible theatre.'[55] The resources and opportunities of the Empire meant that Britain could never be little or driven by mean motives.

Second, Empire, as a glorious and exotic symbol of British power, served as an imaginative idea, which could enthuse all classes in a shared sense of achievement. Here was a new faith, a new social glue, which could bind the Two or more nations together and allow the Conservatives to appeal to the sentiments of Englishmen, as opposed to the selfish calculus of Liberal utilitarianism. 'He recognized,' observes Sichel, 'that a united empire implies a united nation; and that, as he always maintained, Parliament represents national opinion and that colonial opinion and sentiment at last formed part of it.'[56] Empire, with its myths, heroisms, colours and responsibilities, offered the prospect of a politics of vision and power, a Romantic politics that provided scope for a man of destiny and ambition like Disraeli and which transcended and thereby rendered impotent the tawdry profit and loss calculus of utilitarian liberalism. It was no accident that Disraeli prefaced his call to Empire with the allegation that the Whigs had been systematically loosening the ties of the Empire. For they had, argued Disraeli in his Crystal Palace speech, 'looked upon the colonies of England, looked even on our connection with India, as a burden upon this country, viewing everything in a financial aspect and totally passing by those moral and political considerations which make nations great and by the influence of which alone men are distinguished from animals.'

Empire, then, was the apotheosis of Disraelian Conservatism. It would be wrong to say, as do Monypenny and Buckle, that it was from Disraeli's 1872 speech that 'the modern conception of the British Empire largely took its rise'.[57] The future of Britain's relations with its colonies was already being actively discussed.[58] In an important article of 1870, the historian and early biographer of Disraeli, J.A. Froude, had argued that the colonies were a source of strength for Britain and condemned the perceived wish of the Liberal government to see them separate from the Mother Country.[59] Disraeli had himself criticized the Liberals for wanting to abrogate the Empire in 1863.[60] In 1870, Derby found Disraeli 'full of the movement now going on in favour of systematic and closer relation with the colonies...'[61] 'What was novel,' writes Smith, 'was his promoting empire to the centre of the Conservative platform which he was constructing, not only as an issue on which the Liberals seemed vulnerable, but as one which could perform a vital integrating function in providing for all classes a common symbol of national stature, a common source of national prosperity and a common object of national pride and endeavour.'[62] For a political generation, the 'spirit of the times', writes Blake, had been running with the Liberals; now 'for the first time it was giving a fair wind to the Tories'.[63] Just as the young Disraeli escaped from the limitations of his early years through his Levantine journey, so the mature Disraeli made his

rhetoric

final bid to escape the stultifying middle class politics of profit and loss, pleasure and pain, by the imaginative evocation of Empire, a sphere in which the Romantic and aristocratic virtues of adventure, service and military valour at last coalesced against the rich backdrop of eastern bazaars and Arabian camel trains, exotic religions, and grateful natives.

6. The Tory interpretation of history

Disraeli's concepts of a balanced constitution, of the shared interests of aristocracy and people, of popular Toryism and of the selfish objectives of the Whig oligarchy, provided plentiful materials for a re-interpretation of English history and he himself made a significant start upon such a project. The Whigs might possess the present; but if Disraeli had his way they would not own the future – and neither would their myths rule the past.

Disraeli took history seriously. Peter Jupp argues that he was well read in the – admittedly limited – literature available.[64] A large part of the political sections of his novels are given over to his reflections on modern English history and, as we have observed, the basic framework of his political consciousness was historicist, in that he always sought to understand contemporary events or institutions in the light of what he took to be their origins and history. Accordingly, it was of some importance to him that England's history had been seriously misrepresented and that only by dispelling 'the mysteries with which for nearly three centuries it has been the labour of party writers to involve a national history' could contemporary England be understood and its social evils remedied. These mysteries Disraeli set out to dispel and nowhere was his iconoclasm more strikingly exhibited.

> If the history of England be ever written by one who has the knowledge and the courage and both qualities are equally requisite for the undertaking, the world would be more astonished than when reading the Roman annals of Niebuhr. Generally speaking, all the great events have been distorted, most of the important causes concealed, some of the principal characters never appear and all who figure are so misunderstood and misrepresented, that the result is a complete mystification.[65]

The results of Disraeli's historical labours are generally labelled 'the Tory interpretation of history'. It first took shape in the 1820s, was extended in the *Vindication of the English Constitution* and assumed its final form in the novels of the 1840s. Thereafter, notes Jupp, it 'remained substantially the same until his death'.[66] What did this entail? Vincent remarks that Disraeli took the popular Whig interpretation of history and turned it to Tory ends.[67] Now, according to the Whig theory, English history had been characterized since the days of the *Magna Carta* by the gradual extension and deepening of civil, political and economic liberty. Bit by bit, the arbitrary powers of kings and nobles had been chipped away and Englishmen of all ranks had grown to enjoy basic freedoms – to accumulate property, to speak their minds, to be judged by their peers in accordance with the rule of law and so on. The end result was a country possessing significant liberty and this process was continuing; for example, the 1832 Reform Act had recently extended the right to vote to the propertied middle class.

Disraeli agreed with the Whigs that England was a distinctively free country and that these freedoms had accrued over centuries. 'Our free government has been the growth of ages and brooding centuries have watched over and tended its perilous birth and feeble infancy.'[68] Where he differed was in two main areas.

On the mechanism by which liberty was secured in England

As we have seen, Disraeli saw liberty as consisting in community self-government at local level. The social hierarchies of England were not at odds with individual liberty but in fact sustained it by setting up gradations of influence and power within which individuals could find protection and meaning. A crucial dimension of this pluralistic society was the balance within the constitution of the diverse 'estates' of the realm – the monarchy, aristocracy, Commons, Church and poor. The development of liberty in England implied the appropriate balance between these estates and it followed that when the Whigs saw the reduction in the power of the monarch as directly correlated with the extension of liberty, Disraeli disagreed. A monarch possessed of duties and privileges was *one* aspect of a well-balanced and healthy community. The same applied to the other estates. In other words, liberty was about balancing the interests of the various estates of England.

This had been successfully achieved in England's past, or so Disraeli implied, though he was never explicit as to *when*; probably in the reign of Henry VI, or perhaps in that of James I. Anyhow, what is important is that Disraeli believed that a period of social harmony based upon pluralism had been achieved in the past and that its central bulwark was the territorial constitution, i.e. the connection between possession of land and the discharge of political responsibilities.

On the tendencies of modern history

Where the Whigs saw the events following the Glorious Revolution of 1688 as bringing to perfection the liberties of Englishmen, with the final taming of the powers of the monarch, Disraeli saw this as a period of regression in which traditional liberties were imperilled. Since 1688, the delicate balance of the constitution had been undermined. The monarchy had lost its ancient authority and power had increasingly been concentrated amongst the great Whig aristocrats, using the Cabinet and the Commons as their instruments.

The result of the Whigs endeavours, most obvious during the reigns of the first two Hanoverian monarchs, had been to create a 'high aristocratic republic on the model of the Venetian' in which the monarch was reduced to a cipher or doge. This new governing elite had proceeded to corrupt and enervate the nation, introducing innovations such as the national debt (which allowed a small group of City financiers to get rich at the public's expense), commercial restriction and an anti-French foreign policy, and was now, in the 1830s and 1840s, consolidating its disastrous hold upon the nation with the Reform Act, the New Poor Law and the Municipal Corporations Act, deploying, in their armoury, the theoretic doctrines of utilitarian liberalism.

From this perspective then, Disraeli was able to argue that the Whigs, far from being the friends of English liberty, were its greatest enemies, as they were set upon the centralization of power in ways that ran contrary to the devolution and balance of powers that were the true guarantees of English freedom. It was, in truth, the Tories who were – or ought to be – the real friends of liberty. The country party, grounded upon the squires of England, understood the importance of local self-government, revered the Church of England, respected the monarch, opposed the machinations of commercial finance, and believed in the reciprocal exercise of rights and duties between the landed rich and the rural poor. The Tories, then, represented the majority opinion in England and would break the grip of the Whig elite, restore balance to the constitution, free the monarch to rule, and oversee the wellbeing of the poor. Of course, the Tories of the 1800s, 1810s and 1820s had signally failed to do this – but it was just this that proved they were not true Tories at all but a 'factious elite' of pseudo-Tories who had 'shuffled themselves into power by clinging to the skirts' of the last great Tory statesman – Pitt the Younger.[69] Peel had reinvigorated the Tory party in the wake of the crushing defeat of the Reform Act. He gave it a new name – the Conservative party – and a new ideology – the pragmatic reform of established institutions. But for Disraeli, this was no ideology at all, merely another formulation of the Whig-utilitarian calculus of pleasure and pain and certainly did not represent the return to 'true' Tory principles that were the only way forward for the party in an age of social disintegration and popular forces.

England's history, then, was one of liberty, but a liberty driven and sustained by processes that only true Tories (read Disraeli) understood and which only Tories (led by Disraeli) could be relied upon to sustain. Toryism, he hoped, would yet 'rise from the tomb over which Bolingbroke shed his last tear, to bring back strength to the crown, liberty to the subject and to announce that power has only one duty: to secure the social welfare of the PEOPLE'.[70] Toryism was, in other words, the popular cause of English liberty, or would be if Disraeli had his way, for the Toryism he described had never really existed. What Vincent says of Coningsby holds for Disraeli's reflections upon Toryism more generally: 'By restricting true Toryism to a definition peculiar to the author, all actual Tories were placed firmly in the wrong.'[71]

Critical Reflections on Disraeli's Conservatism

To critically analyse all Disraeli asserted would take us far beyond the parameters of this study. At one extreme, it would involve us in an assessment of Conservative thought as such; and at another, into the quirks of Disraeli's personality and the Romanticized world he constructed for himself. We shall consequently confine ourselves to such specific observations as emerge directly from the content of Disraeli's ideas and the context in which he elaborated them.

Disraeli had identified a real problem – the decline of local self-government in Britain and the corresponding rise of bureaucratic centralized government. These undeniable developments were to have considerable effects on the British national character. They were to change, indeed, the character of British national life forever. Disraeli was definitely on to something. But his diagnosis of the *causes* of this process was hopelessly misplaced. The decline of corporate self-governing Britain was a long-term trend, reflecting underlying economic and social dynamics. As regionalized economies broke down, as agriculture became ever more commercialized, as guilds decayed, as communications improved, as new industries and urban centres emerged, the old fabric of British administration was destroyed. At the same time, the rise of modern centralized bureaucracy was a trend observable across Europe and was, in fact, in only its early stages in the mid-19th century. Now one is reluctant to use the word 'inevitable' since Disraeli was a practising politician and had to operate on the principle that the future was open and amenable to personal influence. Yet, we can be fairly certain that the tendencies Disraeli perceived were due to forces far more extensive and weighty than simply the factional ambition of a Whig elite. The idea is unsustainable and, in fact, Disraeli did little to actually prove his case. What he essentially did was point to the observed tendencies to centralized government, note that they had occurred while the Whigs were in the ascendancy, and then explain the former by the latter. But the fact that, as he admitted, these forces had been underway since at least Tudor times – a key moment being the suppression of the monasteries – and that they had occurred under Tory as well as Whig governments, that they were to continue under Disraeli's own administrations, and accelerated after the last Whig had quit the scene, showed that more was involved than the selfish ambition of a handful of Whig magnates.

The second major flaw in Disraeli's thinking was his naïve conception of the landed interest. Agrarian relations in Britain would not have evolved in the way that Disraeli deplored, with the enclosures of the open fields, the dismemberment of the commons, the hiring of labour by the day, the clearances of the Highlands and the conversion of arable land into sheep runs, if landlords had always shown a selfless devotion to social duty. Unfortunately, real landlords sought to maximize rents and increase productivity and this gave them a personal interest in the very commercial forces that were eating the heart out of traditional rural life. Indeed, the question must be posed whether Disraeli himself really believed in the peculiar virtues of the landed aristocracy. *Coningsby* and *Sybil* were essentially anti-aristocratic novels, in which great territorial magnates are satirised and subject to some withering analysis. Consider a passage like the following:

> When Henry VII called his first Parliament, there were only twenty-nine temporal peers to be found and even some of them took their seats illegally, for they had been attainted. Of these twenty-nine not five remain and they, as the Howards, for example, are not Norman nobility. We owe the English peerage to three sources: the spoliation of the Church, the open and flagrant sale of honours by the elder Stuarts and the borough mongering of our own times. Those are the three main sources of the existing peerage of England and in my opinion, disgraceful ones.[72]

Well might Smith observe that in his 1840s trilogy, Disraeli questioned 'the foundations of aristocratic politics', doubting the ability of a regenerated aristocracy to renovate the nation's politics, society and faith.[73] The frailties and failures of the existing landed aristocracy caused Disraeli to call for a real governing aristocracy, an idea he probably derived from Carlyle. An aristocracy formed from 'among those men whom the nation recognizes as the most eminent for virtue, talent and property and, if you please, birth and standing in the land. They guide opinion and therefore they govern.' Now the idea of aristocracy as government by the best opens up a very different social dynamic to government by hereditary titled landlords. True, it is inegalitarian, but founded on meritocracy, with the true rulers rising to the fore by dint of talent and energy and opening the way for men like Gladstone, Peel, Burke and, of course, Disraeli. There can be little doubt that this rather cynical attitude towards the existing aristocracy was Disraeli's true opinion. He knew he was superior to them in ability; yet he knew that they would never accept him as an equal. There was much perception in Prince Albert's judgement that Disraeli was at heart a democrat with the potential to be 'one of the most dangerous men in Europe'.[74] Nevertheless, as his career progressed, this more radical conception of natural leadership fell into abeyance, partly, no doubt, as he became a country squire in his own right and the acknowledged leader of the country party – Disraeli was always open to seduction by the venerable claims of title and landed wealth. But in addition, the idea of maintaining the traditional class and landed structure of England made more political sense than a vague and rather indeterminate call for government by the brightest and best. This was a rather simplistic formula which led either, as in the case of Carlyle, to the worship of the Strong Man, or, in the case of Gladstone, to competitive civil service examinations and the rise of the technocratic class – something from which the Romantic Disraeli recoiled. Disraeli was not blind to the weaknesses and absurdities of the aristocratic classes. But ultimately, he could not avoid seeing them as too much a part of the somewhat muddled fabric of the English nation he genuinely loved. As he acknowledged at the beginning of his career, he had a taste for picturesque ruins and if he could prop them up for his lifetime he would not have been misemployed.

It is ironic, therefore, that the fabric of aristocratic England entered its period of most rapid decay when Disraeli himself became Prime Minister in the 1870s. The cause of that decay was the arrival of cheap foodstuff from the Americas and the Antipodes. Wheat, lamb, beef, dairy products, wool: all began to flood the English market, pushing down agricultural prices by up to a half, and with them the rents that had funded not only the lifestyle of the upper classes but also, as Disraeli had observed, the great institutions of England like the Church, the universities and local justice. What made this so ironic was that Peel's policy of allowing free food imports, which had had relatively little impact on prices in the 1850s and 1860s, only exerted its destructive effects on the rural economy during the premiership of Disraeli – the very man who had led Conservative resistance to Peel and who had staked so much of his political capital on the pivotal role of the landed elite. The only hope of restoring rural prosperity was to re-impose taxes on food imports (as was done, for example, in France and Germany), but Disraeli, always a lukewarm supporter of the Corn Laws and quick to declare protection damned, had no intention of taking up such an electorally damaging policy. The apostle of the territorial constitution and the country party he had come to lead proved as ready as any Whig or political economist to see British agriculture hung out to dry.

A further weakness in Disraeli's Conservative vision was the idea of Empire. It seems strange to label as a weakness that which was surely Disraeli's most distinctive political contribution – his awakening of the British to the grandeur and benefits of their empire and the harnessing of that great entity to the fortunes of the Conservative party – an association that was to yield considerable political advantages over the following thirty years. Politically, the summoning of the spirit of empire was a stroke of genius and provided, at last, an ideology that could make real the project of One Nation Conservatism. But the fact remains that imperialism as an ideology was incompatible with the rest of Disraeli's political system and with the very spirit of Englishness that he set out to preserve. It was an exotic species, entirely alien to the domestic fauna of the British Isles. What Disraeli basically stood for was a medieval hierarchical society organized along corporatist principles; a nation of country squires, deferential peasants, village schools, Cathedral closes, Oxford colleges, almshouses and patrician aristocrats. Now it was simply impossible to graft so modern and all-consuming an entity as an Empire onto this medieval stock. Little England and *Pax Britannica* were irreconcilable and the latter could only be sustained at the expense of the former. The reason for this is simple. If a nation is to build and sustain a far flung empire against the competition of other rival states and, in some instances, the wishes of the colonial peoples, then it needed to be continually at the forefront of economic, technological and social change. It needed to be a thoroughly dynamic country, for otherwise its power would ebb and with it, its imperial pretensions. Britain in the early 19th century was such a dynamic society and this was how it had been able to build up a large empire. But it was precisely this dynamism that Disraeli regretted as it had broken up traditional forms of social and political organization, created new classes, shifted people from villages into overcrowded cities and so on. It was not the hamlets of England that provided the resources for imperial expansion and defence, but the industrial cities like Manchester, Newcastle, and Glasgow, whose impact on the traditional character of England Disraeli decried. Now, if the Empire were to be sustained, the pace of internal change must continually accelerate to ensure that Britain remained the most economically advanced country. This may or may not have been possible – the evidence shows that it was not. Yet what is certain is that such economic and technological dynamism was incompatible with the structured organic society governed by traditionary influences that Disraeli loved and wished to preserve. Young America, not Young England, would be the model for the nation's future. Empire, in short, would dissolve the very social organism it was intended to unify. Disraeli did not live to see these results, but he should have foreseen them as this had been the prevalent view at the time of his entry into politics and, as Chancellor of the Exchequer, he had been a characteristic Little Englander in his attitude to defence spending. What he did do was lumber Conservatism with an exotic imperial legacy that was to prove, in the 20th century, a liability even after the Empire itself had been liquidated.

Conclusion

It is difficult not to sympathize with much of Disraeli's criticisms of the social and political tendencies of the 18th and 19th centuries. We are all too familiar with the insidious spread of bureaucracy into every area of life, the widening distance between ruler and ruled, the sense of powerlessness which the average individuals feels as they watch the political elite legislate on their behalf, implementing policies which seem to vary little whichever party wins the election. The reforming liberal elite, it seems, are always with us. As a reaction, there has been, in recent years, increased interest in communitarian approaches to political organization, with calls for decision making to be devolved to local communities, to regions, to cities, and to religious and ethnic groups. Though modern communitarians hardly make reference to Disraeli, there is no doubt that his continual advocacy of devolution of power, of pluralism within a state, and of the importance to individual well-being of active participation within small, local, communities, all make him one of the most important precursors of a decentralizing approach to politics. Blake well remarks that those seeking a lesson from Disraeli to the modern Conservative party would be best advised to look at this aspect of his philosophy.[75]

However, most commentators have, with reason, been rather less impressed with the practical alternatives Disraeli himself put forward to counter the regrettable tendencies he delineated. Blake describes his solutions as 'vague and imprecise'[76] and it is difficult not to agree. When analysed, Disraeli's programme barely appears to extend beyond the highly sentimental language in which it was expressed. Little wonder, then, that when he finally attained power in 1874, he seemed unsure what to do with it. But this, counters Vincent, is precisely the point. Disraeli's object, he contends, was to 'find an attitude rather than a policy' and that attitude was 'class peace, merging into mutual affection'.[77] Disraeli's only real social policy, he continues, is 'the achievement of an era of good feeling'. From this perspective, Disraeli almost partook of the character of his fellow novelist, Charles Dickens, seeking to unite the people of Britain through a warm sense of fellow feeling – bidding all, rich and poor, factory owner and labourer, to warm themselves by the side of a fire radiating the heat of august institutions and the warm breezes of Empire. Disraelian politics was, ultimately, a politics of sentiment and sentimentality.

There is an important sense in which this is true. Disraeli *did* want to bring people together and achieve unity in difference, and this unity, since it could not be material – for 'this is a country of classes and a country of classes it will ever remain' – had to be psychological. What he wanted to do was not so much change reality as change perceptions of reality, to awaken people to the true moral, political and spiritual significance of the world they inhabited. It was in this, rather than in the unconvincing appeals to a crumbling rural idyll, that his contribution to modern Conservatism lay. For it was in the creation and manipulation of perceptions that words, imagery, and symbolic gestures came into their own as the chief resources of the Conservative politician and who better to deploy them than the artistic genius who had almost wandered into politics in the 1830s? Deploy them he did for a period of over forty years, whether in platform speeches, as at Manchester and Crystal Palace, from the floor of the Commons, through newspapers from *The Representative* to *The Press*, in theatrical moves like the purchase of the Suez Canal shares and the proclamation of Victoria as Empress of India, or in those novels that were closest to his own inclinations. 'Political culture,' observes Vincent, 'is a question of platitudes, but they must be the right platitudes; and uttering the right platitudes requires genius.'[78] And here Disraeli did manifest that genius that he, for one, was always sure he possessed. For what Disraeli brought into existence was less a system of Conservative principles than a Conservative culture and one which proved remarkably successful and enduring.

Disraeli deeply valued the England he knew (or believed he knew) and saw that if this England were to survive, it had to be likewise revered and loved by all the English people. It was not sufficient for a minority to profit from a social system and sing its praises while leaving the majority to sift for themselves – cold, underfed, excluded. History showed that this was not sustainable. The poor would make their voices felt, if only eventually, through the ballot box. 'The palace is not safe,' he remarked, 'when the cottage is not happy.' Even before then, the fact that such a large part of the population was neglected generated a pervading sense of unease, a restlessness which meant that nothing felt truly secure, that everything became, in a sense, provisional and contingent. It was this sense of insecurity that the Whigs were able to exploit to push through measures like the Reform Act and (by the agency of Peel) the repeal of the Corn Laws.

What frustrated Disraeli was that the upper classes failed to appreciate that the poor were not a threat or an irrelevance; they were, in truth, an asset. If the landed elite would only reach out to them and cultivate them and support them, then a coalition could be formed which would secure forever the essence of England. If, by contrast, they were left abandoned and neglected, it was inevitable that they would be used by the discontented middle class reformers and cosmopolitan Whigs to give 'democratic' legitimacy for their theoretic schemes – to the detriment of the institutions and liberties of England. For under the Whigs, national unity would be sustained by the ever-strengthening agency of a centralized state. 'It is always the state and never society – always machinery and never sympathy'. Warm and friendly feelings between peoples of different classes and backgrounds, a shared and reciprocal interest in each other's affairs, and familiarity bred of regular contact, all this really would, Disraeli believed, sustain class relations, stabilize society, and ensure that diversity, inequality and social harmony would all go together.

It was to this realization that Disraeli wished to awaken the upper classes since their advantages of wealth, education, leisure and culture meant that the onus was upon them to initiate the process. The chief agency to which he looked was a widened and popularized Toryism – a spirit of Tory Democracy which, if evolved, would permanently dish the Whigs and uphold the rich, varied, multilayered and venerable character of England. As Disraeli declared in 1872, summarizing the beliefs of his career:

> The Tory party, unless it is a national party, is nothing. It is not a confederacy of nobles, it is not a democratic multitude; it is a party formed from all the numerous classes of this realm – classes alike and equal before the law, but whose different conditions and different aims give vigour and variety to our national life.

However, words were not, by themselves, sufficient, as Disraeli acknowledged when he moved from literature to politics and when he abandoned Young England for his duel with Peel. Few individuals are motivated primarily by class interests and require personal material inducements to behave in ways furthering the social good. The landed elite had few pressing reasons to concern themselves with the condition of the urban poor and exhortations from Disraeli were not going to overcome this deficiency. If this were to occur, significant economic and social engineering would be required of the kind later championed by Joseph Chamberlain at the time of his Tariff Reform campaign. But Disraeli lacked the energy, intellectual stamina, or even inclination for such an enterprise. Politically, too, he was too sagacious. When Chamberlain sought to give specific articulation to the kind of social imperialism implied in Disraeli's ideas of the 1870s, the result was electoral disaster for the Conservatives. Disraeli was a politician who, while professing an ideology, regarded it as a symbol, an ornament, a credential which, if it ever threatened to become a liability rather than an asset, was to be jettisoned. Disraeli was a politician *and* a thinker, but his thought was subservient to his political career and it was this which always came first.

Historians' Debate: Disraeli's Ideology

The question of what (if anything) Disraeli actually believed troubled contemporaries and has continued to stimulate debate amongst historians. Did Disraeli's political conduct reflect an underlying commitment to certain fixed goals, such as the maintenance of the 'aristocratic settlement' and the need to unite the nation around a 'One Nation' agenda, or was his thinking essentially tactical, reflecting an opportunistic pursuit of his own advancement?

Some writers have seen a consistent ideological theme running through Disraeli's career.

Kebbel

[Disraeli] by the force of his character and the breadth of his sympathies, had regained for the principle of authority much of that popular affection which had been gradually estranged from it; had taught the people of England that the classes which they had been educated to distrust were still worthy of their allegiance; and had awakened them at the same time to a sense of the greatness, the beneficence and the priceless national value of the Empire they had inherited from their fathers.[79]

But of the real political faith, the innermost convictions with regard to the problems of the present and the history of the past, which inspired Mr Disraeli through his long parliamentary career, he has left us the fullest and frankest exposition in the well-known trilogy comprised under the titles of *Coningsby*, *Sybil* and *Tancred*. Combining the views therein set forth…with the effect upon his mind of long practical experience in the conduct of affairs, we are able to…see that his policy, however externally different at one time from what it appeared at another, was always true in reality to the cardinal principles which he had adopted in his early manhood.[80]

Apjohn

[In the *Vindication of the English Constitution* Disraeli] indicated the notion which he subsequently elaborated in a fuller manner and which has undoubtedly been his most consistent political idea – that of a Tory democracy, the union of the landed and moneyed gentry with the aspirants for radical reforms, against what he called the Whig oligarchy…in enunciating, elaborating and making use of that idea, from his entrance into political life down to the present moment, he does merit the claim for consistency.[81]

Walton

We cannot usefully make retrospective judgements about Disraeli's sincerity. But we can [identify] enduring principles which underlay Disraeli's political behaviour… The Conservative Party was Disraeli's vehicle for restoring England to its "natural" state of aristocratic rule, responsible government and social harmony. He sought to strengthen the traditional institutions of national and local government, combining a strong monarchy with a revitalized church, a powerful House of Lords and a healthy measure of independence for local government… He saw the rule of the propertied, with due respect for the rights of the poor and due opportunity for the self-advancement of the ambitious, as the best guarantee of traditional liberties as well as of the rights of property.[82]

Jenkins

There are two respects…in which it is possible to argue that Disraeli displayed great consistency throughout his career. Firstly, there is little reason to doubt that Disraeli was consistent in his overall political objective… He sought personal glory, of course, but in doing so he dedicated himself to the preservation of the territorial aristocracy, whose traditional political leadership

Disraeli believed was both a guarantee of the rights and liberties of the people, great and small and the foundation of Britain's greatness among the nations of the world.

Second, there is a remarkable continuity in the rhetoric which Disraeli employed, from the time of his first attempts to gain entry to the House of Commons in the 1830s, right up until his death. Disraeli's essential message, invariably, was that the party to which he adhered was the 'national' party and that its mission was to thwart the sinister and pernicious designs of the opposing party. This 'national' party invariably stood for the maintenance of traditional institutions like the Crown, the Church and the House of Lords and it was resolved to uphold the empire of England, but it also wished to ameliorate (in ways usually unspecified) the condition of the people.'[83]

Others have argued that Disraeli had no consistent ideology, being driven by the pursuit of power only.

Froude
Disraeli had no personal interest in any of the great questions which divided English opinion. He owned no land; he was unconnected with trade; he had none of the hereditary prepossessions of a native Englishman. He was merely a volunteer on the side with which, as a man of intellect, he had most natural sympathy. He took a brief from the Conservatives, without remuneration in money, but trusting to win fame, if not fortune, in an occupation for which he knew he was qualified.[84]

The affectations which so strongly characterized his public appearances were but a dress deliberately assumed, to be thrown off when he left the stage like a theatrical wardrobe.[85]

Cromer
Aspiring to rise to power through the agency of the Conservatives, whose narrow-minded conventional conservatism he despised and to whose defects he was keenly alive, he wisely judged that it was a necessity, if his programme were to be executed, that the association of political power with landed possessions should be the sheet anchor of his system...'[86]

He was certainly a man of genius and he used that genius to found a political school based on extreme self-seeking opportunism.[87]

He cared, in fact, little for principles of any kind, provided the goal of his ambition could be reached. Throughout his career his main object was to rule his countrymen...[88]

Machin
He was completely without any ideological preconceptions which might have made loyal service to ideals a more compelling demand than even rising to a powerful position. To Disraeli, the prospect of gaining power was always

superior to any demand to vindicate ideals or to maintain loyalty to leaders. It is, indeed, difficult to say what ideals he had.[89]

Recently, historians have come to emphasize the way in which Disraeli used ideas as part of a politics of the imagination.

Feuchtwanger

There was something very modern or even post-modern about his preoccupation with image, his belief that rhetoric and words could construct and deconstruct reality, his courting of publicity and celebrity at all costs. Life was a game and he would play it to the full... In giving his party, through a few well-chosen phrases, the image of imperial patriotism and social concern Disraeli exercised more lasting influence than the makers of social and legislative arrangements that were soon overtaken by events and forgotten.[90]

Jenkins

The value of imagination in politics is a recurring theme in Disraeli's thought. In 1833 he wrote that 'imagination governs mankind'. His ultimate indictment of Peel was that he was without 'imagination or any inspiring qualities'. In 1870, he said that Young England had "recognized imagination in the government of nations as a quality not less important than reason." ... Through his writings... Disraeli evolved an idiosyncratic view of English history which permitted him to create a suitable political vehicle out of the Conservative party. By claiming a unique insight both into the national past...as well as into its future destiny, Disraeli was effectively asserting his right to be the leader of the people, rather like a magus or wise man.[91]

V

OPPOSITION AGAIN, 1868–1874

The prospect before Disraeli in 1868 was depressing. He was consigned again to the opposition benches, where he had spent most of the previous two decades. Across the floor sat, not the old Whig-Tory 'pantaloon' Palmerston, but Gladstone, at the peak of his powers and with a majority of over 100. Disraeli was 64 and his health was less than good. His prestige within the Conservatives had been dealt a new blow as the party suffered a mauling at the hands of the electorate he had so nonchalantly expanded. The Conservatives had not won a majority since 1841 and the slow steady advance from the ruin of 1846 seemed to have been wiped away. Disraeli might have been expected to contemplate retirement, but the thought seems barely to have crossed his mind. Having staked his abilities on the game of power, he had really nothing to retire to. To withdraw from politics would have meant giving up the stuff of life and Disraeli was not yet ready to do that. Besides, Disraeli had an oriental patience. Was the world not littered with the ruins of fallen empires? Had not Peel's majority of 1841, almost equally commanding, self-destructed within five years?

Disraeli made little attempt to resist the early force of Gladstone's reforming zeal. As he remarked to Stanley, 'I think on our part there should be, at the present, the utmost reserve and quietness'[1] and such a strategy exactly suited his own fragile health. He did speak against the disestablishment of the Irish Church, stating his belief in the union of Church and State and condemned the 'spoliation' of the Church's property as motivated by the jealousy of the other faiths. But still, the government had a majority of 114. He did not vote against Gladstone's Irish land reforms, seeking unsuccessfully to amend them in Committee, while he gave his broad support to Forster's Education Bill which created, for the first time in England, a national system of elementary education. When the Franco-Prussian war overturned the equilibrium of Europe in 1870–1871, he supported, too, the government's policy of neutrality, though he did criticize the neglect of Britain's own defences. Thus, in the first years of Gladstone's government, Disraeli adopted a policy of watchful, but not antagonistic, opposition, offering advice and pressing amendments, but avoiding explicit confrontation of the kind that might draw his opponents closer together. By 1870, he was pinning his hopes on a 'disruption' in the government ranks as Gladstone proved 'useless to the Radicals' – an event he anticipated in the next two to three years.[2]

Politically underemployed, Disraeli returned to literature and in May 1870, published *Lothair*, his first novel since 1847 and the first by a former Prime Minister. It was an immense success, the reading world being gripped by what his publishers called '*Lothair*-mania'. Sales were extensive in Britain, America and across Europe and by 1876, the novel had yielded Disraeli some £7,500.[3] The aristocratic world had lost none of its enchantment for Disraeli. Inspired by the recent conversion of the Marquis of Bute to Catholicism, the novel (set in the years 1866–1868) records the spiritual conflicts that beset Lothair, a young orphaned nobleman. Brought up in Scotland as a Presbyterian, upon his entry into Society, Lothair is courted by three powerful forces – the Catholic Church, revolutionary atheism and the Church of England – each represented by a fascinating woman, with whom the hero falls successively in love. After being almost killed while fighting alongside Garibaldi's Italian nationalists as they march on Rome, and being nursed to health by a Catholic woman, Lothair returns to England and the arms of Lady Corisande, a good Anglican woman and daughter of a Duke.

As a literary work, *Lothair* was, wrote Froude in 1890, 'immeasurably superior to anything of the kind which he had produced' for, while set against a political backdrop, it had no didactic purpose and accordingly came closer to genuine art.'[4] Yet politically, the novel did Disraeli no favours. 'How could Parliamentarians,' ask Monypenny and Buckle, 'be expected to trust an ex-Premier who…instead of occupying his leisure time…in classical, historical, or constitutional studies, produced a gaudy romance of the peerage, so written as to make it almost impossible to say how much was ironical or satirical and how much soberly intended?' For more conventional Conservatives, *Lothair* only 'revived all the former doubts as to whether a Jewish literary man, so dowered with imagination and so unconventional in his outlook, was the proper person to lead a Conservative party to victory'.[5]

Indeed, throughout the years 1868–1872, Disraeli's place as Conservative leader was far from secure. He had never commanded the respect or affection of his party. Everyone acknowledged his talent, but talent to what end? Most would have been inclined to say to his own, rather than the party's, advancement. Certainly, the party had little to show for his long years as leader in the Commons and his one signal triumph, the Reform Act of 1867, had apparently left the Conservatives in a position as bad as that to which he had helped bring them in 1846. For two decades, the sheltering presence of Lord

Derby had kept Disraeli at the forefront of the party. But with Derby now having quit the scene, was it not time for Disraeli to do the same? His most articulate critic was Lord Salisbury, who had left the Cabinet in opposition to the Reform Bill, which he had, with apparent prescience, dubbed an act of parliamentary suicide. Salisbury's view of Disraeli was about as low as it could be. He was, he said, a 'mere political gamester', an 'adventurer without principles and honesty'. 'And in an age of singularly reckless statesman, he is I think beyond question the one who is least restrained by fear or scruple.' Given such opinions, it was close to humiliating for Disraeli when, in 1869, the Conservative peers seriously considered appointing Salisbury to lead them in the Lords. This Disraeli could not countenance, writing to Lord Cairns:

> The leader in the Lords must be one who shares my entire confidence and must act in complete concert with myself. I do not know that Lord Salisbury and myself are even on speaking terms.[6]

Fortunately for Disraeli, Salisbury withdrew himself from the running. The following year, he declined the leadership again, though pointedly emphasising that 'he was not to be reckoned with as a follower of Disraeli'.[7]

Yet pressure on Disraeli's leadership did not abate. Besides the impact of *Lothair*, there was general disquiet at his relaxed approach to opposition, his willingness to await events rather than take the initiative in attacking the government. Even supporters, like Lord Cairns, began to feel the party might be served if Disraeli made way for his aristocratic friend Lord Stanley, who had recently succeeded his father as the fifteenth Earl Derby. Wealthy, accomplished, respectable and predictably moderate (and already having been offered the throne of Greece), he was a leader who could attract the middle class and Whig support that the party needed. Disraeli's own Chief Whip speculated that Derby's appointment could deliver 40 or 50 seats to the Conservatives. Why could Disraeli not serve under Derby as he had done his father, leading the party in the Commons while Derby sat in the Lords?[8] Yet such plots faced a substantial obstacle. Derby was Disraeli's closest political friend and there is no evidence that he was tempted to challenge for the leadership; he refused, even, the Tory leadership in the House of Lords. Subsequent events were to confirm Derby's own doubts concerning his capacity for leadership.

But Derby was not Disraeli's greatest asset – that, says Vincent, was Gladstone. Gladstone's position in 1868 seemed unassailable. He was leading a talented Liberal administration that combined the best traditions of Whig-Liberal reformism and Peelite efficiency and was committed to a programme of much needed modernising reform. With a majority of over 100, his government seemed set for a period of parliamentary hegemony and there was little Disraeli could do but wait for the political constellation to shift in his favour. It has to be said that Disraeli did little to bring this about, confirming the impression he had given since the 1860s of having run out of ideas as opposition leader – not to say energy, being often absent from the House owing to ill-health. Fortunately, Gladstone did most of the work for him. Just as his mentor Peel had broken up the Tory majority in the 1840s by pushing ahead of his party with his reform agenda, so did Gladstone's reforms gradually reveal the fissures that underlay his apparently imposing majority. The Liberal party showed itself to be the coalition of Whigs, Radicals, Anglicans, non-conformists, Liberals and Irish MPs that it was and Gladstone was unable to keep his party together. Tempers frayed, legislation was lost and majorities fell. This was the situation Disraeli revelled in and he played his part in exacerbating Liberal divisions, though all the while careful not to provide Gladstone with a pretext for uniting his party in opposition to a Conservative threat. By 1871, Gladstone's government was in trouble and Disraeli, now seeing that power might, after all, be 'again within his reach', bestirred himself and demonstrated there was life, yet, in his Conservative vision. During 1871, he made a series of effective attacks on Gladstone's government in the Commons. More significantly, in 1872, he took the Conservative case to the country. Unlike Gladstone, Disraeli made very few speeches to large crowds or outside his own constituency. Yet during 1872, he did so on two occasions to considerable effect.

The first occurred in Manchester in April 1872. Lancashire was a Conservative county, the party winning all the County seats in 1868. More significantly, it was the one true stronghold of 'borough Conservatism', the Conservatives accounting for 24 of the 36 borough seats in the area. Here, at least, the Tory working man was a reality and Gorst, the party organizer, was keen for Disraeli to visit the region. On 3 April 1872, he addressed to a rally of Lancashire Conservatives a speech of three-and-a-quarter hours, consuming, in the process, two bottles of brandy and by the end of which speaker and audience were in a state of exhaustion. To the student of Disraeli's political thought, this speech contains nothing new. The breakdown of the contents of the speech, given in Table 2, is instructive.

In many ways, it was a reversion to the arguments of the 1830s and 1840s. 'What was the Conservative programme?' – to maintain the constitution of Britain, which was itself the embodiment of the experience of the race. As in the 1830s, he singled out the monarchy, House of Lords and Church of England as central to the constitution. In the 1830s, he had raised the spectre of a Whig oligarchy dismantling these institutions in the interests of their

Table 2: Content breakdown of Disraeli's speech

Subject	Share of Speech (%)
Defence of the Monarchy	20
Defence of House of Lords	15
Justification of 1867 Reform Act	2
Defence of Establishment of Church of England	9
Criticism of Gladstone's Radicalism	2
Improved condition of the people	14
Social Reform	4
Ireland	4
Criticism of Gladstone's army and Navy reforms	4
Criticism of Gladstone's restless Domestic Policy	1.7
Foreign Policy	16
Other material	8.3

own aggrandizement. Now it was the left-wing of Gladstone's Commons majority which was pushing him towards the same end. The Venetian oligarchy had given way to progressive radicalism, but the result was the same. Britain's long-matured institutions, so essential to its prosperity and liberties, were in danger. The speech is best remembered for Disraeli's reference to the importance of social reform, but his remarks on this subject were both limited and ambiguous. Yes, he did devote four per cent of his speech to the theme of sanitary reform. But prior to this, he spent 14 per cent of his time celebrating the improved condition of the working man since the 1840s:

> I take the period 1832–1872 and ask what the working classes have realized in this time? Immense results. Their progress has not in any way been inferior to that of any other class…their wages have been raised and their hours of daily toil have been diminished – the means of leisure, which is the great source of civilization, have been increased.[9]

The condition of the Lancashire working class in 1870 was worlds apart from that in 1840. The debates over the 'condition of England question' were a mere memory. Receding into the past with them, Disraeli implied, were the remedies of Young England. Sanitary reform was a response, not to a social system in crisis, but to issues arising from the supply of public goods in an expanding economy. While some state intervention in the market system would be required, the problems motivating this intervention were radically different from those of the 'Hungry Forties'.

> Gentlemen, I think public attention as regards these [social] matters ought to be concentrated upon sanitary legislation. That is a wide subject and, if properly treated, comprises almost every consideration which has a just claim upon legislative interference. Pure air, pure water, the inspection of unhealthy habitations, the adulteration of food, these and many kindred matters may be legitimately dealt with by the Legislature... After all, the first consideration of a Minister should be the health of the people.[10]

This was as far as Disraeli went in setting down the programme of a Conservative government. Like most 19th century politicians, he had neither the inclination nor the bureaucratic resources to develop a detailed programme in opposition. That social reform was the one area of future legislation he canvassed gives to it some significance, though this was to become more apparent later than it was at the time.

Having outlined in general and typically vague terms the Conservative policy, he turned to a critique of Gladstone's government which, he argued, had been constructed on the principle of disruptive change for change's sake. 'Not satiated with the spoliation and anarchy of Ireland, they began to attack every institution and every interest, every class and every calling in the country.' But such destructive energy exacted a toll, which Disraeli satirised in a famous simile:

> As time advanced it was not difficult to perceive that extravagance was being substituted for energy by the Government. The unnatural stimulus was subsiding. Their paroxysms ended in prostration. Some took refuge in melancholy and their eminent chief [Gladstone] alternated between a menace and a sigh. As I sat opposite the Treasury Bench the Ministers reminded me of one of those marine landscapes not very uncommon on the coasts of South America. You behold a range of exhausted volcanoes. Not a flame flickers on a single pallid crest. But the situation is still dangerous. There are occasional earthquakes and ever and anon the dark rumbling of the sea.[11]

On 24 June 1872, he followed up this speech with another, still more important, to the new National Union of Conservative Associations at London's Crystal Palace. Here, notes Blake, he returned to his familiar theme that whereas the Liberals were a party of 'continental' or 'cosmopolitan' ideas, it was the Conservatives who were the truly 'national', patriotic party and as such appealed to the true sentiments of the working class. They appreciated the importance of social reform for the working class, but they also realized that the working man was not interested in social issues alone. He was a natural conservative:

> The working class are proud of belonging to a great country and wish to maintain its greatness – that they are proud of belonging to an Imperial country and are resolved to maintain, if they can, their empire – that they believe on the whole that the greatness and the empire of England are to be attributed to the ancient institutions of the land.

For the last forty years, Disraeli contended, the Liberals had been working systematically to denigrate the British Empire and effect its disintegration. While it was right to grant self-government to the settler colonies, this should have taken place within the context of a 'great policy of Imperial consolidation'. It ought to have been accompanied by an 'Imperial tariff', a military code regulating colonial defence, and the introduction of 'some representative council in the metropolis' which would have brought the colonies into closer relations with the home government.[12] However, the Liberals' disintegrationist agenda had not prevailed owing to the loyalty of the colonies to the Mother Country and 'no Minister in this country will do his duty who neglects any opportunity of reconstructing as much as possible our Colonial Empire and of responding to those distant sympathies which may yet become the source of incalculable strength and happiness to this land'.[13]

Taken together, the Manchester and Crystal Palace speeches were of vital importance for Disraeli's career and the evolution of Conservatism. For Disraeli had finally succeeded in grafting his own set of ideas, which had always been viewed with wariness by traditional Tories, onto the stock root of mainstream Conservatism and in so doing, had at last provided the Conservative party with a coherent and comprehensive ideology, almost, one might say, for the first time in its history and certainly since the Peelite debacle of the 1840s. The Conservatives, on Disraeli's account, were the party of the national interest, for they upheld the institutions essential to liberty and prosperity, advocated social reform in the interests of the working class, and celebrated the British Empire, at once the symbol and guarantor of British national greatness. With these speeches, Disraeli simultaneously squashed any remaining doubts within the party concerning his fitness to lead the Conservatives and increased the pressure on Gladstone's faltering government.

Yet if 1872 was a year of political success for Disraeli, personally it was one of sadness for, in December, his wife Mary Anne died. With her death he lost his closest friend of 33 years. More prosaically, he also lost his Grosvenor Gate home (which his wife had inherited from her first husband for her lifetime only) and £5,000 pa. Above all, he lost the feminine companionship that was so central to his existence. 'I owe everything to woman' he had once remarked. 'A female friend, amiable, clever and devoted, is a possession more valuable than parks and palaces; and without such a muse, few men can succeed in life, none be content.' Soon Disraeli found a new outlet for his romantic ardour in two sisters, whom he had known since the 1830s – the Ladies Bradford and Chesterfield. He proposed (unsuccessfully) to the latter, but it was to the married Lady Bradford to whom he was most devoted, writing to her, even when Prime Minister, two or three times a day. 'Your letters to me are like manna in the wilderness: when I think how little I see of the person I most think of, it makes me not only sad, but sometimes savage.'[14] As he lamented in 1874: 'I am certain there is no greater misfortune, than to have a heart that will not grow old.'

By 1873, Gladstone's government was increasingly beset by accidents, scandals and internal dissension. The Liberal majority began to weaken until on 12 March 1873, a Bill to establish a University of Ireland at Dublin to which Catholic colleges could affiliate was narrowly defeated by a combination of Conservatives, Irish Catholics and dissident Liberals. Gladstone, treating it as a vote of confidence, resigned and Victoria invited Disraeli to form a government. It was a repeat of the many previous occasions when Liberal governments had gradually subsided amidst the fracturing of their initial majority, the Conservatives stepping forward to form a short-lived administration, only to be replaced by a rejuvenated Liberal party at the next election. But there was this crucial difference in 1873 – Disraeli replied to the Queen that he was unable to undertake to form a government in the present parliament and that 'Mr Gladstone ought to remain in and continue to carry on the government.' Why did Disraeli turn down office when offered it? Besides his general distaste for the idea of forming yet another minority government, he saw that the Conservatives would only benefit if Gladstone were forced to return. Gladstone's government was weakening, divided and increasingly ineffectual. The current of public opinion was running towards the Conservatives. In 1871, the Liberals lost six by-elections; in 1872, they lost seven. If the Conservatives assumed office, they would have to deal with all the problems left by Gladstone, who would be left free to rally his forces against the government. Better, by far, to leave Gladstone in the uncomfortable bed he had made for himself.

Disraeli's forbearance before the temptations of office was one of the great strategic decisions of his career. As Gladstone's government was forced to resume office, its difficulties increased and its reputation and popularity fell still further. 'The firm is insolvent,' reflected Disraeli, 'and will soon be bankrupt.' The stock-taking occurred quicker than anticipated. In January 1874, Gladstone unexpectedly dissolved Parliament and called a general election, promising that, if re-elected, he would abolish income tax. It was a bold move but did him little good. Though Disraeli expected a finely balanced parliament, the election was, in fact, a Conservative triumph:

> Conservatives 350
> Liberals 245
> Irish Home Rulers 57

The Conservatives had broken through the 300 barrier and had an overall majority of 48, their majority of 110 in England being partially offset by Liberal majorities in Scotland and Wales. They had a big majority over the Liberals in the County seats, while in the 114 large Boroughs with populations over 50,000, their share of the seats rose from 25 to 44.[15] How far did Disraeli contribute to this dramatic reversal of fortunes? It is generally said, with much truth, that it was Gladstone who lost the 1874 election rather than Disraeli who won it. For Gladstone's reform programme had, over time, antagonized one after another of the powerful interest groups and institutions of the country, including the Church of England, the armed forces and the brewers. Yet he had also alienated key sections of his own support, notably the religious Nonconformists and the trade unions. Gladstone, undoubtedly, was the chief architect of his own demise.

Still, Disraeli's personal role was not inconsiderable and made itself felt in two main areas. First, while Gladstone had antagonized different interest groups, it was Disraeli who seized upon this fact and generalized it into an indictment of Gladstone's whole system of administration. In a much reported pronouncement of 1873, he described how:

> For nearly five years the present Ministers have harassed every trade, worried every profession and assailed or menaced every class, institution and species of property in the country. Occasionally they have varied this state of civil warfare by perpetrating some job which outraged public opinion, or by stumbling into mistakes which have been always discreditable and sometimes ruinous. All this they call a policy and seem quite proud of it; but the country has, I think, made up its mind to close this career of plundering and blundering.[16]

It was these disruptive and dangerous tendencies of Gladstone and his more radical supporters that provided the substance of Disraeli's election 'manifesto'. He repeated his allegation that no British institution was safe if the Liberals were returned, and called upon the electorate to return him with a majority to resist every proposal that might impair the nation's strength or weaken 'her imperial sway'. Ironically, Disraeli was now, comments Blake, 'playing the role of Peel in the 1830s, a rallying point for the forces of property disturbed at excessive innovation though ready to accept the need for cautious piecemeal reform'.[17]

Second, while the Liberals had neglected their party organization, the Conservatives, under Disraeli's direction, had greatly improved theirs. With the new popular electorate created by the 1867 Reform Act, Disraeli realized that a more sophisticated party organization would be required in the future. To this end, he appointed in 1870, the talented Conservative barrister John Gorst chief election agent and placed him in charge of a new Conservative Central Office. The formation of local Conservative Associations was promoted, these in turn being organized into a Conservative National Union. Each association was encouraged to select a candidate from an approved central register well before the election was called. Where, in 1868, the Conservatives had failed to contest 213 Liberal seats, in 1874, this number had fallen to 150. Although Gorst was chiefly responsible for energizing the system of party organization, it was Disraeli who appointed and directed him and monitored progress. It was Disraeli who put the National Union 'on the map' with speeches arranged through its auspices at Manchester and Crystal Palace.[18] Thus, write Monypenny and Buckle, during the years of opposition 'when he appeared to colleagues and followers to be apathetic, he had been quietly…creating a machine which was to lead the party to the victory of 1874 and to be the forerunner of the great party organizations of today'.[19]

Thus, while Gladstone, through his controversial Liberal leadership, had provided the Conservatives with their opportunity in 1874, it was Disraeli who, by his patience, his decision not to take office in 1873, his enunciation of an alternative Conservative vision, his characterization of the government as one of restless plundering, and his behind-the-scenes work to build up a formidable party organization, who ensured that the Conservatives were in a position to exploit the Liberal's gathering unpopularity.

Historians' Debate: **Did Disraeli win the 1874 election – or did Gladstone lose it?**

How far was Disraeli, and the improved party organization he initiated, responsible for the Conservative election victory of 1874? The general view of historians has been that Disraeli's Conservatives were the largely passive beneficiaries of a reaction against Gladstone's reformism and Liberal divisions.

Blake

Often after a period of strenuous reform a moment arrives quite suddenly when the British people tires of being improved. The winter of 1873–1874 was just such an occasion.[20]

Machin
In the election the Conservatives benefited more from Liberal disharmony than from any positive policies of their own. Disraeli's lofty expressions in his speeches of 1872 had not been translated into any definite, detailed intentions. His election manifesto was fairly unconstructive.[21]

Jenkins
One explanation that is frequently offered for the remarkable Conservative triumph in 1874 is that it was largely attributable to the improved state of the party's organization in the constituencies. This was allegedly due to the efforts of J.E. Gorst, who was appointed as Principal Agent by Disraeli in 1870. Some scepticism has recently been expressed by historians, however, concerning the significance of Gorst's contribution to the victory... The most one can say is that Gorst had worked hard to build up the electoral organization in the larger boroughs and that the Conservatives did relatively well in those constituencies – but one cannot simply assume that *ergo* it was Gorst's machinery that delivered the gains.[22]

Coleman
The dominant mood in 1874 was a widespread desire for stability and normality after the strains and stresses of Liberal rule. Liberal disintegration was far more in evidence than Tory resurgence and in many constituencies it was the fall or division of the Liberal vote since 1868, not any surge of the Tory vote, that led to seats changing hands.[23]

However, several writers argue that it was not enough that the Liberals be divided. It was Disraeli's achievement that the Conservatives could take advantage of Liberal weakness.

Kebbel
The people had begun to recognize...that under all the objectionable policy attributed to Toryism...there lay a fund of national sentiment and loyalty to English ideas not equally discernible in their rivals. Great revulsions of popular feeling are seldom attributable to specific grievances. These may fire the train, but more general causes must have laid it.[24]

Walton
Gorst and the new Conservative Central Office probably played a significant part in the 1874 election victory...'[25]

Marriott
His success in 1874 was due, primarily perhaps, to the blunders, unpopularity and internal dissensions of his opponents. But not wholly. It was due partly to a gradual inclination of the mind and instinct of the electorate towards the objects for which modern Conservatism was to stand. Those objects had been in the last few years clearly re-stated and defined by the leader who was

now, in the late evening of his days, to reap the tardy reward of patience and sagacity... The Manchester speech...followed by one at the Crystal Palace...may be said to have defined the principles of the New Toryism and to have prepared the way for the victory at the Polls in 1874.[26]

Jenkins

There can be little doubt that the key to explaining the Conservatives' electoral breakthrough is to be found in the drift towards Conservatism on the part of the middle classes... All these groups may well have found much to approve of in Disraeli's rhetoric about upholding the ancient institutions of the country and maintaining Britain's imperial strength and perhaps a little sanitary reform would not necessarily have been considered a bad thing. Disraeli is therefore reasonably entitled to receive credit for having created his own brand of 'Conservatism' by the 1870s...[27]

VI

PRIME MINISTER, 1874–1880:
DOMESTIC POLICY

Disraeli's Second Ministry (1874–1880) was the first Conservative government with a clear majority since Peel. Its election represented a triumph for Disraeli, though the risk of anti-climax was correspondingly all the more real. Now 69 years old and frequently ill, it was not even clear he could continue. Yet continue he did for six years. The resultant ministry has been a source of great controversy, the issue essentially resolving itself into whether it can be seen as representing a distinctively Disraelian brand of Conservatism, or whether its policies and legislation were a pragmatic response to events, owing little to any underlying Conservative ideology. Behind this question lies another still more fundamental one – was Disraeli a conviction politician, with a political philosophy that guided his actions over the long sweep of his career, or was he, as critics alleged, an opportunist, whose chief principle was his own advancement?

By the early 1870s, Disraelian Conservatism had apparently formed itself into three main elements. First, the use of social reform to regulate the *laissez faire* economy to improve the condition of the people and bind sections of the new working class electorate to the Conservative party; second, the use of government to strengthen Britain's established institutions of church and state in the belief that these institutions, far from being the inefficient bastions of privilege and maladministration, were the key to the nation's well-being and liberties; third, the assertion of British power and interests on the international stage and the pursuit of measures to consolidate and celebrate the British Empire. Thus stated, Disraeli had a reasonably clear vision of what he wished to achieve, finally implementing the ideas he had been advocating since his attack on Peel in the 1840s or even earlier. This conception was articulated by Monypenny and

Buckle and has since received influential support from Paul Smith, who writes that:

> The years from 1874 saw the application to opportunity of the idea of conserving British institutions and the British empire by the action of a national party, integrative in its composition, its conduct and its creed, which he had been preaching all his life.'[1]

Yet these perspectives have been subject to much critical analysis since the 1960s, the picture emerging being one of a tired and ill premier who followed the hand-to-mouth tactics of expediency he had perfected in opposition, left the details and initiative to others, who, in Vincent's words, 'did nothing in particular and did it moderately well', and whose real legacy was to make the Conservatives a safe refuge for members of the propertied classes alienated by Gladstone's growing radicalism.

The Government

Disraeli's government was highly regarded in terms of ability. The appointment of Lord Derby, the son of the former leader and Disraeli's friend since the 1830s, as Foreign Secretary was a natural one – though not, in the end, happy in its results. More successful was Stafford Northcote's tenure as Chancellor of the Exchequer. Northcote, a modest, undemonstrative man, had a strong financial background – a former President of the Board of Trade, he had worked with Peel and Gladstone in the 1840s and had even written a standard text on *Financial Policy*.[2] Disraeli was to describe him as 'my right hand, my most trusted counsellor'. The Home Secretary was Richard Cross, a lawyer and banker who had never held office before and whose appointment was considered a bold experiment. However, he represented the important Conservative county of Lancashire, enjoyed the backing of Derby, and proved an effective administrator. Gathorne Hardy, one of the few Conservatives who was a strong orator, was appointed War Secretary, while Lord Salisbury, once Disraeli's most articulate critic but a man of considerable ability and weight within the Conservative party, agreed to become Secretary of State for India – so drawing, notes Blake, the sting from the party's Right.[3] The most sentimental appointment was that of Lord John Manners, the former soul of Young England, to the undemanding post of Postmaster General. Overall, the Cabinet was cohesive until fissures opened over the question of near-Eastern policy in the years 1876–1878. Yet Disraeli never had the problem of maintaining party unity amidst the kind of centrifugal tendencies that beset Gladstone. His government was one of few in the 19th century to run nearly to the limit of its natural term.

Unfortunately, given Disraeli's long, eventful and sometimes inspired rise to power, one is inclined to be disappointed by what he actually did with it. Richard Cross, the new Home Secretary, recorded his impressions:

> From all his speeches I had quite expected that his mind was full of legislative schemes, but such did not prove to be the case; on the contrary he had to entirely rely on the suggestions of his colleagues and, as they themselves had only just come in to office and that suddenly, there was some difficulty in framing the Queen's speech.[4]

Readers of the debate on the Queen's speech, wrote a Liberal journalist in 1880, 'must have been astonished to find that the men they had elected to save the country from the destructive policy of the Liberal ministry, had…no other policy to substitute for theirs'.[5]

There were several reasons for this:

1. Disraeli had never possessed the restless drive and energy of a Palmerston or Gladstone. His constitution had always been more delicate and by 1874, he was suffering from gout, asthma and bronchial trouble. 'Power! It has come to me too late,' he lamented. 'There were days when, on waking, I felt I could move dynasties and governments; but that has passed away.'[6] For most of his time in office, he was afflicted by pain and disability and there were numerous occasions in which he was unable to take his seat in the Commons, eventually being forced to quit that scene for the less demanding benches of the House of Lords (assuming in the process the title of Earl of Beaconsfield).

2. Disraeli did not possess a 'legislative' or 'administrative' mind. He was the opposite of Peel. His talent says Blake was in the sphere of imagination, ideas and presentation. He never applied himself to the mastery of detail necessary for the implementation of practical legislation. The chaos surrounding his greatest legislative achievement – the 1867 Reform Act – testifies to that. As Bagehot observed: 'The solid part of his mind – the part fit for regulating bills and clauses – is as inferior to that of an ordinary man of decent ability as the light and imaginative part is supreme…'[7] He saw his job as that of setting the tone for his administration, leaving it to Ministers to formulate concrete measures.

3. The idea that governments took office with a fully elaborated programme of legislation which they then proceeded to implement was alien to the 19th century. Gladstone's 1868 government was an exception to this rule. The whole point of Disraeli's criticism of Gladstone was that he had reformed and interfered too much. 'As to our own policy,' he commented the year before taking office, 'it is to uphold the institutions of the country and to arrest that course of feverish criticism and unnecessary change, too long in vogue.'[8]

Still, Disraeli's government accomplished much. We shall, in the light of Disraeli's articulated programme, consider its achievements in three areas – social reform, support for established institutions and foreign and imperial policy.

Social Reform

In 1874, the moment was right, says Smith, for the pursuit of the uncontentious social improvement which the Conservatives represented as being blocked by Gladstone's disruptive 'violence'.[9] Gladstone had won the working class vote and used it to reform the institutions of the country and tackle the problem of Ireland. Neither issue, Disraeli believed, was of much interest to the working class. What they really wanted were measures to enhance the quality of their lives, such as improved sanitation, better accommodation, regulation of factory conditions, and the right to organize trade unions. As Disraeli remarked in response to a Liberal motion to extend the county franchise in 1874, 'when the disposition of the country is favourable, beyond any preceding time that I can recall, to a successful consideration of the social wants of the great body of the people, I think it would be most unwise to encourage this fever for organic change'.[10] Social reform was to be used as a block to further constitutional upheaval and a means of outbidding Gladstone in securing working class support.

However, Disraeli had little room for manoeuvre. There were two sets of constraints. First, economic; the mid-Victorian economic boom had begun to give way to the Great Depression, putting downward pressure on government revenues and increasing resistance to the idea of paying more tax and especially local property taxes, the level of which formed, said Northcote in 1874, 'the object of the highest national interest at the present time'.[11] Where total government revenue had grown at £2.5 million each year between 1869 and 1873, between 1873 and 1877 the annual growth was only £1.5 million.[12] By 1876, the government's budget was heading into deficit and Northcote was forced to raise income tax. In 1878, the government's income actually fell. Fiscal considerations alone virtually ruled out an extensive social programme driven from the centre. Second, ideological; there was a strong bias within Victorian politics and culture against measures of social reform. As Ghosh points out, the concept of social reform was a novelty in the 1870s. It was a necessary but inferior activity, complicated but unglamorous and not a proper area for controversy. If pushed beyond consensus, it soon fell foul of a number of taboos. It took responsibility away from individuals and undermined self-help; it would discriminate against the (virtuous) propertied on behalf of the (less virtuous) propertyless. These were not things that the Conservative party, representing substantial property owners, was for.

Disraeli had done something to relax the ideological restraint by his decision to flag-up social reform as a Conservative policy in the lead up to the election – presenting it as a distinctly Conservative measure which would deflect interest from institutional and electoral reform and win working class support for the Conservatives. Of course, it was all rather little and rather late. In the 1840s, he had done far more to raise a social reform agenda, but had been short on specifics and had, in any case, let the matter drop in the 1850s and 1860s. The economic restraint was partly of his making. For many years, he had championed the cause of the over-burdened local tax payer. Here, at least, he moved quickly to shift the parameters. In the government's first budget in 1874, the problem of 'excessive' local taxation was resolved by increased Treasury grants to local authorities to assist them in the funding of 'national' services such as lunatic asylums, prisons and the police. The Liberals had planned a similar move, but in the context of a reform of local government that was never carried. Exchequer grants to local authorities doubled from £2.7 million in 1874 to £5.7 million in 1878. This was an essential first step to greater social reform activity, which would have to be organized at local level. It began the process of shifting the burden of social welfare spending from landed proprietors to the body of taxpayers as a whole.

The great year for social reform was 1875, with nine important bills helping to fill an otherwise rather empty parliamentary timetable. Disraeli had little to do with the details of these measures, which were the work, chiefly, of the Home Secretary and the Chancellor of the Exchequer. But, as Ghosh emphasizes, he set the reform agenda in his 1872 speeches, pledged his government to legislation in his 1874 Mansion House speech, and oversaw delivery in this area during the 1875 session.[13]

Social Reform Measures

Public Health Act of 1875

This Act consolidated and rationalized the existing patchwork of health legislation, of which the Liberals' incomplete 1872 Health Act was most significant. The Act was largely the work of Richard Cross. It set down the compulsory duties of local authorities to ensure sewage, drainage and water supply; remove nuisances; regulate offensive trades; and deal with contaminated food. (A Rivers Pollution Act the following year prohibited the release of poisonous waste into rivers). Cases of infectious disease were to be notified to the Medical Officer. This Act has been described as 'one of the greatest pieces of legislation in the 19th century'. However, the Act was not innovative in that it built on the investigations and recommendations of Royal Commissions. Enforcement remained a problem since there was a marked reluctance to infringe upon the interests of property owners. For example, the river pollution measure failed to define pollution or provide ways of punishing polluters.

Artisans' Dwellings Act of 1875

This Act was also the work of Cross and it enabled urban local authorities to impose the compulsory purchase of unhealthy slums and oversee their replacement with planned housing for the working class. This activity was to be financed by government loans at low interest, although actual building was to be by the private sector. Disraeli believed this would be a 'very popular and beneficial measure' and called it 'our chief measure'.[14] Its symbolic importance was certainly considerable for it asserted that, in certain circumstances, the rights of the poor to a healthy living environment took precedence over the right of property owners to do what they wished with their own. Its practical consequences were less impressive. It did not compel local authorities to take action; rather, it gave them the power to do so. By 1881, only 10 of the 87 towns to which it applied had made any use of its provisions. It was hedged around by restrictions and was expensive to implement. In practice, it made little difference to the life of slum dwellers. It was far from being a major new departure.

Merchant Shipping Act of 1876

The Merchant Shipping Act was a response to the problem of shipping companies overloading their ships, especially old ships for which, if they sank, they could collect the insurance money. A Royal Commission investigated the matter in 1873, and in 1875 the government brought forward a Bill – but then abandoned it due to pressure of parliamentary time. The Liberal MP Samuel Plimsoll, who was the chief advocate of the measure, was furious and it was his pressure that was mainly responsible for the Bill making its way to the statute book. The result was the 'Plimsoll line', a line painted on the side of every ship to show the maximum loading point. However, the Act allowed the ship owners to decide where to draw the line! The government was reluctant to infringe the economic orthodoxy which left the negotiation of working conditions to the 'free' contract between employer and employee.

Food and Drugs Act of 1875

This followed a report by a select committee and laid down regulations concerning the preparation and adulteration of food. However, its impact was limited since councils were not compelled to appoint the analysts necessary to implement the law. This reflected the widespread desire – shared by Disraeli – to protect the autonomy of local government by not subjecting it to the coercive powers of the state. In practice, this meant relatively little was done since retailers were a powerful group on most town councils.

Trade Union Legislation of 1875

In the longer term, these were the most significant reforms. They sought to define the legal position of labour, which was becoming a bigger political issue with the growth of the trade union movement. Gladstone's government legislated on this issue, but although granting with one hand the legal recognition unions had been demanding, had withdrawn, with the other, the right to picket factory gates, which the trade unionists regarded as an essential tool of their trade. Protests from trade unionists had caused the Liberals to plan a revision of the law on picketing, but this was not in place by the time of the election and Disraeli was keen to exploit this fissure in the relations between the Liberal party and organized labour. To this end, two measures were passed, both of which were largely the work of Cross.

1. *Employers and Workmen Act.* Following upon the recommendations of a Royal Commission in 1874, this replaced the old Master and Servant legislation, removing, thereby, an anomaly whereby workmen could be subject to prosecution in the criminal courts for breech of contract, whereas employers were only liable to a civil action. Both were now subject to civil courts.
2. *Conspiracy and Protection of Property Act.* This measure legalized trade union picketing, provided the acts undertaken were not illegal if carried out by an individual. If it was acceptable for one man to stand outside a factory and request others not to enter, it was acceptable for a thousand to do so. In effect, it gave the green signal to mass primary and secondary picketing. Whether the Cabinet really intended this is doubtful; most of its members knew little about industrial relations and the measure was passed with little discussion, with Disraeli apparently falling asleep during the deliberations.

Disraeli attached much importance to this legislation. 'It is one of those measures that root and consolidate a party. We have settled the long and vexatious contest between Capital and Labour.' He hoped, by this means, to 'gain and retain for the Conservatives the lasting affection of the working classes'.[15] Certainly, the Conspiracy Act settled the legal position of labour for a generation and Alexander MacDonald of the engineering union said that the 'Conservative party has done more for the working classes in five years than the Liberals have done in fifty'. Even so, the Act did not win the trade unions to the Conservatives and certainly didn't settle the conflict between Capital and Labour. Rather, by removing the disabilities of Labour, it allowed that conflict to be conducted on a fairer playing field.[16]

Sandon's Education Act of 1876

This Act was designed to deal with the problem of low school attendance by working class children in rural areas. School Attendance Committees were to be set up to encourage parents to send their children to school, fining parents who did not do so and contributing to their fees in cases of hardship. The government also granted increased subsidies to Church schools. Though the Act helped to improve educational standards in the countryside, this was not its main purpose. Sandon, its author, was a strong Anglican who wished to encourage attendance at existing Church of England schools to avoid the spread of elective Board Schools into the countryside. These boards funded their activities through a local rate and were seen as promoting dissenting religious doctrines. In other words, its chief concern was with preserving the influence of the Church of England and the landed interest.

Miscellaneous Other Acts

Several other acts designed to improve the living conditions of the people were passed by the government. The Factory Act of 1874 reduced the maximum hours of work of women and children from ten-and-a-half to ten per day, with a weekly maximum of 56. This was an attempt to go some way towards meeting the demands for a nine hour day which had been raised by Conservative supporters in the larger urban boroughs, especially in Lancashire.[17] Restricting the hours of work of adult males was considered an unacceptable limitation on freedom of contract, but women and children were regarded as unfree agents and therefore amenable to state regulation. Four years later, the various factory laws passed over the proceeding half-century (numbering around 45) were consolidated into a single Factory Act – which won the praise of the great factory reformer Lord Shaftesbury. Two million people in this country, he said, would bless the day that Cross was appointed Home Secretary. An Enclosure Act of 1876 limited the rights of landowners to enclose common ground, stating that any such enclosure must be shown to be in the public as well as the private interest. Developing this theme, the Epping Forest Act of 1878 ensured that the unenclosed forest east of London be kept free for public use in perpetuity. An Agricultural Holdings Act specified that tenants should be compensated for unexhausted improvements on their farms if their leases expired – but again it was permissive, not compulsory, and would operate only if the landlord agreed in advance!

Assessment of Social Reforms

How are we to view the social legislation of Disraeli's government? Were these measures of real value, or were they largely symbolic? How far do they reflect a distinctly Disraelian Conservatism? Were they the product of a long held 'One Nation' philosophy, or were they a pragmatic response to opportunities?

According to traditional Conservative interpretations, the measures represented the practical application of the social reforming ideas Disraeli had been advocating since his first entry into politics. This was the view of Monypenny and Buckle:

> The aspirations of *Sybil* and 'Young England,' the doctrines in which Disraeli had 'educated' his party for thirty years, the principles laid down in the great speeches of 1872, were translated into legislative form; it was Tory democracy in action.

Disraeli's government 'took the practical pressing needs of the working population one by one and found a remedy for them, without inflicting hardship on any other class, or affecting our historical institutions in any way, save to strengthen their hold on popular affections'.[18]

This view no longer commands general assent. Today, it tends to be argued that, first, Disraeli took little direct interest in the content of the social reforms, and second, that they were limited and piecemeal and did not represent a coherent Conservative social policy. It is, writes Blake, 'an exaggeration to…see in them the fulfilment of some concept of paternalistic Tory democracy which had been adumbrated by Disraeli in opposition to Peel during the 1840s and now at last reached fruition'.[19] They did not challenge orthodox beliefs about the sanctity of property and the very limited role of the state. Social reform 'was not the principal or even a leading secondary preoccupation of Disraeli.' He did not supply a detailed agenda for reform and most of the legislation emerged from existing processes. Several points, in particular, should be noted:

1. Little of it was controversial and it was consistent with Disraeli's election pledge to avoid domestic upheaval. The legislation was largely permissive, not compulsory: 'Permissive legislation,' said Disraeli 'is the characteristic of a free people.' Central government passed responsibility to local authorities, who were empowered to take action, but were unlikely to do so, given ratepayer resistance.
2. Many of the measures were already in the legislative pipeline and happened to emerge in the mid-1870s. For example, the Torrens Act of 1868 would have included similar terms to the Artisan's Dwellings Act,

but its compulsory clauses had been thrown out by the Lords. The measure had been recommended by the Charity Organization Committee, of which Cross was a member, and enjoyed the support of Liberals.

3. The central government did not spend much money. 'The legislation of the 1870s,' says Vincent 'was not a move towards the collectivist state, though it was to some extent a move to collectivist local government.'[20]

4. Most of these measures had little directly to do with Disraeli. He was not much involved with the details of the programme of 1875, being ill for much of the autumn of 1874 when it was being prepared. Most were due to the Home Secretary, Sir Richard Cross. Cross was the prime mover behind the reduction in factory hours, the Artisans Dwellings Act, the Public Health Act, and the Trade Union legislation. The policies were piecemeal in the main and not the result of an overarching programme laid down by the Prime Minister.

5. After 1875, little was done, especially when the real business of government – foreign affairs – came to dominate. As Disraeli's biographers, Monypenny and Buckle acknowledge, from 1876 'foreign policy, which from first to last he maintained to be of primary, if not paramount importance, overshadowed and dwarfed in Beaconsfield's mind all other issues'.[21]

6. Most of the measures made little practical difference and contemporaries did not see them as part of a coherent social programme. Reflecting on the 1875 session, newspapers, commented Derby, 'for the most part speak of it as barren of result'.[22] The Liberal critic and *Daily News* journalist P. Clayden characterized 1875 as a 'year of little schemes. It showed conclusively that the Government could not do anything great'.[23] The following year Bagehot observed that, though presented with the 'most numerous and obedient' majority since Pitt, Disraeli 'did nothing with it... The session just closed will be known in parliamentary annals as one of the least effective or memorable on record...'[24]

It is not difficult to account for the limited nature of the measures. The electorate remained dominated by property owners and it was simply impossible for Disraeli, as a Conservative leader, to infringe upon the rights of property and impose heavier tax burdens in the interests of social justice or working class welfare. Limited measures to win working class votes were acceptable; but Disraeli had no intention of alienating his core support. As it was, Conservative MPs were hardly enthusiastic reformers and Disraeli had to call two party meetings to guarantee support for the Agricultural Holdings Act – which was resented for its concessions on tenants' rights.[25] Besides, although expressing an interest in social amelioration, Disraeli had never seen the State as an engine of social reform. He looked to individuals, and in particular to aristocrats and employers, to recognize the duties of property and lead the nation back into its natural state of unity and freedom from civil strife. Social improvement and stability should come through the actions of privileged individuals (and to some extent the church). The state might be used to right a specific wrong and restore harmony of interests between rich and poor when they were disrupted by vices like greed and pride, but it was not a main instrument of social amelioration. After all, opposition to the centralization of power was a central theme of Disraeli's political perspective.

For Disraeli, 'One Nation' was a call for society to unite behind its natural aristocratic leaders, not a code for social reform. As Paul Smith makes clear: 'Disraeli's popular Toryism…was an idea, an attitude, not a policy and what its progenitor was calling for was a regeneration, not a reconstruction.'

Disraeli's Role

Once the bias against reform is understood, Disraeli's personal contribution to the process can be better assessed. First, by the standards of the time the government did pursue a distinctive social programme. It produced, says Smith, 'a corpus of social legislation unparalleled until the ministries of 1905 and 1945…' According to Blake, the measures 'constitute the biggest instalment of social reform passed by any one government in the 19th century.'[26] For this, Disraeli was ultimately responsible. He could have resisted proposals to reform. What he did do was make time available for reform and provide a benign environment for it. It is true that the details of the Bills owed little to Disraeli, but unlike Gladstone, he was not a restless, interfering Prime Minister, keen to involve himself with the range of government legislation. Such administrative details bored him and he preferred to delegate, leaving ministers free to manage measures relating to their own departments. The key figure was Cross; but Disraeli appointed him and gave him scope to pursue his work.

Second, Disraeli made social reform an acceptable part of the language of Conservatism, extending, thereby, the range of practical politics. He recognized that the working class had to be induced to support the established economic and political order. 'The palace is not safe when the cottage is not happy' he had said in 1848; now, in 1875, he declared social reform to be 'a policy round which the country can rally'. To this end, he sought to remove unnecessary grievances and sustain harmony between rich and poor, employer and employee, which he held to be the natural state of society. The social reform programme was a sustained gesture in this direction and Disraeli promised it, made time for it and publicized it.

Strengthening Institutions

Disraeli attached much importance to the institutions that preserved the balance of the constitution and upheld the system of local self-government. Did he strengthen them in practice?

The Church of England

The Church had found itself under increasing pressure through much of the 19th century. The relative decline in Church attendance; the controversies and schisms associated with the Oxford Movement; the weakening of its hold over education; the disestablishment of its Irish branch and the calls for similar measures of disestablishment in Wales and Scotland – even England itself. Disraeli revered the Church as a 'foundational' English institution. He saw, too, that it was a major interest group with the capacity to sway the votes of its congregations. Since the 1850s, therefore, he had posed at its political friend and now in power, he was in a position to make that support effective. One reflection of this was Sandon's Education Act, designed, as we have seen, to bolster Church schools in rural areas. Another measure was the creation of six new Church bishoprics – described by the Archbishop of Canterbury as 'the greatest ecclesiastical reform since the Reformation'.

Of course, there was always something rather incongruous about Disraeli's pose as the defender of the Faith: he was no Churchman and knew little about internal Church politics. 'Nothing gives me more trouble than the Episcopacy,' he complained. 'There are so many parties, so many "schools of thought" in the Church' – or what he referred to on another occasion as 'Church nonsense.'[27] He was therefore most uncomfortable when he found himself, very early in his ministry, being caught up in a controversy concerning religious ritual. What made the whole thing even more ironic was that the pressure that drove him into this unwanted position came from Queen Victoria. Having spoken of his desire to be guided by her sagacity, he quickly found himself put to a test which, for the good of his future relations with the monarch, he could not be seen to fail.

The issue was the increasing introduction by High Church devotees of the Oxford Movement of 'Catholic' rituals into Church of England services. The Liberal and Evangelical wings of the Church were alarmed by the practice and a Royal Commission had been established in 1867 to consider the matter. Though it reported that some controls were necessary, Gladstone – a prominent High Churchman – had failed to take any action. Disraeli, who would have preferred to follow Gladstone's example, soon found himself under pressure to take a lead from the Archbishop of Canterbury and the Queen – who spoke of 'the duty of the Government to discourage Ritualism in the Church' and said it was her 'earnest wish' that Disraeli's government go as far as it could 'in *satisfying* the *Protestant* feeling of the country'.[28] The question was a fraught one for Disraeli. His Cabinet was divided and included several influential members of the High Church school. Yet he feared that the controversy, if unchecked, would threaten the unity of the Church and he had been alive to the potency of anti-Catholic feeling in England since the 1850s. He had, besides, no wish to displease Victoria at such an early stage of his premiership. In the event, he gave the government's backing to the Archbishop of Canterbury's Public Worship Regulation Bill, speaking forcibly in its favour as a means to 'put down Ritualism' and end the 'mass in masquerade'. He took the opportunity to reaffirm his reverence for the Church, praising it as the embodiment of the Reformation in England. The Bill passed, winning Disraeli the favour of the Queen and the majority of Church and political opinion. A damaging controversy had been arrested, though the Act was divisive in its operation and brought little credit to the Church. More significantly for Disraeli, it alienated sections of High Church opinion from his government and High Churchmen were later prominent critics of his handling of the Eastern Crisis of 1876–1878.

Monarchy

Disraeli attached considerable importance to the institution of monarchy. He regarded it as a symbol of national identity – the embodiment of the British political tradition and the summit of the hierarchical society whose complex gradations he so admired. Above the clash of faction, the patriot monarch was a focal point for all the British people and as such, had the interests of the nation as a whole always before him. To this domestic unifying function, Disraeli added, in the 1870s, the idea of the monarch as the focus for imperial unity. The monarch was the visible and understandable symbol of British power and served to awaken feelings of loyalty amongst the subject peoples.

Thus, by the 1870s, Disraeli had come to see the monarch as embodying the unity of Britain and the Empire. But he knew, too, that the monarch had a more tangible impact upon the functioning of the government. The crown had the capacity to make life difficult for a Prime Minister, to express displeasure, request explanations, veto appointments, even select a Prime Minister. A monarch was a valuable ally to have and since the early 1850s, Disraeli had set about winning the Queen's favour for himself and the Conservative party.

What was his method? It was to distinguish the person of the monarch from the institution of monarchy. Where Gladstone revered the latter, Disraeli targeted the former, making a systematic effort to woo, flatter and entertain Queen Victoria as a woman. He spoke directly to Her Majesty's person, seeking and praising her advice, considering her feelings and prejudices, keeping her informed of his thoughts and actions, sharing with her political gossip and avoiding boring her. In short, he affected the manner of a courtier and rarely can the annals of courtly devotion have yielded such effusions of solicitous homage as Disraeli lavished on the widow of Windsor. 'He lives,' he once declared, 'only for Her and works only for Her and without Her, all is lost.' His 'Sovereign Lady,' he affirmed, possessed 'the utmost devotion of his brain and heart'. The Christmas of 1878 found Disraeli in especially sentimental mood:

> Ever since he has been intimately connected with your Majesty, your Majesty has been to him a guardian Angel and much that he has done that is right, or said that was appropriate, is due to you, Madam. He often thinks how he can repay your Majesty, but he has nothing more to give, having given to your Majesty his duty and heart.[29]

Disraeli did not lay siege to Faery's heart in vain. 'You cannot think,' she wrote to the Prince of Wales, 'how kind he is to me, how attached.'[30] Upon his first visit to Osborne in 1874 Disraeli found her 'wreathed in smiles and as she tattled, glided about the room like a bird... I really thought she was going to embrace me.' Her private secretary recalled that 'the Queen thought that she had never in her life seen so amusing a person...and she was pleased with the audacious way in which he broke through the ice that surrounded her... It is still remembered how much more she used to smile in conversation with him than she did with any other of her Ministers.'[31] A stream of gifts flowed from the Monarch to her devoted Prime Minister – books, statues of John Brown and, above all, the Osborne primroses he so admired. Especially delighted by one such delivery, Disraeli told Victoria how 'in the middle of the night, it occurred to him, that it might be an enchantment and that, perhaps, it was a Faery gift and came from another monarch: Queen Titania, gathering flowers, with her Court, in a soft and sea-girt isle and sending magic blossoms, which, they say, turn the heads of those who receive them.'[32] It was a wrench all the greater for Victoria when the electorate chose in 1880 to separate her from her courtier-Prime Minister: 'Nothing more than trouble and trial await me,' she telegraphed upon hearing the result. 'I consider it a great public misfortune.' 'The grief to her of having to part with the kindest and most devoted as well as one of the wisest Ministers the Queen has ever had, is not to be told.'[33]

Disraeli's intimate friendship with the Queen was the most striking manifestation of his rise to the very pinnacle of British society. 'During a somewhat romantic and imaginative life,' he confided, 'nothing has ever occurred to him so interesting as this confidential correspondence with one so exalted and so inspiring.' Yet in truth he was pushing at an open door. Since the death of Albert in 1861 she had been a withdrawn and lonely figure. Many approached her with respect and awe; few with the disarming solicitude of Disraeli. He was well-placed to do so. His domestic situation was similar: he, too, was a widower and lived a domestically lonely life. 'I love the Queen,' he admitted to a correspondent, 'perhaps the only person in this world left to me that I do love.' He had, further, throughout his life delighted in the company of women and there was nothing he enjoyed more than relating his achievements to a female audience. His sister Sarah, his wife Mary Anne, his Torquay correspondent, the Jewish widow Mrs Brydges Willyams, Lady Londonderry, the Ladies Chesterfield and Bradford, Victoria Queen and Empress – so through Disraeli's life ran the precious thread of female soul mates. Physical passion counted for little; it was the romance of courtship and female favour that he relished.

Politically, too, Victoria was highly sympathetic. Though born a Whig, her politics had for some time been essentially conservative and she was nursing a developing distrust of Gladstone's unstable character. If the alternative to Disraeli was an unpredictable Gladstone leading a party which contained self-confessed Republicans such as Dilke, even the most mundane of Conservatives was bound to appear attractive. And Disraeli was anything but mundane. He took Victoria into the heart of the political world, painting in vivid colours the highs and lows of his premiership. Above all, he opened her eyes to the richness of her Empire, encouraging the Queen to see herself as an imperial sovereign, commanding the allegiance of Princes and Chieftains and inspiring the service of brave Britons engaged in carrying the benefits of Christian civilization around the globe. Victoria, Empress of India, revelled in this role and made it the defining characteristic of the last two decades of her reign.

What did Disraeli gain politically from his cultivation of the Queen? Most obviously, the Queen's open endorsement bolstered his political standing. On several occasions, he persuaded his reluctant monarch to preside over the state opening of parliament. At the height of the Eastern Crisis, she visited him at Hughenden to demonstrate her support for his policy. Disraeli actively used the Queen's authority as a lever to shift recalcitrant colleagues. During the Eastern Crisis, he regularly read Victoria's exhorting letters to his Cabinet. Dissenting ministers were left in no doubt that they were crossing, not only Disraeli, but their Queen. He informed Victoria, too, of the names of those ministers who objected to a resolute policy and the Queen then applied pressure on them during private audiences. There were psychological dividends as well. Disraeli was not the lonely head of an administration; he was the servant of a higher authority in whose name he acted. He shared with the Queen the burdens and responsibilities of office and associated her with his achievements as well as failures, habitually speaking of 'your policy,' 'your forces,' 'your Empire,' and 'your reputation'. Having so long been nominally subordinate to the likes of Lyndhurst, Bentinck and Derby, he was reluctant, even now, to wholly step forth from the shadows. Indeed, he seems genuinely to have appreciated Victoria's political sagacity – which was far from contemptible. Besides, he gained the material trappings of power. Victoria made him an Earl and would have made him a Duke if he had been prepared to accept. Disraeli's appreciation of the potential for hubris held him back, settling for the Order of the Garter instead.

Disraeli was not blind to the Queen's deficiencies – describing her to Derby as 'very troublesome, very wilful and whimsical, like a spoilt child,'[34] and there were risks entailed in his strategy. By flattering the Queen and encouraging her to realize her constitutional importance, Disraeli fed in Victoria a belief in her ability to shape events. The cautious Derby was early concerned: 'Is there not just a risk of encouraging her in too large ideas of her personal power and too great indifference to what the public expects? I only ask; it is for you to judge.'[35] Disraeli judged that it was well worth yielding some influence to the Queen in return for the benefits of Royal favour. The Public Worship and Royal Title Bills were both measures taken up by Disraeli at the behest of the Queen at the cost of short term political difficulties. But having paid the price, Disraeli was at pains to ensure that Victoria did not forget the service he had done her. The Public Worship Act, he told her in 1877, revealed 'the power of the sovereign in this country,' for it 'would never have been introduced, had it not been for your majesty.' Similarly the Royal Titles Act was the Queen's work, he said, and was passed with little support from the Cabinet. On another occasion, he boasted 'of what may be done when the Sovereign and the Minister act together. Witness the Public Worship Act. Witness your Majesty's Imperial Crown'.

Only occasionally did Disraeli and Victoria fail to see eye to eye and on such occasions, writes Strachey, Disraeli could have been forgiven regretting that he had rashly called the genie from out of her bottle.[36] During the Eastern Crisis of 1875–1878, Victoria consistently pushed for a more resolute and confrontational policy than Disraeli was prepared to pursue and he found himself awkwardly situated between a sceptical Cabinet and a doubtless Monarch. His meetings with Victoria became an ordeal: 'if the volcano breaks out again he does not know what he shall do.'[37] It cannot have been a comfortable feeling for Disraeli to meet his Cabinet knowing that in his pocket was a letter from the Queen threatening abdication if forceful meas-ures against Russia were not undertaken. In the event, his tact and patience kept his Cabinet more or less together and his monarch on her throne. His breech with the Queen was still wider over the issue of responsibility for the debacle of the Zulu War. Disraeli had nothing but contempt for Lord Chelmsford, commander of the British forces, who had failed to deliver what he had promised (always the worst failing in Disraeli's eyes) and refused to invite him to his Hughenden home. Victoria, determined to support the 'man on the spot' and unencumbered by electoral considerations, protested with vigour, but Disraeli stood his ground – showing there were limits even to the influence of the Faery.

Such differences were in any case rare and were soon smoothed over. On balance, Disraeli worked harmoniously with his monarch and both emerged from the relationship clear winners. While Victoria gained an amusing flatterer and relished the sense of being at the heart of government and of a great Empire, Disraeli gained the prestige and support of the most exalted personage in the realm and a worthy object for his romantic imagination. It was a happy coincidence of wants which has no parallel in the history of parliamentary monarchy.

The Landed Aristocracy

Disraeli had always held the landed aristocracy to be the foundation of the British tradition of political liberty. It was the independent wealth and digni-fied position of the landed classes which had resisted the oppressive central-ization of government, sustained the various components of the constitution, and ensured a healthy system of local government founded on paternalism. However, he had given little thought to how this territorial constitution might be strengthened, quite the reverse. Far from even preserving the *status quo*, the Reform Act he had pushed through in 1867 for largely opportunistic reasons put the skids under landed politics by creating a mass urban elec-torate which would be marshalled not by titled grandees, as the old Boroughs had been, but by party organizations staffed by middle class activists. In the sphere of agriculture, even so warm a supporter as Sir George Stapledon was forced to admit that he 'at no time put agriculture to the forefront in his measures of practical statesmanship,' he 'never came forward with a creative policy of agricultural reform'.[38]

Prime Minister Disraeli had few plans to materially assist the landed interest. This in itself would not have been especially significant were it not for the fact that, by one of history's sharper ironies, his assumption of office coincided with the beginning of a sustained depression in British agriculture which would eventually transform not merely the rural but the social and political landscape of Britain. As cheap food from North America and Australasia began to arrive in large quantities, Disraeli came under pressure to take measures to relieve the position of farmers and landlords. There were demands for a reduction in taxes on property and agricultural produce; and there was a demand for a restoration of agricultural protection – the cause in which Disraeli had ostensibly helped destroy Peel in 1846.

Disraeli was prepared to go some way towards reducing the tax burden on landed property, a cause which he had himself long championed. In the budget of 1874, the central government took over the responsibility for funding lunatic asylums, police and local prisons, while also in that year, the tax on owning and trading horses was abolished. But beyond this Disraeli was not prepared to go. Due to pressure on revenue, he failed even to repeal the unpopular duty on malt, a decision that surprised and disappointed the County Agricultural Association. Ironically, it was Gladstone who repealed the duty in 1880.

With regard to protection, Disraeli replied that it was simply politically impossible to bring back the Corn Laws. Even in 1846 their *continuance* had brought the Conservatives to the brink of crisis; how much more controversial would be any attempt to bring them back in a Britain even more urban, industrial and wedded to the benefits of free trade and with a working class electorate benefiting from falling food prices? However, beyond rejecting protection, write Monypenny and Buckle, Disraeli propounded 'no remedy of his own for the woeful state of agriculture' and continually lamented the run of bad harvests, not recognizing that the problem was the failure of prices to rise as output fell due to the arrival of imports. He had to be pressed even into appointing a Royal Commission on the problem, which reported after his death.[39] The fact was that Disraeli had given no serious consideration to the problems of agriculture, had an irrepressible optimism that recovery would come, and was not prepared to initiate actions that would carry him beyond the confines of everyday politics. Instead, he took refuge in rhetoric. As demands grew for the break-up of the large estates between small peasant proprietors, Disraeli defended, as he had done for 40 years, the virtues of the 'territorial constitution'.

> The number and variety of classes in England dependent on land are sources of our strength. They have given us the proprietors of the soil, the constructors of our liberty in a great degree and the best security for local government; they have given us the farmers, who cultivate and improve their estates and lastly the agricultural peasant, whose lot is deplored by those not acquainted with it, but who has during the last forty years made more continuous progress than any other class in Her Majesty's dominions.[40]

It was a familiar enough refrain which, in the 1870s, escaped being merely a cliché, by assuming the form of a funeral oration.

Historians' Debate: Disraeli and Social Reform

One of the most controversial aspects of the Conservative government of 1874–1880 was the importance and meaning of its Social Reform legislation. Was it the product of a distinctly Disraelian Conservatism, part of a Tory Democracy agenda with roots traceable to the Young England movement of the 1840s, or was it a piecemeal response to pressing social problems that could just as easily have been implemented by a Liberal government?

Tory apologists at the time and some subsequent historians have advocated the view that it was the embodiment of Disraeli's long-term concern with an inclusive politics.

Marriott

It is impossible to deny that with the author of *Sybil* social reform was a matter of longstanding conviction and genuine enthusiasm… It is true that critics of the later day, accustomed to bolder departures from the principle of *laissez-faire*, are apt to deride the legislation of these years as halting and indecisive…vitiated by reluctance to confer upon public authorities compulsory powers. Even if it be admitted that the later is the best way, it does not follow that the former was not good in itself and at the time the best possible. The legislative and administrative achievements of the first three years of the Disraeli Government generously fulfilled, not the specific promises, for these were notably absent, but the general spirit of the programme laid before the electorate by the Tory leader.[41]

Murray

Underlying the wavering of his political course was the fixed maxim that institutions like the Church, the Crown and the landed aristocracy were trustees for the people. Under his guidance the triad 'Altar, Throne and Cottage' was definitely inscribed on the banners of the Conservative party… He did not think the masses fit to govern; he did think they ought to be governed for their own benefit and not for that of any class or oligarchy…his desire for social improvement was sincere and unchanging.[42]

Southgate

In office with power, the Conservatives redeemed Disraeli's promise of social reform… In view of the record it seems captious of Lord Blake to hold that the Government had no programme and 'Disraeli had little idea what to do', especially as he admits that this was the biggest instalment of social reform in the nineteenth century. Disraeli hoped that social reform was 'a policy round which the country could rally', even that the Conservatives would 'retain…the lasting affection of the working classes.'[43]

Stapledon

…there can be no denying the fact that, stoutly supported by his shrewd Home Secretary Richard A. Cross, Disraeli in his second administration was responsible for a wealth of first class 'health of the people' legislation.[44]

Most recent historians see the social reforms as being motivated, not by ideology, but by a need to find practical solutions to generally recognized social problems. There was nothing distinctly 'Disraelian' about them and their objects were limited.

Feuchtwanger

...all historians are now agreed that the social legislation was neither the result of a coherent programme nor of a distinctive ideological orientation different from the prevailing orthodoxy of economic liberalism. It filled the gap left by constitutional reform. Disraeli's part in it was slight and he sometimes dozed when it was being discussed in cabinet...[45]

Jenkins

Certainly, there was to be no question of the Conservatives embarking upon a systematic exercise in paternalistic social reform, inspired by the sort of 'One Nation' principles that Disraeli had laid down in his Young England days. Disraeli may still occasionally have used language reminiscent of his earlier views...but in reality his government's response to such matters was influenced by the prevailing doctrines of political economy. A generation of Conservative administrators had grown up – men like Northcote and Cross, who were imbued with the teachings of mid-Victorian *laissez faire* Liberalism – and there was little to suggest that Disraeli dissented from such thinking.

In order to assess the contribution made by the Conservatives in the field of social reform, it has to be appreciated that most of their Bills were really the product of the administrative machine and might just as easily have been implemented by another government.[46]

Walton

Most recent historians have followed Paul Smith and indeed Lord Blake himself, in viewing the 'One Nation' interpretation with considerable scepticism. The legislation itself was of varying quality. Some of it was inherited from the previous government and merely happened to emerge from the administrative pipeline in the mid-1870s. Some was effectively imposed on the government by outside agitation...specific policies were the work of individual ministers and emerged piecemeal, rather than expressing a great overarching programme laid down by the prime minister. Most of the measures fell outside the conventional patterns of party conflict and their connections with 'Young England' were at best rhetorical... This was, then, limited and piecemeal social reform...offering no opposition to established orthodoxies about the sanctity of property and the (very narrow) extent of the legitimate role of the state in the economy.[47]

However, some historians, most notably Ghosh, argue that in the context of the 1870s, Disraeli's concern with social reform did mark a distinct development in the style of 'Liberal Conservatism' and helped ensure that social policy did not become a contentious class based issue in British politics.

...Disraeli and hence the ministry, had definite intention as to social reform and his recurrence to the ideas voiced in 1867–1868 and 1872 was more or less automatic... Disraeli's aim over the next twelve months was thus to show by all means, visual and substantial, that a programme of 'necessary and adequate' social measures was being carried out. The 1875 session records one of Disraeli's most untypical triumphs – the execution according to timetable of his pledge to legislate *en masse* on social topics.[48]

What made the social legislation of 1875 remarkable was not its detailed origins, which were technical, bipartisan and conventional, but a series of political factors – advance pledges, the focusing of legislative strategy, the management of Parliament and the presentation of the whole... The measure of the success of 'Disraelian' social reform is thus...the *absence* of social policy as a central issue before 1900 and the continual primacy of institutional questions in politics.[49]

VII

PRIME MINISTER: FOREIGN AND IMPERIAL POLICY

Disraeli realized that foreign policy would be one of the key areas in which the government's reputation would be made or lost. His goal since the 1840s had been to restore the Conservatives to power on the basis of wide national support and an effective foreign policy was central to defining this 'national' approach to politics. The political situation favoured such a bid. Gladstone's 1868 Liberal government was widely seen as pursuing a weak foreign policy – watching from the sidelines as the European balance of power was transformed by the rise of Prussia and loosening the ties between Britain and its Empire. If the Liberals had abandoned the overtly national foreign policy associated with Palmerston, then that tradition would be taken up by the Conservatives. If Gladstone saw the Empire as an expensive and somewhat embarrassing institution, then Disraeli would celebrate and consolidate Britain's imperial power. Thus, Disraeli's foreign policy goals were clear. They were to assert British power and interests in Europe and around the world and to strengthen the Empire.

Constraints

If the *goal* of Disraeli's foreign policy was clear, the *means* to achieve it were less so. He was subject to four sets of constraints.

1. *Finance* Disraeli had charged Gladstone with neglecting the nation's defences, and realized that if he were to pursue a more active foreign policy more would have to be spent. Yet he also adhered to the orthodox Victorian belief in low government spending. As Vincent remarks, 'like other Victorian premiers, he was trapped within the pretence that one could have a foreign policy without having a defence policy...'[1] Disraeli did spend Gladstone's carefully assembled surplus on the army and navy

upon assuming office, but the increases were modest and well below what the military wanted. 'I would,' Disraeli wrote to Derby in 1875, be more impressed by the demands for extra spending 'if I could not remember a time when the Commander in Chief had not been seriously alarmed at the state of our armaments…an increase of £300,000 or £400,000 is justifiable, because inevitable… Beyond that we must not go…'[2] By 1876, government revenues were faltering and even the limited military operations that were engaged upon after 1876 put upward pressure on taxes. Quite simply, Britain lacked the military means to intervene in Europe or sustain a wide range of imperial commitments and Disraeli did not confront this problem.

2. *European balance of power* Traditionally, Disraeli had advocated an alliance with France to uphold British interests in Europe. However, Germany's defeat of France in 1870 and her subsequent alliance with Austria and Russia had left France marginalized. 'She is,' commented Disraeli, 'more likely to be partitioned than conquer Europe again.' With Britain isolated, it was not clear how she could assert her interests in Europe. 'Since the fall of France,' remarked Disraeli, '…the conduct of foreign affairs for England has become infinitely more difficult. There is no balance and unless we go out of our way to act with the three Northern Powers, they can act without us, which is not agreeable for a State like England.'[3] The obvious solution would be to 'drive a wedge between the three allies', but this was to prove difficult to effect.[4]

3. *Lord Derby* Disraeli appointed Lord Derby, one of his oldest political friends, as Foreign Secretary. This was a mistake. The main concern of Derby was to avoid foreign intervention. Given that the whole point of Disraeli's foreign policy was to show that Britain was prepared to intervene to assert her interests, there was an obvious conflict between the Prime Minister and Foreign Secretary, which was only resolved with Derby's resignation in 1878.

4. *A lack of clear thinking* Though, says Eldridge, Disraeli was determined to 'do something' in the sphere of foreign policy, it was 'not precisely clear what that "something" was' and 'he possessed no ideas other than the traditional Palmerstonian conception of British interests and approach to defence strategy'.[5] As a result of this limiting factor, Disraeli did not pursue a deliberately conceived foreign policy; the policy initiatives he did eventually take were essentially reactive, a response to events and the initiatives of others.

Disraeli's Foreign Policy in Practice

In trying to make sense of Disraeli's foreign policy, it is customary to distinguish between his *Imperial* policy and his policies towards *Europe and the Eastern*

Question. The division is a useful one – though it should be noted that one of the leading features of Disraeli's administration was the emphasis upon the imperial dimensions of foreign policy.

The Eastern Question and the Balance of Power

Europe in 1874 was dominated by the *Dreikaiserbund* (Three Emperors' League), a loose alliance between Germany, Austria, and Russia formed in 1873. For the German Chancellor, Bismarck, the purpose of the League was to consolidate the position of Germany by maintaining Russian support and keeping France isolated. Though the alliance was vague and bedevilled by Austrio-Russian rivalries, it appeared to signify a serious *imbalance* of power in Europe and Disraeli wanted to undermine it – but precisely how he had little idea. In the event, an opportunity presented itself in 1876 – though in the context of a more serious problem that plunged the government into crisis. This problem was a new act in the ongoing drama of the Eastern Question.

The Eastern Question refers to the problems posed to European diplomacy in the 19th century by the gradual weakening of the Ottoman Empire. The Ottoman Empire occupied the world's most strategically important region, formally including the Balkans region of Europe, Turkey-proper, Asia Minor, Syria, Palestine, Arabia and Egypt. As such, it also dominated the eastern Mediterranean, the most important sea in the world and the historic centre of western civilization. Unfortunately, the Ottoman Empire was in the process of long-term dissolution. It was becoming ever weaker and backward and struggling to maintain its empire in the face of independence movements of subject peoples (the Greeks, for example, had been a key group to struggle to free themselves from Ottoman rule in the 1820s) and from the covetous gaze of other Great Powers.

In July 1875, an uprising, sparked by a combination of economic grievances and nationalist agitation and supported by the governments of Serbia and Montenegro, began amongst the Christian peasants in the Ottoman province of Bosnia-Herzegovina. At the same time, a financial crisis struck the government of Turkey, which was forced to suspend interest payments on the national debt. This, in itself, was a matter of some significance to Britain, which was the chief creditor of the Turkish government. Between 1858 and 1872, nearly £200 million of Turkish bonds had been sold on the London market.[6] It seemed as if the Ottoman Empire might finally be about to dissolve, especially when further rebellions broke out in Bulgaria. Disraeli initially shared this view, noting that the 'end is coming' and not seeing how the power of the Sultan could be maintained.[7] The problem was that Ottoman weakness created a chance for opportunists to pursue their objectives in the region, including Austria and Russia. Since its defeat by Prussia in 1866, Austria had been taking a more direct interest in the Balkans and now put forward a proposal for a programme of reforms in the government of Bosnia, to be supervised by a mixed Christian and Muslim commission. Russia and Prussia agreed, as did Turkey and Britain – Disraeli remarking 'We can't be more Turkish than the Sultan.'

The reforms, however, failed to placate the rebels and, as the crisis in Turkey deepened, Austria and Russia both feared that their rival claims to influence in the region would draw them into war. To try to prevent this, they combined to submit, on 13 May 1876, a new and tougher set of demands known as the Berlin Memorandum. This called on the Sultan to introduce reforms into his government (to be supervised by the Great Powers) and hinted at the use of force if he did not do so within a two-month period. At the same time, they secretly agreed that, if the Ottoman Empire were to disintegrate, Austria should be allowed to occupy Bosnia and Russia, Bessarabia. France and Italy agreed to the Memorandum. But Disraeli refused and instead, ordered the British fleet to Besika Bay. There were three reasons for this:

1. Disraeli wished to break up the alliance of the northern powers; signing the Memorandum would only strengthen it.
2. A Prime Minister intending to reassert Britain's reputation for an active and independent foreign policy could hardly sign a document over whose contents he had not been consulted.
3. Disraeli believed the proposed reforms merely put 'a knife to the throat of Turkey'. They would almost certainly fail, in which case the more 'efficacious' measures referred to would be employed and Britain would be 'drawn, step by step, into participating in a scheme, which would end very soon in the disintegration of Turkey'.[8]

This refusal of Disraeli's government to sign the Memorandum was the chief charge levelled at it by Gladstone. Always an advocate of the Concert of Europe, Gladstone argued that Disraeli's action had fractured the alliance of the European powers and signalled to the Sultan that he could rely on British support against any intervention by the powers in his affairs. The result, he argued, was the adoption by the Turks of an inflexible policy which set in train the conflict of the next two years. Ironically, Queen Victoria concurred, warning that Britain's refusal to sign might encourage the Turks and 'precipitate, rather than prevent, the catastrophe'.

Disraeli's Approach to the Eastern Crisis

Throughout the Eastern Crisis, Disraeli's policy was guided by his determination to uphold Britain's economic and strategic interests as a great imperial power.

The events in Turkey threatened those interests and the chief agency of that threat was either Russia and Austria working together or Russia acting alone. As Disraeli made clear in a speech at the beginning of the crisis, the British government was 'deeply conscious of the nature and magnitude' of Britain's interests in the region and 'those British interests they are resolved to guard and maintain'. 'We...must remember that our connection with the East is not merely an affair of sentiment and tradition, but that we have urgent and substantial and enormous interests which we must guard and keep.'[9]

Disraeli had three specific objectives – break up the alliance of the northern powers and re-establish the balance of power in Europe through British leadership; maintain the Ottoman Empire in the face of the threats to its integrity; and appeal to public opinion by showing that his government was vigilant in upholding British interests.

1. *Balance of power*

Disraeli wanted to break up what he regarded as the 'unnatural' Northern Alliance of Russia, Germany and Austria. This was one reason why he had refused to sign the Berlin Memorandum and he saw that if Austria and Germany were to stand by and allow Russia to occupy Constantinople, then 'the Holy Alliance will be revived in aggravated form and force'. Austria would have Bosnia and Herzegovina, Germany would take Holland and 'France, Belgium and England would be in a position I trust I should never live to witness.'[10] From this perspective, it was necessary to block Russia's ambitions in the Balkans and Eastern Mediterranean and detach her from Austria and Germany.

2. *The Russian threat to Britain's strategic interests*

Like Palmerston before him, Disraeli had no doubt that British interests required the maintenance of the territorial integrity of the Ottoman Empire. If the Turkish Empire were to break up, then Russia would almost certainly move in to fill the power vacuum, dominating south-east Europe, the eastern Mediterranean and Asia Minor. It would then be able to pose a direct threat to Britain's Indian Empire – for two reasons.

(a) The southward advance of Russian power towards the borders of Afghanistan and Persia, which had been going forward since the 1860s, would be facilitated. This advance had caused Disraeli much unease. It contributed to the decision to proclaim the British Empire of India and it motivated the switch to a more forward policy in Afghanistan. If Russia were to dominate Turkey and the eastern Mediterranean, then Britain would lose the capacity to challenge her in the region of the Black Sea – as she had been able to do at the time of the Crimean War. If she chose to, Russia would be able to advance on Afghanistan unhindered.

(b) She would be able to move on to threaten the Suez Canal route to India. The Canal, which had been opened in 1869 and which was already the chief shipping route between Britain and India, flowed through Egypt, which was nominally part of the Ottoman Empire. With Ottoman power gone, Disraeli believed that Egypt would be at Russia's mercy. Now some were already suggesting that it might be better for Britain to abandon Constantinople to Russia and secure her Canal interests by occupying Egypt instead. Disraeli rejected this idea. 'If the Russians had Constantinople, they could at any time march their Army through Syria to the mouth of the Nile and then what would be the use of holding Egypt? Not even the command of the sea could help us in such circumstances. People who talk in this manner must be utterly ignorant of geography. Our strength is on the sea. Constantinople is the key of India and not Egypt and the Suez Canal.'[11]

3. *Public opinion*

Throughout the crisis, Disraeli was haunted by the example of the Crimean War, where the irresolution of the Cabinet eventually brought about the fall of the government. He repeatedly warned his colleagues that if the Conservatives failed to assert British interests in the region, they would be denounced as weak by the public and ousted from office. This was a classically Disraelian preoccupation and was not shared by Derby and most of the other ministers. It also raised the question of *how* Britain would go beyond posturing to action if this were required. After all, Aberdeen's government fell not because of its decision to enter the war but because of the blunders of the campaign. There was no guarantee that these would not be repeated.

The fixed point in Disraeli's Eastern diplomacy was the safeguarding of British interests in Europe and India from a perceived Russian threat. When the Queen questioned his decision to send the fleet to Besika Bay, he replied that it had not been sent 'to protect Christians or Turks (the excuse given before public opinion), but to uphold Your Majesty's Empire'.[12] Yet he was prepared to be flexible over how this was to be achieved. He was willing to countenance some reduction in the Ottoman territories in Europe as long as Constantinople and the Straits were not threatened. He saw, too, that Britain needed to work with other powers to achieve a satisfactory outcome. Thus, while not prepared to work with the *Dreikaiserbund* as a whole, he was prepared to work with its members individually. One option was Germany, but Bismarck's proposals for a partition of the Ottoman Empire between Russia, Austria, France and Britain were too radical for Britain to accept. His preferred ally was Austria, who posed no threat to British strategic interests in the area. But the Austrians, supported by Bismarck, were still seeking to work with Russia while secretly hoping that Russia and the Turks would exhaust themselves in a war, allowing the Austrians to assert their claim to the dominance of Bosnia-Herzegovina. Only when Austria's patience with Russia finally ran out did the possibility of Anglo-Austrian cooperation materialize and bring the crisis to an end. Disraeli was even prepared to consider working with Russia and in June 1876, assured Russia's ambassador to Britain that he was not suspicious of Russia's intentions and acknowledged that Turkey's disappearance from Europe 'was sooner or later inevitable'.[13]

In terms of his publicly stated policy, Disraeli declared his support for the Ottoman Empire and took his stand on the Treaty of Paris of 1856 which had ended the last conflict with Russia in the region (the Crimean War of 1854–1856) and which, comment Monypenny and Buckle, made the support 'of the integrity and independence of the Turkish Empire a principle, not merely of British, but of European policy'.[14] Disraeli was determined not to repeat the mistake of British irresolution in the face of Russian threats which was widely seen as precipitating the Crimean War. He little suspected that the traditions of Palmerstonian diplomacy would now become a liability with the potential to derail his entire foreign policy – even his administration. For, operating in the 1870s were three new variables that transformed the entire context of his diplomacy – the growing appeal of Balkan nationalism; the unacceptable behaviour of the Turks; and the crusading intervention of Gladstone.

The Bulgarian Atrocities

At first, it seemed that Disraeli's decision not to sign the Berlin Memorandum was justified. A coup in Turkey overthrew the Sultan and placed upon the throne his nephew, who was apparently more amenable to reform. In response, the Northern Powers withdrew the Memorandum. 'I look upon the tripartite confederacy to be at an end,' remarked Disraeli. 'It was an unnatural state of affairs and never would have occurred had England maintained, of late years, her just position in public affairs.'[15] However, in the spring of 1876, a full-scale uprising against Turkish rule began in Bulgaria and was followed in July by Serbia and Montenegro's declaration of war on Turkey. Any hope Disraeli might have harboured that the Great Powers would keep out of the conflict was soon confounded when it emerged that in the course of suppressing the Bulgarian uprising, irregular Turkish 'bashi-bazouk' forces had massacred around 12,000 Bulgarian peasants. The killings had occurred in May, but it was not until 23 June 1876, that the Liberal newspaper, the *Daily News*, first published accounts of the atrocities.

Disraeli did not, initially, take the accounts seriously. The government had no intelligence on the matter and appearing in a pro-insurgent paper, they were, he wrote, 'to a great extent invention...their object is to create a cry against the government'.[16] In the Commons, he described reports of the massacres as 'coffee-house babble', adding that the Turks did not use torture, they 'terminated their connection with culprits in a more expeditious manner'. Disraeli's flippant response to the reports caused widespread offence. Although later official investigations caused him to admit the reality of the massacre, he never really took them seriously, believing they disrupted the true interests of British foreign policy, which was the preservation of Turkey.

More significant was the fact that Disraeli was too much of a conservative to have any sympathy with nationalism. Nationalism was, for him, a meaningless idea that was deployed by radicals and subversives, chiefly through the activities of shadowy secret societies, to pursue social and political change. He had never shared the British enthusiasm for the cause of Italian unity and the claims of Serbians, Albanians and Bulgarians moved him not at all. 'Fancy autonomy for Bosnia,' he reflected, 'with a mixed population: autonomy for Ireland would be less absurd…'[17] The whole crisis, he stated in July 1876, was the product of 'secret societies and revolutionary committees'. The Herzegovina affair 'might have been settled in a week' if the Turks had possessed some 'common energy, or perhaps some pocket money even…'[18] Disraeli's failure to comprehend the nature of Balkan nationalism was a huge blind spot and reflected his propensity to retreat into romantic phraseology in the face of disagreeable 19th century realities. The promotion of nationalist ideas had indeed been very often associated with the activities of secret societies, like the Carbonari in Italy, and this was especially true at the time of Disraeli's entry into politics in the 1830s. But by the 1860s and 1870s, nationalist feeling had expanded well beyond the world of secret handshakes and invisible ink. Disraeli may not have liked this fact. The problem was that he refused to acknowledge it. This was not an unusual characteristic of Disraeli's; witness his belief in the aristocratic settlement at a time when Britain was becoming an urban and industrial society. But in Britain, the gulf between appearance and reality could be bridged by rhetoric and, in any case, the consequences of misapprehension were not dire. Unfortunately, the virtues of Disraelian rhetoric were lost on the people of the Balkans and the forces operating in that region did so to far more sinister effect.

Even domestically, the traditional principles of British policy in the East were out of temper with the high moral tone of the mid-Victorian age and the growing force of public opinion. Was it possible for a Britain with a vigorous press, an increasingly democratic electorate, and an image of itself as a Christian nation supportive of the liberties of individuals and small nations to support, on grounds of strategic interest, a degenerate and despotic Turkish Empire? Disraeli believed that it was and in his last speech to the Commons, summoned the concept of Empire to vindicate his policy:

> Those who suppose that England ever would uphold… Turkey from
> blind superstition and from a want of sympathy with the highest

aspirations of humanity, are deceived. What our duty is at this particular moment is to maintain the Empire of England.[19]

All this tumult, he remarked in a letter to Derby, 'is on a false assumption, that we have been, or are, upholding Turkey. All the Turks may be in the Propontis, so far as I'm concerned...'[20] What the government was upholding was British power.

Such naked *realpolitik* was not at all acceptable to Gladstone, for whom it was both misguided and immoral for Britain to look to Turkey to uphold its strategic interests. This he made manifest when, in September 1876, he published his famous pamphlet *The Bulgarian Horrors and the Question of the East*. Gladstone had been in semi-retirement since losing the election in 1874, but the massacre of Christians by Muslim Turks stung him into activity. As he witnessed the growing public campaign against Turkish policy, he saw that the issue was one which would allow him to reconnect with the 'masses' and reassert his leadership of the Liberal party. His hurriedly written pamphlet was a sensation, selling 200,000 copies within a month. The Turks, he declared, were the 'one great anti-human specimens of humanity' and he argued that Bulgaria and the other suppressed nationalities of the Balkans should be given effective autonomy within the Ottoman Empire.

Disraeli was offended by Gladstone's intervention, which confirmed their mutual hatred. Referring to the pamphlet, of which Gladstone had had the 'impudence' to send him a copy, Disraeli wrote that the 'document is passionate and not strong; vindictive and ill-written – that of course. Indeed, in that respect, of all Bulgarian horrors, perhaps the greatest'. In another private letter he wrote:

> Posterity will do justice to that unprincipled maniac Gladstone – extraordinary mixture of envy, vindictiveness, hypocrisy and superstition; and with one commanding characteristic – whether Prime Minister, or Leader of the Opposition, whether preaching, praying, speechifying or scribbling – never a gentleman![21]

Disraeli used scarcely less restrained language in public. Any man, he stated in a speech in Aylesbury, who would take advantage of the public's concern at the Bulgarian atrocities to pursue his own individual ends and suggest a course which 'he must know to be injurious to the interests of the country...is a man whose conduct no language can too strongly condemn'. Disraeli even made the outrageous claim that, as the action Gladstone recommended would lead to 'havoc and ruin', it could 'fairly be described as worse than any of those Bulgarian atrocities which now occupy attention'.[22]

Gladstone's opinions of his rival were no more flattering. Disraeli, he wrote at this time, is a man of 'diabolical cleverness' who is never beaten.

Every reverse, every defeat is to him only an admonition to wait and catch his opportunity of retrieving and more than retrieving his position'. Near the end of his life, Gladstone remarked that 'In past times the Tory party had principles by which it would and did stand for bad and for good. All this Dizzy destroyed'. Gladstone believed that Disraeli's 'crypto-Judaism has had to do with this policy. The Jews of the East *bitterly* hate the Christians; who have not always used them well'. What Disraeli 'hates is Christian liberty and reconstruction'. It was now that Gladstone read Disraeli's novel *Tancred*, in which the hero is urged to magnetize the Queen through his conversation and encourage her to shift the seat of her Empire from Britain to Delhi. In the light of the Royal Titles Bill and Disraeli's flattery of Victoria, could this not be what was happening?[23]

The anti-Turkish agitation led by Gladstone had important consequences for Disraeli's diplomacy. He had wished to present the Russians with a clear message of Britain's unwillingness to tolerate any threat to Turkey's territorial integrity. However, the extent of anti-Turk feeling in Britain raised doubts as to whether Britain really would go to war on behalf of Turkey if Russia intervened in the region. Disraeli's policy of resolute opposition was undermined. On 5 September 1876, Derby warned Britain's ambassador to Constantinople that the 'accounts of outrages and excesses committed by the Turkish troops' had made it 'practically impossible' for Britain to defend the Ottoman Empire against a Russian attack.[24]

By the autumn of 1876, the war between Serbia and Montenegro and the Turks was continuing – with the Turks having the upper hand. This made Great Power intervention on behalf of the Christians all the more likely and Austria, Russia and Germany discussed plans for partitioning the Ottoman Empire. It was in the hope of avoiding this that Disraeli's government proposed a Conference of the Great Powers in Constantinople to consider the future of Turkey in terms of both reform and the maintenance of its territorial integrity. With all sides still keen to avoid all-out war, the proposal was accepted.

Britain, represented at the Conference by the Secretary of State for India, Lord Salisbury, pressed for the amelioration of the condition of the Sultan's Christian subjects in the context of the maintenance of the Ottoman Empire. This was to be achieved by upholding the effective independence of Serbia and Montenegro and acceding administrative autonomy to Bosnia and Bulgaria, with a pledge of additional reforms by the Sultan. But now, a difficulty intervened: when the powers finally placed their relatively weak proposals for reform to the Turks in January 1877, they were rejected and the conference broke up. It is sometimes suggested, for example, by Clayden, that Disraeli contributed to this result by giving the impression to the Turks that Britain would stand by them whatever the outcome. It is truer to say that only direct pressure from Britain could have induced the Sultan to accept the reforms – and this neither Disraeli nor Derby was prepared to apply. Indeed, other factors were at work. Turkish nationalism had been awakened and there was resistance, in Constantinople, to the whole idea of foreign powers interfering in the affairs of the Empire. In addition, the Turks believed that Russia did not really have the stomach for a fight and were happy to call their bluff. Accordingly, when Russia drew up a protocol calling on the Turks to introduce a series of mild reforms, securing, this time, the signature of Britain (the London Protocol), the Turks rejected it.

Russia Declares War on Turkey

Thus, on 24 April 1877, Russia, having first secretly secured Austrian neutrality by acknowledging her right to occupy Bosnia-Herzegovina, declared war on Turkey, claiming it was enforcing the terms of the London Protocol. In reality, Russia's object was to assert her power in the Balkans, secure the return of Bessarabia (lost in the 1856 Treaty of Paris) and create a large independent Bulgarian state subject to Russian influence. Disraeli recognized that it was impossible for Britain to come to Turkey's defence; she had herself signed the Protocol and, in any case, public opinion would not have tolerated war on Turkey's behalf. Britain consequently adopted a position of neutrality in the war, only warning the Russians (in a letter of 6 May 1877) that she would be forced to intervene if any of the following positions were threatened – the Persian Gulf, Egypt, Suez, Constantinople and the Straits. This note, which was accepted by the Russian foreign minister (who specifically said that the acquisition of Constantinople was 'excluded from the views of his Majesty the Emperor') remained the basis of British policy for the next nine months.

Public opinion in Britain was now bitterly divided between the Russophiles – who supported the nationalist, Christian, movements against the Muslim Turks and accordingly sympathized with Russian intervention, and the Turkophiles, who attached more importance to maintaining the Turkish Empire as a bulwark against Russia. Gladstone came to lead the Russophiles, a movement which was strongest in the north of England, Scotland and Wales and which appealed particularly to middle class nonconformists and members of the High Church party still angry with Disraeli for his Public Worship Act. Yet Gladstone did not speak for all Liberals. In the major Commons vote on the handling of the crisis, six Liberals voted with the government and 18 abstained. The supporters of Turkey, stronger in the south and London, included the bulk of the Establishment, mainstream members of the Church of England, aristocratic society and Queen Victoria. A notable convert was the *Daily Telegraph*, formerly a vocal supporter of Gladstone.

Disraeli's sympathies were with the Turkophiles. The upper and lower classes, he told the Cabinet in June 1877, were united against Russia. The middle classes would always be against war – but 'fortunately the middle classes did not now govern'.[25] But, despite the urgent prompting of the Queen, there was little he could do to influence events. More important than divisions amongst public opinion were divisions within his Cabinet. The basic problem Disraeli faced throughout the crisis was the reluctance of the majority of his Cabinet colleagues to support strong measures on behalf of Turkey. Of the 12 members of the Cabinet, only Lord John Manners and Gathorne Hardy were consistent advocates of a firm stance against Russia. Of the remainder, some such as Cross, Northcote and W.H. Smith, were luke-warm, others, including Salisbury, were sceptical, while Carnarvon and Derby were hostile to the idea of even threatening war with Russia. What motivated this reluctance? There was a general disinclination, in view of the Bulgarian atrocities and the state of public opinion, to ally Britain with what Carlyle called 'the unspeakable Turk'.[26] There was consciousness, too, of the depressed condition of the economy and manufacturers were said to be alarmed at the prospect of a war. In the background was a determination to avoid the regrettable events of the Crimean War.

Of the opponents of war, by far the most important was Lord Derby who was, after all, Foreign Secretary. Derby was a moderate and passive individual of liberal sympathies who attached no importance to the maintenance of the Ottoman Empire and who believed that the state of public opinion in Britain and the lack of European allies meant Britain could not 'fight for Turkey again as in 1854–1856'.[27] Thus, while prepared to send dispatches warning the Russians off Britain's strategic interests, he had no intention of taking more resolute action. If Britain sent a force with the cooperation of the Turks, she would become their ally in a war with Russia; if without Turkish support, she would be precipitating a scramble for Ottoman territory. Derby was even prepared to accept a temporary Russian occupation of Constantinople; only a permanent one would be a ground for war. It was here that the essential difference with Disraeli lay, for the Premier was resolved to block any potential Russian entry into Constantinople[28]; and it was a very significant difference as the Russians, who had previously declaimed any intention of occupying Constantinople, were now talking of doing so for temporary strategic reasons.

Out of step with a cautious Cabinet and harassed all the while by a Queen and a Conservative press convinced of the need for action, Disraeli wore down his already precarious health in the attempt to hold his government together and push it towards the measures he deemed essential. For Disraeli saw that, having so publicly warned the Russians against infringing Britain's eastern interests, it was imperative for the credibility of the government's entire approach to foreign policy that the necessary preparations be made for backing up threats with action. He was characteristically worried about public opinion. As Derby reports of a meeting in July 1877, he:

> found him…uneasy and excited: he said matters were critical: the Russians were advancing in Europe and there was nothing to stop them. If they got Constantinople, there would be an outbreak of popular feeling against us, the bulk of the Conservatives would desert us, the Whigs would join in and Gladstone and his friends would say 'if our advice had been taken, all this might have been averted.' The ministry would be upset and that with ignominy.[29]

Although Disraeli feared the results of inaction, he failed to give a decisive lead. He manoeuvred and adjusted, continually trying to reconcile the differences of his 'discordant and unwilling' Cabinet. This was really an impossible task. The most he could do was to persuade his Cabinet to sanction a threat of war *once* Russia had taken Constantinople – once, that is, the key objective of British diplomacy had been relinquished. It was little wonder that the Queen was so perplexed and alarmed. Her letters to Disraeli during this period, in which she repeatedly urged the removal of Derby and the adoption of forceful measures against Russia, are classics of unrestrained emotion.

> In the letter the Queen wrote to Lord Beaconsfield the night Lord Salisbury was here…she *urged so strongly* (and Lord Salisbury agreed) the *importance* of the CZAR knowing that we *will not let him have Constantinople!* Lord Derby and his wife most likely say the *reverse right and left* and RUSSIA GOES ON! It maddens the Queen to feel that all our efforts are being destroyed by the Ministers who ought to carry them out. The Queen must say that she can't stand it![30]

It was at this time that Victoria visited Disraeli at Hughenden to publicly demonstrate her support for her Prime Minister – the first time she had visited the residence of a serving Prime Minister since the days of Peel.

Why did Disraeli not remove the 'negative and sluggish' Derby and pursue a firmer line? There were three factors here.

1. His connections with Derby were strong and of long duration. The two men had grown up politically together and Disraeli felt loath to take action against him: 'My heart,' he wrote to his friend, 'is as much concerned in it as my intelligence and I wish not to conceal, how grievous would be to me the blow, that severed our long connection and faithful friendship.'
2. Disraeli was very concerned to maintain party unity. He owed his position to party and he continued to attach an importance to it, rare at the time. He suspected Salisbury of pro-Russian sympathies and to dismiss Derby over the issue might well precipitate an exodus of senior figures from

the Cabinet. 'A government can only die once,' Disraeli observed and the departure of Derby might threaten just such a life-threatening crisis.

3. Despite his resolute rhetoric, Disraeli knew he could not risk, let alone win, a war with Russia without major allies. These Britain lacked. France, the Crimean ally, was out of the equation and Austria had already – unknown to Disraeli – been squared by Russia and had no wish to bear the brunt of war as a 'British tool'.[31] Only if and when, the Austrians concluded, they could no longer trust the Russians to observe the conventions they had agreed, would Disraeli secure the alliance he needed. Ironically, even the Sultan rejected Disraeli's proposal that a British force be landed on the Gallipoli peninsula. Though he might dream of driving the Russians into the Caspian and invading Russian Armenia, these schemes, remarks Anderson, 'were extravagant futility'.[32]

With the Cabinet divided between war and peace, no firm line was adopted and affairs drifted, the government being spared greater embarrassment by the Turk's plucky resistance of the Russians at Plevna. But this gave way in December 1877 and the Russian advance recommenced. With the moment of truth approaching, the Cabinet was still unable to agree on how to respond. Disraeli, although warning the Cabinet that if they remained inactive 'he foresaw discredit to the government and disaster for the country', had to hint at resignation in order to carry a proposal to summon parliament and secure a vote of credit for war preparations. While the Cabinet fiddled, Victoria burned. 'Oh if the Queen were a man, she would like to go and give those horrid Russians whose word one cannot be trust such a beating.'

Finally, on 23 January 1878, Disraeli persuaded the Cabinet to agree to:

1. The resumption of alliance negotiations with the Austrians – themselves opposed to the idea of Russia occupying Constantinople.
2. Approach parliament for a grant of £6 million for war preparations.
3. The despatch of British ships through the Dardanelles to Constantinople. On 15 February 1878, after further delays and rescinded orders, the British fleet finally anchored off Constantinople.

These measures were enough to force the resignations of Derby and Carnarvon. Carnarvon's resignation was final and Disraeli was inclined to accept Derby's – before doubts set in. Derby's was a name that resonated, not only within the Conservative party and his native Lancashire, but amongst the middle classes more generally. In the City, financial interests were unnerved by the apparent victory of the 'war party' within the Cabinet. Several Cabinet members began to fear the consequences of his loss and the Whips warned that the vote on war credits might be imperilled. 'The retirement of Lord Derby,' Disraeli wrote to the Queen, 'is producing disastrous results on the Conservative party, both in Parliament and out of doors. A general disintegration is taking place... All the Lancashire members and others who represent the chief seats of manufactures and commerce, can no longer be relied on...'[33] Disraeli, the party man, now decided it would be better if Derby stayed after all and emissaries were sent to suggest that he rescind his resignation – which he agreed to do. The whole affair reflected little to the credit of either man. Derby returned with the purely negative hope of 'preventing mischief as long as I can', while Disraeli had exhibited a weakness in leadership, pulling back from the course he considered best when party difficulties reared their head. For better or worse, he was no statesman of the school of Peel or Gladstone.

Faced with the prospect of a war with Britain and even Austria, who were by now alarmed at the prospect of Russia occupying Constantinople and controlling the Straits, the Tsar decided to sue for peace, forcing the Turks to agree to the *Treaty of San Stefano* (March 1878) – 'the fullest practical expression ever given in Russian foreign policy to the Panslav ideal.'[34] For Britain, this Treaty was totally unacceptable, chiefly because:

1. It envisaged the creation of a large Bulgarian state stretching across most of the Southern Balkans to the Aegean and which would be under Russian domination. From such a base the Russians would be able to command the entire Balkans region and occupy Constantinople at will.
2. It ceded territory in Central Asia to Russia, including the eastern portions of Armenia which abutted onto the Black Sea.

These terms, said Disraeli, would abolish 'the dominion of the Ottoman Empire in Europe' and reduce the Sultan 'to a state of absolute subjugation to Russia'. Britain demanded that any Treaty affecting the integrity of Turkey be placed before a Congress of the great powers. When Russia failed to respond, the Cabinet agreed on 27 March 1878, to further measures, including the mobilization of the army reserves and the movement of 7,000 Indian troops to Malta as a clear statement that Britain was prepared to deploy the full weight of her imperial resources in any impending struggle with Russia. This was too much for Derby who belatedly resigned as Foreign Secretary. His replacement was Lord Salisbury who, over the previous months, had gradually moved from being a critic to supporter of Disraeli's approach to the crisis.

With Salisbury's appointment as Foreign Secretary, there was at last a firm and clear-sighted approach to the Eastern problem and a relative coming together of Prime Minister and Foreign Secretary. In some ways, he occupied a position between that of Derby and Disraeli. Salisbury did not think that Britain should make support for the Ottoman Empire the centrepiece of its Eastern policy. This was mainly because Turkey's inhuman methods of government rendered it a no longer effective barrier to Russian expansion.

As he wrote to Disraeli during the atrocity agitation: 'It is clear enough that the traditional Palmerston policy is at an end. We have not the power, even if we had the wish, to give back any of the revolted districts to the *discretionary* power of the Porte.'[35] He was equally sceptical of any Russian threat to Britain's Indian interests, urging those who believed that Russia was close to challenging India to use larger scale maps. His personal preference was for a partition of the Ottoman Empire, with Britain acquiring Egypt. But even if this were not possible, he believed that Britain had to maintain its prestige and thought Derby had been far too weak in his handling of the Russians. In practice, therefore, he was prepared to work with Disraeli to get Russia before a Congress to settle the crisis.

With Britain taking firm measures and Austria making clear its opposition to a large Bulgarian state and anger at the failure of San Stefano to make any reference to her acquisition of Bosnia, the Russians agreed to open negotiations with Britain. The upshot of these and simultaneous negotiations with the Sultan and Austria-Hungary was as follows:

1. The large Bulgarian state envisaged at San Stefano would be divided into two halves separated by the Balkan mountains. The southern part would remain within the Ottoman Empire – though with administrative independence.
2. Britain was to endorse Austria's annexation of Bosnia.
3. Though Russia promised not to acquire any more territory in Asiatic Turkey, she refused to relinquish her gains in East Armenia. This was a setback for Disraeli as it meant that Russia's land threat to India had increased – the very thing he most wished to avoid.
4. To counterbalance Russian gains in Armenia, Britain formed a defensive alliance with Turkey, in which the Turks would cede Cyprus to Britain, to provide a naval base in the eastern Mediterranean. In return, Britain pledged to defend Turkey if attacked by Russia in its Asiatic territories.

By this means, Disraeli claimed, 'the power of England in the Mediterranean will be absolutely increased' and the 'Indian Empire immensely strengthened. Cyprus is the key to Western Asia'. In addition, Turkey, he hoped, 'would be a stronger barrier against Russia than she was before the war'.[36]

The Berlin Congress

The way was now open for a European Congress to ratify the new arrangements and this was held in Berlin in June 1878. The Congress was the climax of Disraeli's career. Although 73 years of age, in poor health and by the end of the Congress, close to collapse, he was determined to go. It enabled him to fulfil the part of a statesman on a European stage, legislating the affairs of the

Continent amidst scenes of ceremony and grandeur. Disraeli was the 'lion of the Congress'. Everyone, says Blake, wanted to meet this romantic and mysterious character whose rise to power fascinated European society and there was a great run on his novels.[37] 'The old Jew,' remarked Bismarck, 'that is the man.'

Most of the main points had already been settled, but Disraeli was determined to get his way on the remaining details – in particular, the right of the Sultan to station troops in Southern Bulgaria, which Russia at first rejected – and adopted an intransigent strategy, threatening to break up the Congress if his demands were not accepted. He made this clear to Bismarck, who proceeded to put pressure upon Russia, which finally gave way. Disraeli's main concession to Russia was to allow it to retain the former Turkish territories of Kars and Batoum on the eastern side of the Black Sea. But the acquisition of Cyprus, which was now made public, more than compensated for this. With Turkish authority now effectively ending at the Balkan mountains, it was agreed that Austria was to administer the territories of Bosnia and Herzegovina.

The Treaty of Berlin was signed on 13 July 1878. Disraeli was by now very weak and it was only with difficulty that his doctor roused him for this last effort, and he headed for London the next day. Arriving at Downing Street he was met by crowds – partly organized by his old friend Lord Henry Lennox – and made his famous boast of obtaining 'peace with honour'. The Treaty was regarded as a victory for Britain and Disraeli was at the height of his fame and prestige. He had stood firm and achieved, without war, his basic objective of keeping Russia out of Constantinople, despite the distractions of Gladstone, Derby, the Queen, and ill-health. The Queen offered him a Dukedom, which he declined, but he did accept the Order of the Garter. 'High and low,' she wrote, 'are delighted, excepting Mr Gladstone who is frantic...' In the Commons vote on the Treaty, the government won a great victory, by 338 votes to 195, with 18 Liberals abstaining and 5 voting for the government.

Assessment

'The Treaty of Berlin,' wrote Monypenny and Buckle, 'is Beaconsfield's main international work; by it his reputation as a European statesman must stand or fall.'[38] What, then, is the verdict regarding Disraeli's handling of the Eastern Crisis?

1. *Peace*

Disraeli accomplished much of what he intended without the need for war. Not a single British life had been lost and little expense had been incurred – a notable contrast with the Crimean War. He had judged truly. Russia had not been prepared to risk war with Britain and Austria and a resolute stand by Britain had helped to bring Russia to the negotiating table. More than this, the Treaty itself not only lifted the prospect of war from Europe but, add Monypenny and Buckle, 'none of the six great European powers – Austria, France, Germany, Great Britain, Italy, Russia – was at war in Europe during the 36 years which intervened between the Treaty and the outbreak of Armageddon in 1914'.[39] Though admitting that peace was not secured in the Balkans, Monypenny and Buckle argue that no arrangement possible in 1878 could have effected that and what conflicts there were confined to the Balkan region.

Against this it has been argued, for example by Seaman, that the peace that prevailed after 1878 had little to do with the Berlin Treaty and that the concession of Bosnia to Austria in the Treaty lit a slow burning fuse that led to the outbreak of the World War in 1914. This was because the Bosnian territories were coveted by Serbia and the rivalry between Serbia and Austria for influence in that region culminated in the assassination in Bosnia of Archduke Ferdinand, the heir to the Austrian throne, by a Serbian-supporting terrorist.[40]

This rebuttal is unconvincing. It is, to begin with, hardly fair to hold the framers of a Treaty in 1878 responsible for events that happened 36 years later and which had much more to do with the evolution of Great Power rivalries in Europe and beyond. Second, it was inevitable that Turkey would be unable to sustain its grip on Bosnia and there was no way that Austria would be prepared to see the creation of a greater Serbia, incorporating Bosnia, on its border – with or without a Treaty of Berlin. Austrio-Serbian rivalry in the Balkans cannot be laid at the door of Disraeli.

2. Blocking the advance of Russia

Monypenny and Buckle contend that, by his actions in 1876–1878, Disraeli had lifted a real and present threat to Britain's imperial interests. Russia's landward advance through European Turkey towards Constantinople and the Mediterranean and through Asia Minor towards Syria and Egypt, had been permanently stopped.

Does this claim stand up? Seaman says no, arguing that Russia had no intention of seizing either Constantinople or the Suez Canal and that an invasion of Egypt through Syria and Palestine, a distance of more than 1,000 miles, was simply not practical strategy. Eldridge agrees, branding Disraeli's fears of Russia 'rather ridiculous and ill-founded'. This is perhaps an exaggeration. As Blake notes, in 1840, an Egyptian army had covered precisely this distance to threaten Constantinople and the *threat* of such an advance if the Ottoman Empire imploded had to be considered. In addition, Russian troops would, he argues, almost certainly have entered Constantinople in

March 1878 if it had not been for British opposition.[41] Even so, it is improbable that the Russians would have sought to occupy Constantinople permanently in the face of the opposition of all the European powers. On the other hand, Disraeli had done nothing to block the more significant advance of Russia in Asia towards Persia and Afghanistan. Indeed, Russia's acquisition of strategic bases at Kars and Batoum weakened Britain's overall position in South West Asia.

3. Cyprus

Through Disraeli's initiative, Britain had acquired in Cyprus a military base in the eastern Mediterranean from which she could oversee her interests in this vital region. In practice, the benefits of this transaction were limited as the island proved 'extremely unhealthy and the shores short of anchorage'.[42] Monypenny and Buckle acknowledge that the island proved of little military value, but point out that this reflected, first, the fact that Russia did not challenge Turkey in Asia – the very point to be achieved – and, second, that in the 1880s Britain, under Gladstone, acquired direct control of Egypt – something Disraeli was not prepared to countenance for fear of alienating France. Even so, Gladstone was surely right to complain that Disraeli had made an 'insane covenant' when he had, on Britain's behalf, made an open-ended commitment to fight single-handed on behalf of Turkey 2,000 miles away in Asia Minor. It was unlikely that any government would have wished to honour such a pledge.

4. A strengthened Turkey

Disraeli had not only ensured that Turkey remained 'part of the acknowledged political system of Europe' but the Treaty of Berlin had strengthened it by overseeing the removal of the outlying provinces it could not govern and which were a source only of instability. A smaller Turkey was stronger and better able to defend her essential interests. In the process, the majority of Turkey's Christian subjects, whose treatment was the pretext for the war, had been removed from Turkish governance.

However, while Turkey was indeed strengthened, the state which chiefly benefited from this was not Britain but Germany. Once Disraeli had fallen from power, Gladstone's government did nothing to maintain friendly links with Turkey and Britain's influence with the Porte was displaced by that of Germany who became Turkey's chief European ally. To this, Monypenny and Buckle reply that Disraeli could not be held responsible for the subsequent actions of statesmen. He could only deal with the situation before him. While this is true, the fact remains that Disraeli's handling of the Eastern Crisis contributed to this subsequent parting of the ways between Britain and Turkey. For, his support for Turkey had been so blatantly founded upon the language of realpolitik and British material interests that he effectively discredited any future policy of supporting Turkey. Disraeli had no understanding of the sensitivities of the British middle class conscience. His failure to comprehend the indignation caused by the Bulgarian atrocities was, says Blake, his worst mistake.[43] Disraeli, complained Derby, 'believes quite thoroughly in "prestige" as all foreigners do...' He had upheld the cause of Turkey in the short run; but he had left it stripped of ethical legitimacy. No future British government would take its stand on the maintenance of the Ottoman Empire. It was Suez and Egypt that were to become the future locus of British policy in the East and this was foreseen by some, such as Clayden, who wrote in 1880 that Disraeli had 'missed the opportunity of establishing a direct British protectorate over Egypt by vaguely assuming an indirect British protectorate over Constantinople'.[44]

5. *The division of Bulgaria*
Disraeli's greatest achievement at the Berlin Congress was to block Russia's proposed creation of a Greater Bulgaria. However his division of Bulgaria into two parts lasted only seven years. In 1885, something approaching the Greater Bulgaria that Disraeli had opposed was inaugurated, with Salisbury' approval. Of course, by then the chief fear of Disraeli – that a Greater Bulgaria would be a mere client state of Russia – had failed to materialize, the Bulgarians having gone from being 'clients and tools' of Russia to being a 'people with a strong sense of individuality and independence'. Yet this was precisely what Gladstone had foreseen when he had remarked that the surest barrier to Russian advance in the Balkans were the breasts of free men.

6. *Breaking up the Emperors' league*
One of Disraeli's key diplomatic goals was to redress the balance of power in Europe by fracturing the Three Emperors' League. This had been successfully achieved during the Eastern Crisis as Austria was gradually detached from her erstwhile ally to adopt a critical position alongside Britain – to the fury of the Tsar. The alliance was shattered. As Disraeli reflected in 1880: 'Next to making a tolerable settlement for the Porte, our great object was to break-up and permanently prevent, the alliance of the three Empires and I maintain there never was a general diplomatic result more completely effected.'[45] Gladstone's Concert of Europe was in fact an alliance of three autocratic powers – Russia, Austria and Germany – and it was, say Monypenny and Buckle, well for the balance of power in Europe and the maintenance of liberty that this alliance was dissolved.

However, the estrangement between Germany, Austria and Russia was only temporary. Fences were soon mended by Bismarck and in 1881, the more robust and formally binding Three Emperors' Alliance was negotiated between the three northern powers – though this too proved short-lived owing to continuing rivalries between Austria and Russia for influence in the

Balkans. It was this long-term strategic conflict between Russia and Austria that drove the northern powers apart – not Disraeli's diplomacy.

7. Disraeli's handling of the crisis

It will be noted that Monypenny and Buckle say that it is by the terms of the Treaty of Berlin that Disraeli must be judged. Posing the issue in this way has the consequence that his wider handling of the crisis is not considered by them, and here it is difficult to be so sanguine. For the relatively successful outcome of the Berlin Congress should not disguise the hesitancy and confusion that bedevilled the early stages of the crisis, when Disraeli failed to provide a strong lead and allowed Derby to remain for far too long in his post, given that he was actively seeking to frustrate the Prime Minister's own policy – even requesting him to withdraw his belated resignation when internal party difficulties threatened. Britain had warned Russia that it would not accept the occupation of Constantinople and yet Disraeli's government did nothing to ensure that the threat could be upheld. If the Russians had broken through at Plevna and marched on Constantinople, there was nothing Britain could have done to stop them and even in 1878, the sending of the fleet through the Dardanelles and the stationing of 7,000 Indian troops at Malta was largely tokenism. A key British objective would have been lost and dislodging Russia from Constantinople and Gallipoli would have been impossible. Disraeli had taken a stand but had not the stomach to make it a reality. His whole policy had witnessed the triumph of style over substance.

Yet any such criticism of Disraeli must be qualified. His options during the crisis were severely circumscribed. Few senior politicians were ready to contemplate a war with Russia – the events of the Crimean War were sufficient warning on that score – and to undertake such a hazardous endeavour on behalf of the massacring Turks found few supporters. The public shared this distaste for war, however much they might wish to see the Russians rebuffed. As the events surrounding Derby's first resignation reveal, Disraeli was far too much a politician to risk the real perils of an eastern campaign without popular or parliamentary backing. Most important, Britain had no allies. She could not realistically block Russia without Austrian support and this was only slowly secured. The only person convinced of the need to contemplate conflict was the Queen and Disraeli, with his previously fulsome praise for Her Majesty's sagacity and protestations of devotion to her Regal Will, was in an awkward position. The divisions in his Cabinet, which so well mirrored the divisions within the nation, then did Disraeli a service, allowing him to pose to his monarch as a man of resolution frustrated by the timidity of his colleagues. As Disraeli admitted to Victoria in 1878, 'there have been terrible opportunities lost and terrible acts of weakness committed, by us during these two years, but the nation was perplexed, bewildered and half-hearted.'[46] It suited Disraeli to bide his time, waiting for the key alliances to form without which war was really unthinkable and in early 1878, they did. At home, Lord Salisbury, the political heavyweight whose opinion mattered most within the Conservative party, was finally secured for the 'resolute-stance party' and the Foreign Secretaryship; while in Europe, Russia's behaviour finally alienated the other powers and yielded the cooperation of Austria – and ultimately Bismarck. It was the exhaustion of Austria's patience with Russia that finally brought the Tsar to the negotiating table.

Conclusion

Thus while, when judged according to his own standards and rhetoric, Disraeli's handling of the crisis often appears dilatory and weak and the long-term results far from convincing, when judged according to the political and diplomatic possibilities, it was very well judged. The outcome of the Berlin Congress differed remarkably little from the bag and baggage policy recommended by Gladstone. Turkish power in the Balkans had been effectively broken. But in terms of domestic politics, the outcome could not have been more different. Disraeli had been obsessed by the public's judgement of his policy. Indeed Derby, when reflecting on Disraeli's motives during the crisis, believed that he was 'ready to adopt any course which seems to be the most likely to be popular'. 'He only desires the credit at home of a spirited policy.'[47] What alarmed him was not so much Russia's move on Constantinople, but the reaction of the Conservative party, the House of Commons, the Queen, and the general public to such an eventuality. As late as January 1878, the government, by its failure to adopt a strategy to deal with Russia's advance, was open to censure by a patriotic public opinion. The transformation in the government's standing which had occurred by June 1878 was Disraeli's greatest personal triumph. He had secured for the Conservatives the neglected heritage of Palmerstonian diplomacy against the unpatriotic cosmopolitanism of the Liberals; he had watched Gladstone re-open Liberal divisions yet again, as sections of front and backbench opinion recoiled from his emotional language and apparent pro-Russian sympathies; he had been seen to assert British power and make her opinion count in the councils of Europe; he had sounded the note of Empire, bringing Indian troops into the European arena and guarding the imperial arteries; he had won the gratitude of his Monarch; and he had secured his legacy as a statesman, making states, drawing frontiers and disposing of peoples amidst gilded salons and the aroma of cigar smoke. This, after all, was what it had all been for since he had first thrown his political hat into the ring in the 1830s. 'To the premier,' wrote Derby, 'the main thing is to please and surprise the public by bold strokes and unexpected moves…' It was here, in the politics of presentation, that the eastern campaign was truly fought and won in a way which tested to the limit Disraeli's political skills. If few wanted war, by 1878, fewer still were prepared to question either the benefits or meaning of 'peace with honour'.

Imperial Policy under Disraeli

Though Disraeli had used Empire as a source of inspirational rhetoric, he did not come to power with any plans to pursue an expansionary imperial policy. It is usually said that he wished rather to consolidate the Empire, but in truth, he had little idea how this might be achieved and even doubted whether it was still possible to 'unite the colonies more closely with England'.[48] He left Colonial policy solely to Carnarvon and the Colonial Office. The ideas of the Crystal Palace speech were not followed up. There was no move towards an imperial customs union or an imperial assembly. The reductions in colonial military commitments made by Gladstone were not reversed. Disraeli did little to encourage ministers who pressed for a more proactive imperial policy. When, for instance, the First Lord of the Admiralty (G. Hunt) recommended raising a loan to pay for the fortification of the navy's colonial coaling stations, he received no support from Disraeli.[49] The island of Fiji was formally annexed in 1874, but this move was made on the initiative of Carnarvon, who was in turn responding reluctantly to a long-running campaign by missionaries, humanitarians, and the governments of Australia and New Zealand. It was in no sense an aggressive act bearing the imprint of Disraeli,[50] who was, says Stembridge, 'no more eager for annexation than Gladstone had been…'[51] Thus, upon becoming Prime Minister, Disraeli did little to expand or intensify Britain's imperial commitments. His two first significant moves were largely symbolic in character.

1. Purchase of Suez Canal shares in 1875
The Suez Canal had been opened by French engineers in 1869. By linking the Mediterranean to the Red Sea and Indian Ocean, it reduced by several weeks the time spent sailing between Britain and India. Soon four-fifths of the traffic passing through the canal was British. More important, it was the route by which troops and supplies passed to and from India. It was thus a crucial imperial link. However, 56 per cent of the canal company shares were held by France, the other 44 per cent being owned by the Khedive – the ruler of Egypt. Accordingly, write Monypenny and Buckle, 'a vital link in British imperial communications was under the control of a foreign company and at the mercy of a foreign ruler'.[52] Disraeli was keen to acquire a stake in the company and in 1874, he initiated an offer to buy out the French owners of the canal, which was making heavy losses, but French public opinion vetoed

the scheme. The following year, a new opportunity arose when the Khedive, who was profligate and encumbered with debts, approached the French with a view to raising a new loan on the security of his shares. The British Cabinet was determined that France should not own the entire company and in November 1875, Britain's consul in Egypt was instructed to offer to buy the shares outright. The Khedive agreed to sell his stake for £4 million. Parliament was not sitting at the time, so to raise the money at short notice, Disraeli despatched his Private Secretary, Montagu Corry, to the house of his old friend Baron Rothschild. Corry told the Baron that he wanted 4 million pounds. 'When?' 'Tomorrow', Corry answered. The Baron chewed on a grape and ejected the skin. 'What is your security?' 'The British Government.' 'You shall have it.'

Disraeli was elated, his triumphant letter to Victoria rather giving the impression that Britain had acquired the entire canal:

> It is just settled: you have it, Madam. The French Government has been out-generaled. They tried too much, offering loans at an usurious rate and with conditions which would have virtually given them the government of Egypt. The Khedive, in despair and disgust, offered your Majesty's Government to purchase his shares outright. He never would listen to such a proposition before. Four millions sterling! And almost immediately. There was only one firm that could do it – Rothschilds. They behaved admirably; advanced the money at a low rate and the entire interest of the Khedive is now yours, Madam.

In practical terms, the purchase made little difference and Disraeli was wide of the mark when he said that possession of the shares 'was necessary to maintain the empire' and would give an 'immense, not to say preponderating, influence in the management of the canal'. The majority of shares were still with the French and the canal's navigation was controlled by international agreements. The company could not have closed it even if it wished. But the purchase did much for Disraeli's prestige. It was just the sort of gesture he enjoyed and served to symbolize Britain's commitment to its Indian Empire.

2. Victoria, Empress of India

The idea that the Queen might assume a position of formal sovereignty over India seems to have been implanted by Disraeli in the wake of the Mutiny and the proclamation of direct British control in 1858. Victoria was struck by the possibility of becoming an Empress – especially when the unification of Germany in 1871 meant that her daughter Vicky, who was married to the heir to the throne of Prussia, was set to become Empress of Germany. Predictably, she made no progress with Gladstone, but rightly saw that

Disraeli would be far more forthcoming. Although initially reluctant to take up the idea, he knew he could not resist for long: 'The Empress Queen demands her Imperial crown... I would have avoided touching upon the matter, but can do so no longer.' With the Prince of Wales just concluding a most successful tour of India, the timing was propitious. Disraeli himself had stated that 'You can only act upon the opinion of Eastern nations through their imagination,' and was more than alive to the potency of ceremonial in government. 'It is only by the amplification of titles that you can often touch and satisfy the imagination of nations; and that is an element which governments must not despise.'[53] To have the Queen declared Empress of India would, he believed, strengthen India's loyalty to Britain and act as a symbol of British prestige and power and serve as a signal to Russia 'that the Parliament of England have resolved to uphold the Empire of India.'

A Royal Titles Bill was accordingly brought forward in 1876, conferring on the Queen the additional title of Empress of India. However, the measure encountered unexpectedly intense opposition, especially in the press. Liberals saw the title of Empress as smacking of absolutist government and it was believed that the historic title of King or Queen would fall into abeyance. But as one contemporary remarked, the new title was for foreign use only.[54]

In India, the assumption of the new title on 1 January 1877 was celebrated in a great assembly of princes or Durbar which lasted fourteen days. 'The Faery,' wrote Disraeli, 'is much excited about the doings at Delhi. They have produced a great effect in India and indeed throughout the world and vindicate triumphantly the policy of the measure which was so virulently, but so fruitlessly, opposed. It has no doubt consolidated our empire there.'[55]

Later Imperial Events

The latter part of Disraeli's premiership saw imperial affairs shift from being an asset to a liability. The country became embroiled in embarrassing wars in South Africa and Afghanistan and these contributed to a developing sense of disillusionment with the government and contributed to its defeat in 1880. The question arises as to how far Disraeli himself and his rhetoric of Empire were responsible for these outcomes. The general verdict is that while Disraeli did set the broad principles of policy that led to war, he was not accountable for the particular actions of imperial administrators that determined the occasion and timing of conflict. They were, it is said, a reflection of Disraeli's lack of control over members of his Cabinet and colonial governments. This is a strange and inconsistent defence. Delegation was Disraeli's management style. He set the course for his government, supplied the supporting rhetoric, and let others get on with the task of implementing it.

On these grounds, Disraeli is held to deserve the credit for the government's achievements. It can hardly be argued that, on the same grounds, Disraeli does not deserve sanction for its failures.

1. South Africa

Disraeli left the details of colonial administration to his colonial secretary, Earl Carnarvon, and his successor, Hicks Beach. Carnarvon was not only an effective and experienced administrator. He was, unlike Disraeli, a proactive imperialist and this was a source of tension within the government. He oversaw the annexation to Britain of the Fiji Islands, supported British involvement in the finances of Egypt, and pressed for increased numbers of troops to be deployed in the colonies. But it was his South African policy that defined his period in office and stored up problems for Disraeli.

South Africa had a small and scattered settler community surrounded by far larger numbers of native tribesmen. It had long been the preferred British policy to bring about a federation of the British and Dutch settler communities and Carnarvon, who had implemented a confederation scheme in Canada in 1867, agreed – as did Disraeli. The British were especially concerned by the situation in the Transvaal. A poor, agricultural, territory founded by the Dutch Boers in an attempt to escape British jurisdiction, its white inhabitants were in a permanent state of conflict with various local tribes, including the Zulus. Unable to control the situation, the Boers' harsh treatment of the natives only provoked wider unrest and it was feared that a native uprising might be ignited across South Africa. Carnarvon was determined to eliminate this source of instability by bringing the Transvaal and ultimately the Orange Free State, under British control. The impetus behind this 'forward policy' was very much his and he asked Disraeli only to concur 'in what may seem a sudden, but is not a hasty or ill-considered measure'. Disraeli was less enthusiastic, but distracted by the Eastern Question and trusting Carnarvon's judgement, he agreed, describing the annexation of the Transvaal as a 'geographical necessity'. What he failed to appreciate were the risks involved in pushing forward so aggressively when, as Eldridge observes, 'none of the conditions for a successful federation seemed to exist'.[56]

To implement his federation scheme Carnarvon appointed the experienced Indian administrator, Sir Bartle Frere, as High Commissioner for South Africa. Frere arrived in South Africa in April 1877, but at the same time, a British delegation to the Transvaal announced the annexation of the state to Britain. The Dutch Boers were hardly enthusiastic and the Transvaal parliament protested against the unilateral declaration. However, the bulk of the local inhabitants, realising their vulnerable position in the face of increasing native unrest, acquiesced with the move – for the time being. But by 1880, their anger was growing, with public declarations that they were not subjects of the Queen and a general refusal to pay taxes. The annexation, in short, was unpopular and resented and was shortly afterwards abandoned by Gladstone's government after the first Boer War.

Yet, annexation first precipitated a conflict, not with the Boers, but with the native Zulu population. The Zulus, under their chief Cetewayo, were a martial tribe who had been involved in a long-running war with the Boers. Unfortunately, the annexation of the Transvaal meant that a war with the Boers was a war with Britain. Frere quickly became convinced that lifting the native threat was essential to carrying through his plans for a federation. The stage was set for war. The problem was the same as that which was arising simultaneously under Lytton in India, namely, a colonial administrator, sent out to do a job, was prepared to take measures which did not always meet with approval in London where wider concerns and problems had to be considered. For in Europe, the Eastern Crisis was entering a critical stage and the government was extremely reluctant to enter into a war in South Africa. Carnarvon warned: 'A native war is just now impossible and you must avoid it.' Yet, Carnarvon then resigned in opposition to Disraeli's eastern policy. His successor, Hicks Beach, knew little about South Africa and struggled to control Frere. Telegraph messages between Britain and South Africa took a minimum of 16 days to arrive and Frere never spelt out clearly his intentions. When, on 30 September 1878, Frere requested that reinforcements be sent out so he could put an end to Zulu 'pretensions', Beach, with the backing of the Cabinet, initially refused the troops and told him to avoid war. But Frere pushed on regardless and the Cabinet, fearing the consequences of failing to support a British administrator in the field, reluctantly dispatched additional troops in November 1878 for defensive purposes only. Frere, believing that the British had to demonstrate their authority in South Africa, ignored this qualification and, on 11 December 1878, submitted an ultimatum to the Zulus demanding that they demobilize their forces, accept a permanent British Resident in their territory, and change their marriage law, under which a warrior could only marry once he had shed blood in battle. When the ultimatum expired on 9 January 1879, Frere declared war. The Zulu war was Frere's responsibility, not the government's and certainly not Disraeli's. Even so, Hicks Beach was optimistic about its outcome, writing to Disraeli that 'there is, I hope, a good prospect...of the war being short and successful, like the Afghan campaign...though Frere's policy – especially in the matter of cost – is extremely inconvenient to us at the present moment, I am sanguine as to its success and think we shall be able, without much difficulty, to defend its main principles here'.[57]

The Afghan comparison soon proved more apposite than Beach could have anticipated. For Frere's war started disastrously. On 22 January 1879, a Zulu army of 20,000 destroyed a British force of 1,200 at a camp at Ishandhlwana.

When the news arrived in Britain in February 1879 it caused a great outcry and the Government's prestige fell still further. Reinforcements had to be sent and the drain on finances and manpower disturbed Disraeli. In fact, he became depressed and his health deteriorated. 'It will change everything,' he wrote to the Queen, 'reduce our Continental influence and embarrass our finances.' More bad news followed when the son of the former French Emperor Napoleon III, who had volunteered to serve in the British forces in an unofficial capacity and against Disraeli's opposition, was killed in an ambush. The Queen was much distressed and the government's reputation took another blow.[58]

Disraeli vacillated on the course to pursue. His decision was weak and unconvincing. He could either have given strong backing to Frere and his policy or ordered his recall. The Cabinet, and probably Disraeli, favoured the latter, but Queen Victoria and Hicks Beach continued to have faith in Frere's abilities and Disraeli felt unable to overrule them.[59] The result was an unsatisfactory compromise. Frere was reprimanded for disobedience but allowed to remain in his post. The Liberals in the Commons made much of this inconsistency, Sir William Harcourt reading out the text of an imaginary letter from Hicks Beach to Frere:

> Dear Sir Bartle Frere. I cannot think you are right. Indeed I think you are very wrong; but after all you know a great deal better than I do. I hope you won't do what you are going to do; but if you do I hope it will turn out well.

Additional forces under Sir Garnet Wolseley were eventually dispatched, but by the time they arrived, the Zulus had been crushed.

Overall, Disraeli was critical of Frere's conduct and said privately that he ought to be impeached. In so far as he was responsible for the war, it was in giving Carnarvon such a free hand in colonial policy and in not monitoring more closely the correspondence between Hicks Beach and Frere during 1878. According to Walton:

> The African events were emphatically not part of a new aggressive policy of militaristic aggrandizement: rather, they resulted from a series of blunders and miscalculations involving inadequate responses to external circumstances.[60]

This is something of an exaggeration. The forcible annexation of the Transvaal, itself part of a wider scheme of Federation under the British flag, was an act of imperial expansion. A native war then became, as Disraeli admitted, at some stage inevitable.[61] But he was not responsible either for the timing of the conflict or the failure to make the required military preparations. Here, it was Frere and the British Commander, Lord Chelmsford, who were culpable. Even so, as Victoria justly observed, 'with our enormous Empire, we must always be prepared for such contingencies...'[62]

2. India and Afghanistan

The part of the Empire to which Disraeli attached most importance was India. He was fascinated by India and thought its possession was Britain's chief claim to being a great world power. He therefore supported the growing trend by which the protection of Britain's interests in India shaped its foreign and imperial policy. The routes to India had to be protected from rival powers, especially Russia. The purchase of the Suez shares, the Royal Titles Bill and the Eastern question were all manifestations of concern with Britain's position in India.

A more specific concern was with the North West Frontier between India and Afghanistan. For centuries, invaders had entered India by this route and the British feared that Russia, gradually advancing into Central Asia and establishing contacts with the Ameer, could eventually occupy Afghanistan and so threaten British rule in India. The question then, was what to do about Afghanistan? There were two schools of thought:

(a) *Masterly inactivity*. Britain should keep out of Afghanistan, with its inaccessible mountains and warring tribes, and take its defensive position on the Indus River.
(b) *Forward policy*. Britain should take an active role in Afghanistan and effectively dominate its foreign policy.

Disraeli feared Russian intervention and favoured a forward policy. Thus, when the Viceroy, Lord Northbrook, resigned in 1876, unhappy with the pressure to push Britain's presence in Afghanistan, Disraeli sought to place at the head of the Government of India someone capable of carrying forward an interventionist policy. His choice eventually fell upon Lord Lytton, British Minister at Lisbon and son of his old friend Bulwer Lytton. As he remarked to Salisbury in 1877:

> I have no doubt whatever, as to our course; we must, completely and unflinchingly, support Lytton. We chose him for this very kind of business. Had it been a routine age, we might have made, what might be called, a more prudent selection, but we foresaw what would occur and indeed saw what was occurring; we wanted a man of ambition, imagination, some vanity and much will – and we have got him.[63]

Lytton's secret brief was to persuade the Ameer to receive a British military delegation and accept the stationing of British agents on his northern border to monitor Russian activity. In return, Britain was to provide financial subsidies and help defend Afghanistan if attacked. For two years, Lytton unsuccessfully laboured to secure these terms – the Ameer preferring to negotiate with the

Russians. Worse still, in July 1878, the political temperature was raised when the Ameer accepted the arrival of a Russian military delegation in Kabul – itself a counterblast to Britain's decision to send Indian Army troops to Malta. For Lytton, it was unacceptable for the ruler of Afghanistan to enter-tain Russian officers in Kabul. He decided it was time to prosecute his forward policy with more vigour by not only sending a British military mission to Kabul but insisting that the Ameer dismiss the Russian delegation. The India Office endorsed the first but not the second of these moves.

Disraeli's response to this initiative was confused. Most historians have concurred with Blake that Disraeli's responsibility for what happened next was 'minimal'.[64] In truth, the matter is less clear. Disraeli was in two minds about the Afghan situation. In terms of instinct and general principle, he was at one with the Viceroy. 'With Lytton's general policy,' he wrote to the Secretary of State for India, Lord Cranbrook, 'I entirely agree. I have always been opposed to and deplored, "masterly inactivity".' In a speech at the Lord Mayor's banquet in November, Disraeli observed that British India's North West Frontier was 'a haphazard and not a scientific one', providing the oppor-tunity for enemies to 'embarrass and disturb our dominion…'[65] However, he seems to have regarded the Russian presence in Kabul in 1878 as a remnant of the Eastern Crisis and hoped that, following the Treaty of Berlin, it would cease of its own accord. But this was far from certain. Even after the Treaty had been signed, he was very concerned that Russia should actually comply with its terms and withdraw from occupied territory. From this perspective, Afghanistan became yet another test of British resolve; standing up to Russia in Afghanistan would then form part of a policy of demonstrating to the Russians that Britain was determined to hold her to her treaty commitments. As ever, he was alive to the domestic political ramifications:

> I am convinced the country require that we shall act with decision and firmness on this Afghan question. So far as I can judge, the feel-ing is strong and rising, in the country. So long as they thought there was 'Peace with Honour' the conduct of the Government was popular, but if they find there is no peace, they will soon be apt to conclude there is also no honour.[66]

Thus, whether viewed from the perspective of general policy, or of the latter stages of the Eastern Crisis, a firm stance towards Afghanistan was necessary. But the motives were subtly different and Disraeli did not keep this distinc-tion in his head. While Russia might withdraw its mission as part of a general winding down of the Eastern Crisis, the problem of the 'scientific frontier' and the Ameer's apparently pro-Russian policy would remain. This was the situation with which the Viceroy had to deal. Sent out to press a forward policy in Afghanistan, he had not only failed to make any progress, but

Britain had lost ground to the Russians and the mere fact of the mission having been accepted, even if it were subsequently withdrawn, was a major setback. Viewed from India, Lytton felt that Britain had to show it was in earnest. Disraeli agreed. The problem was that, having only just avoided a war with Russia over Constantinople, there was no desire amongst the Cabinet to risk a war with Afghanistan and possibly Russia over a matter as apparently trivial as the presence of a Russian mission in Kabul.

To try to avoid the possibility of conflict, the Foreign Office had agreed on 19 August 1878, to send a despatch to Russia protesting at the presence of the Kabul mission. Unfortunately, Lytton was not informed of this until 13 September 1878, by which time plans for a British military mission were well advanced. He was told, first, not to send a mission until the outcome of the protest to Russia was clear and second, that any mission should not advance up the Khyber Pass to Kabul but should only proceed to Candahar, well away from the capital. Lytton's initial response was to delay the mission. But on 21 September 1878, he told it to proceed via the Khyber Pass to Kabul. Neither step had been sanctioned by London.

Disraeli, as well as his Indian Secretary, supported Lytton's action. On 17 September 1878, he had written to Cranbrook that 'there is no doubt that there should be no delay in the Mission' and on the day after the mission was sent he gave it his blessing:

> ...there are occasions when prudence is not wisdom. And this is one. There are times for action. We must control and even create events. No doubt our Envoy will make the best terms he can. He will, of course, not show all his cards at once, but I am clearly of opinion that what we want, at this present moment, is to prove our ascendancy in Afghanistan and, to accomplish that, we must not stick at trifles...[67]

Disraeli knew that the majority of the Cabinet, and in particular Lord Salisbury, strongly disapproved and it is likely that he looked to Lytton to take the initiative and allow him to present the Cabinet (which was not then meeting) with a *fait accompli* when it reassembled in the autumn. The idea that Disraeli was only remotely responsible for events in Afghanistan simply cannot be sustained. It was a bold imperial move of the kind that Disraeli relished.

The problem was that the mission, far from demonstrating British ascendancy in Afghanistan, was turned back at the border – an incident highly damaging to British prestige. Disraeli, now exposed to Cabinet criticism, was angry that Lytton had failed to carry through his initiative: 'I am not satisfied with the position,' he wrote to Cranbrook, 'as nothing could justify Lytton's course except he was prepared to act and was in a situation which justified the responsibility of disobeying the orders of H.M. Government.'[68] Still, Disraeli saw that there could be no going back and continued to give

Lytton his support. An ultimatum was now sent to the Ameer, demanding that he accept a permanent British mission in Kabul and when no reply was received, British forces were sent into Afghanistan on 21 November 1878. After a series of British victories, the Ameer fled to Turkestan – where his appeals for Russian aid evoked no response. His son assumed the throne and in May 1879, he accepted British control of his foreign policy, and agreed to the establishment of a British mission, headed by Sir Louis Cavagnari, at Kabul. It seemed a highly successful outcome. 'The check to Russia,' wrote Disraeli to Victoria, 'to use a very mild expression, is complete.' To Lytton he wrote that 'greatly owing to your energy and foresight, we have secured a scientific and adequate frontier for our Indian Empire'.[69] While in the House of Lords, he declared that 'we have secured that frontier which I hope and believe will render our Indian Empire invulnerable...'

But, as others were to discover, if there was one thing the Afghans hated more than each other it was foreigners. On 3 September 1879, mutinous Afghan soldiers rose up and massacred the entire British mission. It was a humiliating blow for Lytton and the government and appeared to vindicate the earlier 'masterly inactivity' approach. For British prestige, it was necessary that the massacre be avenged and a new army, under Roberts, entered Afghanistan and took Kabul, crushing all resistance. The situation was thus salvaged. What, exactly, to do with Afghanistan was unclear and the Cabinet resolved to establish British control in the southern hills, leaving the Afghans to settle their own affairs in Kabul and the north of the country. Thus were matters left when the Conservatives fell from power.

Assessment

Was there a case to answer for events in Afghanistan? Clearly the policy pursued was highly risky and the massacre was a major setback for Disraeli and his government. Was Disraeli responsible to any significant degree? The answer must be yes. He was determined to pursue a forward policy in Afghanistan and selected Lord Lytton as the man to implement it. When the policy apparently succeeded he was fulsome in his praise. 'It will always be to me a source of real satisfaction that I had the opportunity of placing you on the throne of the Gt. Mogul.'[70]

It is usually argued that Disraeli was not responsible for the actual crisis provoked when Lytton's mission was rebuffed by the Ameer. This is not convincing. Disraeli understood the reasons for Lytton's intervention and gave it his blessing. The problem was that the Afghan issue became embroiled in the wider question of the Eastern Crisis and Anglo-Russian relations. The Russian mission was indeed prompted by the events in the Near East. From this, Disraeli and Salisbury (and most of the Cabinet) drew differing conclusions. For Disraeli it was vital to take a firm stand against Russia in Afghanistan if the achievement of his Berlin diplomacy were to be consolidated. As in the Balkans, this meant a possibility of war, though Disraeli again believed that Russia would back down in the face of British resolve. The Cabinet took the opposite view. Having narrowly avoided a calamitous war with Russia over Constantinople, they were not prepared to risk another over Kabul. Here, Disraeli was fortunate. The crisis broke while the Cabinet was in its summer recess. Salisbury wished to avoid conflict and Disraeli, from the perspective of his eastern diplomacy, was happy to agree to the sending of a protest note to the Russians. But the bigger game was still afoot on the borders of Britain's greatest imperial possession and whether viewed from Calcutta or 10 Downing Street, the mere withdrawal of the Russian mission would not have been enough. Lytton had been sent to India to secure the admission of a British mission to Afghanistan and monitor the northern Afghan border. Not only had neither been achieved, but the Ameer was in consultation with the Russians who were present in Kabul! This was not acceptable to the Government of India. Britain had to assert its power in Afghanistan and this is what Lytton did. Although Disraeli affected annoyance in correspondence with Salisbury and was genuinely angry when Lytton's mission sought entry via the Khyber Pass and allowed itself to be stopped, he essentially supported the Viceroy's bold move and basked in the apparently successful outcome. It was not justified to lay the blame for the massacre at Lytton's door and Disraeli did not do so. The overall outcome of the Afghan intervention was about as good as could be expected in such a treacherous environment.

Assessment of Disraeli's Foreign Policy

Since the 1850s, Disraeli had seen foreign policy as an area in which party differences were most clearly displayed. Where domestic policy was dominated – except at the margins – by consensus, attitudes to foreign policy differed widely. Disraeli, drawn to the possibilities of diplomatic intrigue, great power relations, and imperial exotica, was resolved to make his mark in this area. During the 1850s and early 1860s, when Palmerston dominated the scene, Disraeli was a critic of aggressive and expensive foreign initiatives and posed as a prudent Little Englander. This position helped inflict defeats in the Commons but had little resonance with the public. From the 1860s, Gladstone's policies of conciliation, non-intervention and scepticism towards the boons of Empire, pushed Disraeli into the more attractive position of advocate of Empire and defender of British prestige.

It was on this platform that Disraeli assumed office in 1874. Yet the change was more one of presentation than substance. Disraeli had no real idea how to assert British power in Europe or strengthen the Empire. Even if he had, he would have discovered that his capacity to effect significant change was non-existent. In an age of great continental armies, of settler colonies keen to govern themselves, and domestic resistance to increased taxation, there was little scope for assertions of British power. In such a context, Disraeli prudently opted for symbolic measures, such as the proclamation of the Queen as Empress of India.

However, two things then ensured that foreign policy would thrust itself forward to dominate the last years of Disraeli's period in office. The first was the Eastern Question. Here, Disraeli was reacting to an external crisis and what is notable is the moderation of his initial reaction. He took no precipitate action and worked, fairly successfully, with his extremely cautious Foreign Secretary. Given the limited resources at his disposal, Disraeli played his hand as well as could be expected and the Treaty of Berlin was a genuine success for Disraeli.

In imperial policy, too, a series of crises intruded, but here, Disraeli was partly responsible. If he did not initiate either the Zulu or Afghan wars, he appointed the men who did, gave his general backing to the policies they pursued, and helped generate a culture of imperial expansion. Given Disraeli's distaste for administrative detail and the slow communications between London and the periphery, it was always likely that the 'men on the spot' would take initiatives London was reluctant to endorse. Indeed, it was through just such localized initiatives that the Empire had been built up in the first place. Disraeli understood and tolerated this; it was the cost and damage caused by the *failure* of these initiatives that troubled him.

In the sphere of foreign policy, Disraeli's tenure of office was broadly successful. Britain counted for more in the counsels of Europe and the Empire had been celebrated – if not greatly strengthened. Even so, the failure was in the area that concerned Disraeli the most – public opinion. He had sought to make foreign policy a vote winner for the Tories and had manoeuvred skilfully to seize the domestic legacy of Palmerston's nationalism and combine it with visions of imperial glory. In his 'election manifesto' of 1880, he claimed that the government had seen off the attempt by the Liberals to 'enfeeble our colonies by their policy of decomposition' and had asserted 'the presence, not to say ascendancy, of England in the councils of Europe'. Of course, practice fell short of rhetoric – but this had happened under Palmerston also. The failure was, in fact, one of presentation. Quite simply, Disraeli was trumped by Gladstone. Just as Disraeli had puffed up his achievements, Gladstone greatly exaggerated the recklessness, wickedness and profligacy of his policies. The contest was one of appearance not reality, rhetoric not sober calculation. This had conventionally been Disraeli's home ground and it was, therefore, all the more galling that he should be beaten by Gladstone, who had ensured that by 1880, foreign policy was a liability for the Conservatives.

The Last Years of Disraeli's Government 1878–1880

1878 saw the high point of Disraeli's Premiership and of his career. The remaining months of his government were ones of declining fortunes. This decline had several aspects:

Foreign Policy Failures

Far from being an asset to the government, imperial initiatives in Afghanistan and South Africa proved an embarrassing liability. The public may have been attracted by rhetorical visions of imperial grandeur; but they had little appetite for the military risks and expenditure imperial commitments implied.

Health Problems

Disraeli's health, not good even in 1874, only deteriorated over time. Plagued by gout, asthma, and bronchitis, weeks went past when he rarely ventured out of doors. Social functions and dinners left his constitution shattered. To escape the demands of life in the Commons he had taken refuge in the Lords in 1876 as the Earl of Beaconsfield – leaving the task of defending the government and countering a resurgent Gladstone to his less accomplished deputies. From 1878, it was enough Disraeli could do to perform his basic tasks as Prime Minister: he had no energy left to give new direction to his government.

Economic Problems

These were the most important factors sapping the credibility of Disraeli's government. Here, Disraeli was unlucky. His arrival in office saw the end of the mid-Victorian boom and the commencement of the Great Depression. Economic growth faltered and a period of falling prices began, which was to last for a period of over 20 years. Business confidence fell and Britain had, for the first time, a sense of the beginnings of economic decline. None of this was Disraeli's fault, but his government could hardly escape the consequences of the public's sense of economic malaise and he himself frankly admitted that it was not 'prepared with any remedial measures...'[71]

Agricultural Depression

This was especially ironic and damaging. During the 1870s, cheap grain began to arrive as the plains of North America were opened up to British consumers by railway and steam ship. This development coincided with a run of bad harvests, but where, in previous years, reduced output would have meant higher prices, now the gap was merely filled by imports. The result was a severe agricultural depression, which continued into the 20th century. 'The stars in their courses have fought against me,' Disraeli lamented. As the party of the landed interest, this was obviously a blow for the Conservatives. 'I think,' Disraeli wrote, 'the agricultural bankruptcy must finish us.'[72] Worse still, it signalled the beginning of the end for the great territorial aristocracy that Disraeli had entered politics to defend. Rural society, which had underpinned Britain's national greatness, began to disintegrate. Landlord rents fell, removing the funds that had subsidized their political and social activities. Dissension within rural communities increased. Tenant farmers wanted greater rent reductions while the labourers, who profited from cheaper bread, left the land. The number of labourers in English agriculture fell by one-third in the period 1870–1914. Disraeli was very concerned at this threat to the organic rural society he had praised. But there was no political prospect of protecting agriculture behind tariffs, even had Disraeli not been a believer in free trade.

Financial Problems

Economic depression reduced government revenue at a time when spending on military operations was increasing. The Zulu war alone cost £500,000 a month. Disraeli, although recognising that 'it is difficult to carry through a commanding policy with a failing Exchequer', was reluctant to increase taxation for political reasons (income tax already having increased by three pence in the pound since 1874) and the result was rising government deficits. In 1879–1880, the deficit was £3.35 million, funded by borrowing and raids on the sinking fund. This broke the rules of 19th century budgetary finance and gave additional ammunition to Gladstone's attack upon the government as extravagant and incompetent.[73]

Loss of Reforming Impetus

By 1877, the government's programme of social reform had ground to a halt. Time and energy were increasingly taken up with the more serious (and prestigious) business of foreign and imperial affairs, while the economic depression reduced the money available for reform measures. The government was forced to cut back the money devoted to education and grants to local authorities. Indeed, the consequences of Disraeli's relaxed approach to parliamentary management were making themselves felt. Individual ministers brought forward bills which competed for time, with the result that few made it to the statute book. Legislation to reform county government was one such casualty. 'There has been,' wrote Clayden in 1880, 'no order, no discipline, no head.'[74]

Gladstone Resurgent

The Balkan Crisis had terminated Gladstone's always unconvincing retirement and in 1879, he launched his famous Midlothian Campaign, denouncing the government before large audiences for its arrogant and immoral policy abroad and its incompetent and profligate conduct at home. It was a powerful attack. Disraeli lacked the strength and temperament to respond. Although believing in the power of words and ideas in politics, his arena had always been Parliament and the political world of London. He could do little to counter Gladstone's direct appeal to the mass audiences of the provinces, merely describing it as 'wearisome rhetoric' and a 'waste of powder and shot'. Wearisome it may have been, but wasteful it was not.

The 1880 Election

Under the combined weight of these blows, the government, says Smith, effectively died on its feet. The only question was when to call an election. This was eventually called for 31 March 1880 after some favourable by-election results gave the government grounds for optimism. Disraeli articulated no particular policy for the campaign. Essentially, he repeated the strategy of 1874, portraying the Conservatives as the party of established interests and order against the disruptive objectives of the Liberals. He did, however, raise the issue of Ireland, suggesting that the Liberals would fail to resist the growing forces of nationalism and home rule. Though prescient, Ireland was hardly a winning 'cry' for the Conservatives as they had done little about the Irish problem and lacked any clear policy. Besides, the public was sick of the issue and had other things on its mind besides the 'imperial character of this realm'. The basic fact was that the economy was in a poor condition. Governments overseeing slow growth, falling prices and wages, depressed confidence and deficit budgets rarely win elections. Foreign policy, far from distracting from these problems, had worsened them by the late 1870s and this was exploited by Gladstone who made the government's disruptive, extravagant and immoral foreign policy his chief target in his election campaign.

Disraeli, suspecting a narrow result, was taken aback at the scale of the Liberal triumph:

Liberals 353
Conservatives 238
Home Rule Irish 61

The Liberals thus had a majority of 115 over the Conservatives and an overall majority of 54. The Conservatives did badly everywhere, losing 100 seats in all, but especially in Scotland, where they won only six seats and in Wales, where they mustered only two. Even in the Counties, the Conservatives lost 29 seats as rural voters gave vent to their frustration at their economic plight. The average swing against them was 5 per cent.[75] The gains of 1874 had been reversed and with only 24 of the 114 larger Borough seats, they were again tending to become a party of the agrarian interest.

Why did the Conservatives lose in 1880?

Disraeli was not the first disappointed candidate to blame forces beyond his control for his failure. 'I think, as far as I can collect, "hard times" was the cry against us. The suffering wanted a change – no matter what, they are sick of waiting.'[76] He could have equally well pointed to the fact that the Liberals, divided and fractious in 1874, had recovered their unity in 1880 and with it, their 'natural' 19th century majority. There is much to be said for the idea that a reaction to the Liberals was almost inevitable in 1880.

Yet Disraeli cannot escape responsibility for the surprisingly heavy defeat. Despite a lifetime's devotion to the territorial constitution, he had no policy for agriculture beyond praying for a return to good harvests. Foreign policy had become a liability after Berlin. Here, as we have seen, Disraeli played a large role. In India he encouraged, while in South Africa he sanctioned, the forward policies that led to disaster. His imperialist rhetoric raised expectations and encouraged subordinates and Disraeli failed to comprehend that asserting Britain's authority at the periphery of the Empire was a hazardous operation that required a clear preponderance of military strength. It was not enough to entrust these matters to over-confident consuls with inadequate forces. Gladstone systematically outperformed Disraeli on the platform. As a peer, Disraeli was barred by convention from engaging in active campaigning. But there was no precedent for Gladstone's campaign either and Disraeli lacked the strength, ideas, or inclination to mount a reply. By shifting the agenda onto the terrain of political ethics, Gladstone cleverly cut the ground from beneath the Conservative appeal. How could a policy be in British interests if it were also morally wrong? Disraeli's amoral foreign policy played into Gladstone's hands and provided him with an emotional focus around which the Liberals could rally. A final factor was party organization. Having developed a superior party organization in 1874, the Conservatives committed the classic mistake of allowing it to languish once in office. Gorst had resigned from his directing role at Conservative Central Office and Disraeli, preoccupied as he was, had failed to secure an adequate replacement. By 1880, party organization was another element shifting the balance towards the Liberals.

Final Days

Disraeli was now old and ill and had just lost a general election and it might be thought that retirement was inevitable. But the party wished him to remain Leader and Disraeli, with his tenacious love of politics not yet exhausted, was ready to oblige. Of course, he appreciated the realities confronting the party:

> The situation requires youth and energy. When they are found – and they will be found – I shall make my bow. In the meantime I must act as if I were still young and vigorous and take all steps in my power to sustain the spirit and restore the discipline of the Tory party. They have existed for more than a century and a half as an organized political connection and having survived the loss of the American colonies, the first Napoleon and Lord Grey's Reform Act, they must not be snuffed out… You see I prophesy as becomes one in the sunset of life – or rather I should say the twilight of existence.[77]

Disraeli once remarked that if I want to read a novel, I write one. With leisure once more on his hands, he turned again to literature and finished a manuscript he had commenced before 1874 and which he now published under the title *Endymion*. It was 55 years since his first novel was published. Disraeli believed that he owed 'everything to woman' and the novel's theme was the role of noble women in the career of one Endymion, who rises from a middle class background to become Prime Minister. Outside of the light the work sheds on the period of Disraeli's entry into politics, it is of little importance. But the fact of one of the leading statesmen of Europe publishing a romantic novel was itself a sensation and Longman paid a record sum of £10,000 – around £600,000 today – for the rights.

No sooner was one novel completed than another was begun. Called *Falconet*, its hero, Joseph Toplady Falconet, was modelled on Gladstone. The opening pages provide an effective and witty satire on the early career of Gladstone and it is rather to be regretted that the novel was never completed.

On 15 March 1881, Disraeli delivered his last speech in the Lords. Plagued by ill health, he was very susceptible to the weather. He remarked at this time: 'I am blind and deaf. I only live for climate and I never get it.' In late March 1881, he caught a chill in the cold east wind. The result was intensified bronchitis and from then on his health steadily declined. He realized the end was near. But his wit remained. He was pleased to correct the Hansard text for his last speech to Parliament, saying: 'I will not go down to posterity talking bad grammar'. When it was suggested that the Queen might be called for he replied: 'No it is better not. She would only ask me to take a message to Albert'. His last recorded words were: 'I had rather live but I am not afraid to die'. On 19 April 1881, he sat forward in his bed as if to begin speaking in the Commons. But no words came and he lay back and died.

Victoria was deeply saddened. Writing to Disraeli's personal secretary, she said:

> I can scarcely see for my fast falling tears… Never had I so kind and devoted a Minister and very few such devoted friends. His affection-ate sympathy, his wise counsel – *all* were so invaluable even out of office. I have lost *so* many dear and valued friends but none whose loss will be more keenly felt. To England and to the *World* his loss is *immense* and at such a moment. God's will be done. I have learnt to say this but the bitterness and the suffering are not the less severe. As yet I cannot realize it.

Disraeli was buried with his wife in the vault outside Hughenden church. Protocol then forbade a monarch from attending the funeral of one of her subjects. But the Queen insisted on subsequently visiting the grave and took tea in Disraeli's library at Hughenden. She also arranged for a marble monu-ment to be erected inside the church with the words 'Kings love him that speaketh right'.

Historians' Debate: Disraeli and Imperialism

How consistent was Disraeli's attachment to the doctrines of imperialism? How coherent were the policies he formulated on its basis?

Some historians, basing themselves on certain negative comments regarding the Empire made by Disraeli himself, have questioned the extent and motives of his imperialism.

Disraeli

These wretched colonies will all be independent, too, in a few years and are a millstone around our necks.[78]

What is the use of these colonial dead-weights which *we do not govern?*… Leave the Canadians to defend themselves, recall the African squadron, give up the Settlements on the west coast of Africa and we shall make a saving which will, at the same time, enable us to build ships and have a good budget.[79]

Bodelsen

The assertion sometimes made that Disraeli was one of the founders, even the founder, of British Imperialism will, then, hardly stand the test of an examination of his correspondence, speeches and colonial policy. In the first place one seems to be justified, in the light of his utterances before the

Crystal Palace speech and of subsequent events, to say that Disraeli was never really much concerned about colonial questions for their own sake...his utterances on the colonial questions before 1872 are closely connected with considerations for the welfare of the Tory party and it seems safe to say that his advocacy of Imperialism in the Crystal Palace speech was due less to a conviction of the greatness of the cause than to a desire to add a popular plank to the Conservative platform.

That he initiated the connection between Imperialism and Conservatism is undeniable. But apart from that, his contributions to Imperialism seem to be of questionable value. His criticism of the colonial policy of the Liberals...shows a considerable ignorance of colonial conditions. Any attempt to resume Imperial control of these subjects would, so far from conducing to the closer unity of the Empire, probably have resulted in declarations of independence on the part of the colonies.[80]

Bentley
The government lacked any coherent Imperial policy and neither Disraeli nor his ministers held any ideology about Imperial expansion except insofar as they believed history showed it to be a bad and dangerous thing.[81]

However, since the 1960s, historians have defended the consistency of Disraeli's interest in the Empire.

Stembridge
[Disraeli] spoke too often of the importance of the Empire to British strength and prestige for historians to doubt his sincerity or to believe that he was simply an opportunist mouthing the popular slogans of the moment.[82]

Eldridge
True, Disraeli was not interested in the self-governing colonies, the government of indigenous peoples, or expansion in the tropics, except in so far as these problems impinged on Great Britain's foreign policy and its prestige as a world power. It was the part the possession of empire could play in assisting Great Britain's role in world affairs that had interested him. The key to Disraeli's imperial ideas lay in the conduct of Indian business and in his handling of the Eastern Question crisis when, in speech after speech, a new vision of empire emerged: of a centralized military empire backing up the strength of Great Britain in her role as a world power, providing both resources and armies beyond the control of parliament.[83]

Feuchtwanger
Disraeli himself had, as the Chancellor of the Exchequer, sometimes viewed relations with the colonies from the financial aspect, but on the whole he

could claim that his remarks at the Free Trade Hall and the Crystal Palace were consistent with attitudes he had always taken.[84]

Jenkins
[Though Disraeli did make anti-imperial remarks in the 1850s] it is necessary to set such comments in their immediate context. It then becomes clear that Disraeli, as Chancellor of the Exchequer, was expressing momentary irritation at the financial burden imposed upon Britain by the cost of defending her colonies and the complications in British foreign policy sometimes caused by her colonial commitments – specifically, in the case of his 1852 outburst, the way that relations with the USA were being strained because of a fisheries dispute between the USA and Canada. From a more general perspective, it can be argued that Disraeli actually displayed a consistent concern with the importance of maintaining the Empire, which he regarded as an essential pillar supporting Britain's status as a great power in the eyes of the world.[85]

Walton
If we trace Disraeli's views on the British Empire through his writings and speeches more carefully, we find that the views he expressed in 1872 are consistent with his declared attitudes over many years. The empire had not been a strong or sustained priority for him, admittedly, but he can be acquitted of opportunistically tailoring his speeches to fit the (anyway uncertain) temper of the times.[86]

Even so, it is generally accepted that Disraeli, in his 1874–1880 government, did not seek to expand the Empire in the way Liberal critics like Gladstone alleged.

Feuchtwanger
In spite of his public image as the champion of imperialism he had in fact no consistent imperial and colonial policy and certainly no general policy of expansion.[87]

Eldridge
With the so-called 'forward movements' of the early years of his administration he had almost nothing to do. The decisions extending British influence in various parts of the world were not even part of a consistent Conservative philosophy, but merely the outcomes of earlier events. For the 'forward movements' of the later years of his administration Disraeli also had little responsibility... The actions of men on the spot, very often in flagrant disregard of the instructions of Her Majesty's Government, were more responsible for the Zulu and Afghan wars than the vacillation of Disraeli and his Cabinet.[88]

Smith

He had raised the banner of empire in 1872 on a consolidatory, not an expansionist, basis. He used empire as an inspirational vision and a device of incantatory rhetoric, and he had a firm if occasionally naïve confidence in its ability to weigh in the European balance of power, but, as prime minister, he showed little inclination to do anything about it...The forward movements of empire were the result, not of Disraeli's imperialism, but of his excessively loose control of the cabinet...[89]

VIII

DISRAELI AND THE ART OF POLITICS

How are we to judge Disraeli? This question really implies another; by what standard are we to judge his career? Surely we shall require one since Disraeli was a peculiar politician, whether viewed from his or any other time. Indeed, assessments of Disraeli have generally been deficient owing to the selection of inappropriate standards.

For Disraeli, politics was a mode of life, a manner of living, which, if approached correctly, was one of the highest available to man for it partook of the character of art. 'This,' he said of the Congress of Berlin, 'is a wondrous scene; life in its highest form.' Disraeli had aspired to be a literary artist – a poet and novelist capable of embodying the progressive forces and shaping the destinies of his age. By common assent, including his own, he failed. He lacked the literary ability necessary and had not the patience required for the kind of laborious application characteristic of his father. The idea of legislating from beyond the grave had no appeal to a man who craved the literary celebrity of the young Byron. 'I am only truly great in action' he wrote and sought a sphere in which he could excel and realize his creative potential. He found it in politics. For what he saw in the 1830s was that politics, viewed through the refracting lens of genius, was a grand drama in which individuals of vision and courage manipulated men and shaped the fate of nations. Politics was an art and, as such, was an end in itself. It was indeed the greatest game, played for the highest odds and requiring the exercise of the widest range of qualities, ranging from the forensic application of reason to the emotive animal spirits, and played out amidst the raw material of individual egos, sectional interests, rival states, and the rise and fall of empires. Politics was not about ideology, although ideology would occupy a place within the crafted political career. It was not about continual business, for art requires silences and knowledge of when to act and when not. It was not a pursuit of one goal, for such would be distorting and inharmonious and lead to a stifling dogmatism. It was not about the defence of lost causes; a character might embrace martyrdom for some principle, but a political artist would be unwise to write himself out of the flow of events. Blake observes that for Disraeli, politics was the art of the possible; the art of the impossible had no more appeal than the grave.

Disraeli's writing is the key to this. Commentators have approached his novels looking for some key to his political action. There is none. Yet, there was still, in Disraeli's mind, an intimate association between his politics and his novels. Each inspired the other. 'My books,' he wrote, 'are the history of my life…the psychological development of my character.'[1] When he ceased being Prime Minister, he wrote a novel. But when in office and he 'had at last my dream', he left off writing since it had become unnecessary; as he wrote in his diary in 1833 'I wish to *act* what I *write*.'[2]

Disraeli, then, saw his life as an artistic expression through the medium of the governance of men and women. This provides us with our standard. How did Disraeli seek to pursue politics as an art and how successful was he?

Personality

At the heart of politics were people. For Disraeli, it was the human element that saved politics from being a mere affair of 'stationary'. In its absence 'it is pens and paper who are in communication, not human beings'.[3] His 'way of looking at politics,' reflected Derby, 'is always a personal one.'[4] The key to the correct management of men was the 'perception and observation of character'. Disraeli prided himself upon this: 'I can read characters at a glance…'[5] There is some irony here. As a novelist, he was a poor creator of characters and peopled his books with figures freely borrowed from real life. They rarely live as literary creations. But Disraeli was an acute and quick observer of the world in which he moved or even, in his younger days, barely glimpsed. He loved to analyze character and frequently deployed that perception to good effect. No one, he believed, understood Peel better and he was proud of the portrait of Peel he painted in his *Lord George Bentinck*. But equally important, he *used* that insight with devastating effect in his attacks on Peel during the years 1844–1846, striking, with remorseless accuracy, at Peel's weak points – his pomposity, sensitivity, fear of ridicule and lack of humour. By this means, an insignificant backbencher, for whom few, even on his own side, had a good thought, played his part in bringing down a man who Disraeli himself called the greatest parliamentarian in history. Well might Bagehot observe that 'when he has confined his efforts to showing how well he understands both the weak and strong points of those around him, he has been terrible and quite unsurpassed'.[6]

There were numerous other examples. Having overturned Peel, he needed an ally with the capacity to command respect on the Tory backbenches. He found one in Bentinck, a man as unlike Disraeli in temperament, background and interests as it is possible to imagine. If there was to be cooperation, the flexibility would all have to be Disraeli's. He played his part with such skill that by the time of his early death, Bentinck was not only recommending that Disraeli be his successor as leader of the Protectionists but was prepared to buy him a country house. A passage from Disraeli's brilliant biography of his chief captures the skill with which Disraeli read Bentinck's character and played his part. Bentinck, having decided to devote his life to politics, had sold the stable of horses which had for long been his passion. One of those horses had gone on to win the Derby. That evening Disraeli came upon a disconsolate Bentinck in the House of Commons library:

He gave a sort of superb groan. 'All my life I have been trying for this and for what have I sacrificed it!' he murmured.

> It was in vain to offer solace.
> 'You don't know what the Derby is,' he moaned out.
> 'Yes, I do; it is the blue ribbon of the turf.'
> 'It is the blue ribbon of the turf,' he slowly repeated to himself and sitting down at the table, he buried himself in a folio of statistics.[7]

Disraeli knew little enough about racing. Yet he knew Bentinck well enough to judge precisely the phrase that would capture the countryman's sense of desolation.

There are numerous other examples of Disraeli's capacity to read and manipulate personality. He managed to work with Lord Derby for twenty years, though that grand aristocrat began with an ingrained dislike of the less than respectable adventurer. Though there was never any love between the two men, Disraeli survived in Derby's shadow to emerge as Prime Minister when he quit the scene. Disraeli perceived that Lord Salisbury, another equally grand aristocrat, could undermine his hold on the Conservative party and correctly judged that he could be disarmed as a critic by a place in the Cabinet and, within that body, slowly but surely secured him as a key ally. Above all, Disraeli understood the emotional needs of Queen Victoria and systematically won her allegiance through pen and word and deed from the 1850s onwards. By 1880, he was easily her favourite Prime Minister since Melbourne and she shed tears at his departure. Gladstone was always shocked at the ease with which Disraeli glided through the salons of High Society and ingratiated himself with Dukes, Duchesses, and Princes. He was indeed perfectly at ease in such environments, despite the disadvantages of race and background. Yet Disraeli did not merely transcend these limitations; he turned his ability to judge characters, however grand, to his advantage.

Naturally Disraeli made mistakes. Sentimentality was a weakness and he had, said Derby, an 'entire absence of vindictiveness'.[8] Blake notes that a good

Prime Minister must be a good butcher. Disraeli was far from this. He proved overly indulgent of his old friend Lord Stanley, permitting him to remain at the Foreign Office though he was actively resisting his chief's own eastern policy. Lord Henry Lennox was another whom Disraeli continued to indulge long after their earlier friendship had cooled. Sir Charles Adderley, having shown his ineffectiveness during the Plimsoll agitation, was allowed to remain as President of the Board of Trade for a further three years.[9] But on balance, Disraeli judged right, using his understanding and interest in personality to advance his political career.

Ideology

Disraeli needed an ideology, if only to give his career meaning. Most of the established political class imbibed their political ideology from the familiar trappings of privilege – Eton, Oxford, county society, the officers' mess and so on. They had no need to reason it out for themselves and few took the trouble to. This did not apply to Disraeli. He had to construct his own ideological system, to create his own political meaning. This gave him room for manoeuvre and in the early stage of his career he took it, swinging between Radicalism, Toryism and various mixtures of the two. Yet Disraeli, though an imaginative thinker, was not a creative one. We have already commented upon his inability to create living characters in his novels – or, for that matter, living plots. The same was true of his political thinking. Rather than develop a new political system, he adopted the easier expedient of expounding an ideology of the *status quo*, taking refuge in his own outsider's idealization of the existing landed system, painting its charms in broad brush strokes and rhetorical flourishes. Not having been born into the landed establishment, he took a voyeuristic delight in its manifestations and suffused its doings in a romantic glow. During the 1830s, he took up the position of official ideologue of the landed class. To be sure, the landed aristocracy were not sure that they wanted such a being – the whole point of Toryism was that it was a natural outgrowth of the customary order and they were certainly unconvinced that the man to do the job was Disraeli. Properly speaking, the fact that the territorial constitution found itself championed in extravagant and somewhat vulgar terms by a literary and urban Jew was in itself a symptom of that system's decay. 'Save me from my friends' was no doubt a reflection of many a backwoods Tory in the 1840s. But this would not have concerned Disraeli, for his philosophy of the landed constitution more than served his interest. It gave him the ideological grounding he desired with the minimum of effort. Disraeli was intellectually indolent. He did not investigate the real character of rural affairs with any closeness. He never altered his conception of the sociology and economics of the countryside, notwithstanding the tremendous changes that were going on all the while. He made no effort to develop a strategy in response to the agricultural crisis of the 1870s. He merely repeated the old clichés that had served his ends in the 1840s. Disraeli is sometimes criticized for political inconsistency. But in matters of political philosophy, he was extremely rigid. Having made a caricature for himself in the 1830s, he remained true to it for the rest of his adult life.

Disraeli was not conscious of any tension here. His ideology enabled him to play a part and justified, to himself, the social system which he wished to preserve – chiefly because it sustained the arena in which he could excel. There was no question of his seeking to implement policy on the basis of his ideals. They were impossibly vague and, in any case, that was not the point. This is why debates concerning the degree of conformity between Disraeli's ideas and his political actions are so wide off the mark. His purpose was to manage a set of political circumstances, not implement some body of 'truths'; or as Smith puts it, Disraeli constructed a 'web' of ideas which helped to define a world he could inhabit and through which define and realize his genius.[10] His vision of an organic rural society was never meant to be a depiction of reality and even less was it an engine of policy. It was a psychological device, a literary creation which lived in his imagination and served him well at key moments of his career. It justified his decision to throw his lot in with the Tories. It won him the leadership of Young England. It gave a spurious legitimacy to his attacks on Peel. It enabled him to claim some consistency during the long days of opposition, while all the time, he was shifting his party into the paths opened for it by the despised Peel. Rather less was heard of it in the 1870s, for by then Disraeli had discovered the merits of the alien concept of Empire and when, shortly afterwards, he found himself in power, he had no need for a vision which, if taken literally, would only embarrass his government. As the landed interest, which it had been his life work to sustain, disintegrated around him, Disraeli was content to merely adjust the burden of local taxation and reduce the tax on horses.

Of course, to espouse an ideology with an at best tenuous connection with reality was risky for a practising politician and especially in one operating amidst such a rapidly changing society. Disraeli was fortunate to get away with it. By the 1870s, reality was breaking in and he had no response beyond lamentation. But it had served his time and his purposes and that was what mattered. He had caught and profited from the mid-Victorian equipoise. Disraeli is often described, for example by Vincent, as an unlucky politician, and in detailed matters of timing this was often true. But a politician is fortunate indeed if he can articulate the same political philosophy for a period of over 40 years and still find himself in power at the end of it.

Conflict

Any successful drama requires antagonism. Conflict, struggle, the clash of men and movements – these are the stuff of dramatic art and this Disraeli understood. He was a reactive politician, thriving on challenges and crises. Throughout his career he delighted in drawing exaggerated contrasts and pitching one idea against its opposite. Upon his first entry into public affairs, he portrayed the political issue of his time as one of a Whig elite versus popular democracy. An oligarchy of Whig grandees was endeavouring to tighten its exclusive grip on the politics of England while deploying the language of reform. The Tories, Disraeli claimed, were the true party of the 'people'. Neither proposition was very plausible, but as a tactic for appealing to the always excluded majority, it had political merit. Later, the clash between unpatriotic Liberal radicalism and patriotic Tory imperialism would play a similar role. Disraeli was a reactive politician. It was opposition that awoke him from his temperamental lethargy. The note of Empire, for example, was roused by the perceived tendency of liberalism to dissolve imperial ties. It was the Liberal's Reform Bill of 1866 that provoked the Tory Reform Bill of 1867 and Gladstone's personality that, by reaction, gave that measure its final form. Generally, Disraeli picked and fought his battles well. The one exception was his greatest foe of all – Gladstone, a fact that Disraeli could not wish away and which he could never overcome. For Gladstone was a political master whose powers exceeded Disraeli's own. True, Disraeli frequently held his own against Gladstone and scored some satisfying victories – such as the 1866–1867 Reform controversies and the 1874 election. He also knew how to counterpoise his own natural calmness to Gladstone's irritable and excitable character. But Gladstone had reserves and dimensions to his politics that Disraeli could not match, such as intellectual vigour, administrative skill, a capacity to evolve with circumstances, sheer brute energy. In 1852, he destroyed Disraeli's budget and brought down a government. In 1876–1880, he assaulted Disraeli's foreign policy and terminated his tenure of office. The personal rivalry between these two men supplied a dialectic which drove both to higher levels – but in the end it was Gladstone, not Disraeli, who occupied the stage.

Timing

Gladstone was given to reflecting upon the importance of timing, of catching the tide in the affairs of men, to successful politics and believed that he had a special gift in this respect. The same could not be claimed for Disraeli, but he did deploy well-judged timing to good effect at certain critical moments in his career. He timed well his attacks upon Peel in the period 1844–1846.

He was quick, possibly overly so, to abandon protection once the Corn Laws had been repealed. He utilised electoral reform as the ideal weapon with which to exploit Liberal divisions in the wake of Palmerston's death. In 1872, the decision to unfurl the banner of Empire was a master stroke, whether judged from the perspective of Disraeli's own languishing career, the interests of the Conservative party, or the strategic politics of Europe. In 1873, he astutely declined to take office from an expectant Queen – and Gladstone.

Yet, failures to judge political times aright are equally apparent. We can cite numerous particular circumstances – his decision to apply to Peel for office in 1841; his belief that Palmerston's time had passed in 1855; the slowness of his response to the Bulgarian atrocities; his failure to part with Derby until the Eastern crisis had almost run its course; the decision to delay calling a general election until 1880. But of greater significance are two more strategic failings. First, Disraeli allowed himself to be too often the victim of events. For all his reflections upon the role of a great statesman moulding the destiny of nations, Disraeli signally failed to live up to his ideal; or rather he did so in his imagination, not in his reality. Disraeli simply lacked the physical energy or intellectual power to shape events. Conscious of his incapacity, he made a virtue of it, priding himself on his oriental patience, his preparedness to wait for events to turn in his favour. While Liberal ministers held forth, Disraeli characteristically sat motionless for long hours on the Commons front bench, his hat sunk over his eyes, occasionally reaching for his monocle to check on the passage of time on the clock, before resuming his reveries. Of course, for much of the mid-Victorian period, Disraeli could do little else but wait and his patience received its reward. The wheel did eventually turn in his favour. Still, this was not inevitable. A Liberal victory in 1874 would have ended Disraeli's career in failure. More important, patience was frequently a policy of drift. Disraeli sleepwalked through the 1850s, the decade when he ought to have been at the peak of his powers. We know what he could do when he bestirred himself – 1845 and 1867 show us that. But in a career of over 40 years, such moments stand out as islands of activity in an otherwise rather flat sea. The fact was, as Derby reflected in 1875, 'he requires the excitement of an attack, or of an emergency of some sort, to raise him.'

Second, Disraeli lacked foresight.[11] He was slow to perceive and respond to new trends and did little to win the future for himself or his party. There was a chronic short-termism in his thinking. With him, reflected Derby in 1871, 'a temporary success is an end in itself: he either does not care, or thinks it useless to struggle, for distant results: and indeed will sacrifice these for the advantage of the moment...'[12] He knew about the rising force of the working class, he spoke of the democratic principle in the 1830s, and highlighted the existence of the two nations in the 1840s. But he failed to recognize the political significance of this situation. Socially he may have acknowledged two nations; politically he was only interested in the first and having secured his place in upper class society, rarely ventured beyond the London clubs and salons and the country houses of the aristocracy. That the franchise was bound to be extended to include sections of the working class was generally accepted. Yet during the 1850s and early 1860s, when parliamentary affairs brought few dividends, Disraeli did nothing to win the new electorate to the Conservatives and seemed to believe that the second nation would remain content with aristocratic paternalism. Indeed, though he gave large sections of the urban working class the vote in 1867, he made no effort to develop policies to appeal to them and fatalistically accepted that they would vote Liberal – consoling himself with a re-jigging of parliamentary boundaries. Tory Democracy was quickly seen to be the way forward and later Tories liked to believe that this had been understood by Disraeli. But as numerous historians have shown, this was a myth. Their hero possessed no such perspicacity. Though Gladstone's background and education was far more patrician, he made no such mistake and showed that it was possible to develop a populist appeal within the framework of Victorian politics.

Strategy

Taken in the round, Disraeli's career was a dramatic triumph. From derided beginnings, with none of the advantages of place or position, he managed to form the necessary alliances to enter parliament as a Tory. Once in his seat, he managed to break the rules that would have kept him a marginal figure. Confronted with the resulting scene of desolation, he practically rebuilt the party, working in the shadow of Derby, but all the while laying the foundations for his own advance. Eventually, in the late 1860s, the kaleidoscope shifted in his favour and he seized his chance. The Reform Bill was carried, Derby retired, the Queen was secured, Gladstone imploded, and Disraeli brought forth a programme of Empire and social reform. Thus was he able to take the occupancy of the inheritance he had created. More than any other 19th century Prime Minister, he was the author of his own achievements. Well might Randolph Churchill summarize his career: 'Failure, failure, partial success, renewed failure, ultimate and complete triumph.'

Nevertheless, there was too much passivity and good fortune in Disraeli's rise to power to make it a true reflection of political art. The 1840s were his creative decade. Having cleared the ground of Peel and most of the other talented members of the Conservative party, he essentially sat and waited until he eventually profited from the actions of others. If Palmerston had not died in 1865 and if Gladstone had not fragmented the Liberal majority in 1873–1874, Disraeli would not have been Prime Minister. That is to say,

Disraeli did not create a winning situation in 1874, though he certainly exploited and profited from it. This was not a contemptible achievement. But patience and safety were hardly qualities that would have recommended themselves to the romantic man of fame that was Disraeli in his youth. Ironically, Disraeli owed his ultimate success not to his own wayward genius but to Gladstone's. It took a man of Gladstone's unpredictable and driving character to persuade the middle class that Disraeli was a safe pair of hands.

Presentation

Disraeli well understood the role of presentation in political success and here he played his part to perfection. He was indeed a great actor and during his career adopted a series of personae. 'You must dress,' reflected Disraeli, 'according to your age, your pursuits, your object in life… In youth a little fancy is rather expected, but, if political life be your object, it should be avoided, at least after one and twenty.' In the 1830s, during his first assault on London society, he affected the airs of the young urban dandy. In the late 1840s, having assumed a leading position in the Tory party, his dress became far more sombre, with browns and blacks: 'The British people,' he wrote, 'being subject to fogs and possessing a powerful Middle Class, require grave statesmen.' As squire of Hughenden, he assumed the mantle of pillar of county society – regular in attendance at Sunday worship, magistrate, and counsellor to his tenant farmers. Disraeli never convinced as a countryman, but he embraced his role with studied alacrity and ensured that his leadership of the country party was not too incongruous. Indeed, Disraeli was at ease in all forms of society and here his sense of being an outsider was an advantage. Disraeli, one must remember, was the son of a Jew and the grandson of an Italian and had attended neither public school nor university. He loved England but was not English. He was aware of the distinction and subtly cultivated and played with it throughout his career. It gave him a sense of detachment, of ironic distance, which is the true characteristic of the artist. Despite having been born and raised in England and travelling only rarely beyond its borders, he was still able to respond to the offer of a cigar in the following terms: 'You English once had a great man who discovered tobacco, on which you English now live; and potatoes on which your Irish live; and you cut off his head.'[13] 'You English', 'your Irish': curious affectations of speech for a leader of the Conservative party. Disraeli always felt that he had chosen to become a Conservative just as he had chosen to champion the cause of English nationality. This element of contingency and volition meant that, though forced for much of his career to play court to aristocrats and princes, he retained his sense of integrity; he had sold his talents, not his soul. It meant, too, that he could enter social situations without the awkward class baggage of which otherwise more favoured men such as Peel and Gladstone could never wholly divest themselves. Technically he was middle class; but this counted for little when compared to his exoticism, his singularity, his Judaism. He was truly *sui generis*. Some, such as Carlyle, always loathed the Hebrew conjuror; most grew to be fascinated by this sphinx-like individual who spoke in epigrams.

For most of his career, the House of Commons was Disraeli's stage and here too, he proved himself an accomplished performer. 'Mr Disraeli,' wrote Bagehot in 1859, 'has made himself a *power* in the House of Commons exactly by this art.'[14] As a young man, he had believed that he could wipe the floor of the greatest debaters of his day. He never quite did this, but he did hold his own and sustain, almost single-handed, the Conservative cause against an array of Liberal talent and on more than one occasion did indeed storm the government defences – even if Derby did not always exploit his victories. As a parliamentarian, he won the respect of all sides of the House and when he finally departed for the Lords, the Commons was felt to be a poorer place. 'To the imagination of the younger men,' wrote the Liberal, Sir William Harcourt, on his departure, 'your life will always have a special fascination. For them you have enlarged the horizon of the possibilities of the future.'[15] His oratorical style evolved in tandem with his demeanour. In his younger years, he deliberately sought after an elaborate style of speaking which, though not generally recommending itself to the more prosaic world of the Commons made a devastating impact in the Corn Law debates of 1845–1846. Subsequently, his style became more subdued, downbeat even, and it was, noticed one observer, increasingly his habit to 'reserve all his wit and brilliancy' for the last fifteen minutes of a speech. Then he would show that 'he still possesses that power of sarcasm and wit which so galled Sir Robert Peel in the Corn Law struggle'.[16] His speeches were usually relatively short and delivered in what Blake describes as a 'cool worldly tone', as if he were 'a sophisticated man of the world addressing an assembly of like-minded persons'.[17] It was the natural demeanour for someone to adopt who had to oppose more than he had to defend, who was rarely emotionally engaged in the issues under debate, and who faced in the likes of Gladstone and Bright men of evangelical fervour. His gestures, too, were studied and increasingly formulaic – as Sir Henry Lucy observed:

> The merest tyro in the House knows a moment beforehand when Mr Disraeli is approaching what he regards as a convenient place in his speech for dropping in the phrase-gem he pretends to have just found in a odd corner of his mind. They see him leading up to it; they note the disappearance of the hands in the direction of the coat tail pock-ets, sometimes in search of a pocket handkerchief, which is brought

out and shaken with a light and careless air, oftenest to extend the coat tails, whilst with body gently rocked to and fro and an affected hesitancy of speech, he produces his *bon mot*. For the style of repartee in which Mr Disraeli indulges – which may be described generally as a sort of solemn chaffing, varied by strokes of polished sarcasm – this manner is admirable, in proportion as it has seldom been observed.[18]

Disraeli was not an orator by nature. He had none of Gladstone's relish for speaking outside parliament and dreaded such annual rituals as the Lord Mayor's banquet, when he was expected to articulate government policy. It was another of the personas he found himself called upon to adopt and it was a mark of his achievement that he carried on within the Commons the often fruitless task of leading the Conservatives with resilience and deter- mination. He knew what could and could not be done and what he did was usually well-judged and expressed in language appropriately laced with sarcasm and wit. Nobody else in parliamentary history has sustained the burdens of a party's future for so long and in such inhospitable circumstances; well might Blake describe him as not merely an 'impresario and an actor manager', but a 'superb parliamentarian, one of the half-dozen greatest in our history'.[19]

What of his message? Here, too, Disraeli understood the importance of image and appearance. The key to political success, he often claimed, was the ability to engage with the imagination of the population. Political communi- ties were bound by the affections and it was the job of the political leaders to stimulate sentiments of loyalty, reverence and devotion. They must stir the emotions of the electorate and this was to be achieved by the appropriate images and phrases. His chief charge against Peel is that he had failed to do this and he was determined not to make the same mistake. From the 1840s onwards, he created a conception of Conservatism which was potent with associations. The Conservatives stood for the established hierarchy of Britain; for a nation unified by active patriotism; for the symbolic majesty of the Crown; for a foreign policy that would uphold British prestige around the world; for pride in the British Empire. It was through these ideas that Disraeli supplied modern Conservatism with its sense of an ideology. It was also the means by which he hoped, by engendering emotional cohesion, to sustain the traditional class system against the disintegrating influence of industrial- ization and liberal individualism. In terms of presentational appeal, Disraeli accomplished very much. It was his personal legacy to the Conservative party. What he did not do and had not the intellectual stamina to achieve was the embodiment of these ideas in sustained measures. Disraeli's Conservatism stood for certain things, but did very little to secure them. By 1880, not much had been done to reinvigorate the territorial constitution

or consolidate the Empire or enhance the life of the working class. Disraeli
dealt in images, ideas, emotions, and speculations. The gulf separating
appearance from reality was considerable. But Disraeli would not have
accepted this distinction; thinking, in Disraeli's world, made it so. His success
was in this respect modern – even post-modern. It was a matter of art and
imagination – the artifice of Carlyle's 'Hebrew conjuror'. Like all art, it was
personal and subjective. It existed, ultimately, in Disraeli's own mind. That
was why he considered himself indispensable. Like Napoleon III, his associate in the days before either had power, he had no real followers in his own
lifetime and like the Second Empire, his own vanished, in 1880, as
Gladstone remarked, like some magic castle in an Italian romance.

Conclusion

Was Disraeli a success? By his own criteria he was, unreservedly. His career
had a satisfying narrative. Notwithstanding his despised beginnings and the
at best grudging acknowledgement of his talents by friend and foe alike, he
went on to attain the Prime Ministership, to rise to an Earldom, to win the
devotion of a monarch and, at Berlin, to shape the destinies of nations.
No politician has ever travelled quite so far. He showed, reflected
Monypenny and Buckle, 'that there is no eminence to which genius, aided by
courage, resolution, patience, industry and "happy chance" may not
attain...'[20] The romance of Disraeli's career is undeniable. 'He was,' wrote
one of his earliest biographers in 1881, 'unique in his generation and in his
century; a man without parallel and, in the path which he marked out
for himself, without a rival.'[21] Yet, what is equally striking is its self-
consciousness. From start to finish, Disraeli was the author of his own career.
This was true not only metaphorically but literally. The accounts we have of
Disraeli's adventures and achievements, from his early attempts to enter
parliament, his role in the Young England confederacy, his contribution to
the fall of Peel, his working partnership with Bentinck, his opposition strata-
gems, his parliamentary triumphs, his skill at piloting through the Reform
Act, of the ideas of One Nation Conservatism and social reform, of the decision to unfurl the flag of Empire, of the trials and tribulations of the Eastern
Question and of the climax of Berlin – all derive, very largely, from Disraeli's
own version of events. This in itself tells us much. It serves as a reminder – if
such be needed – of Disraeli's profound egotism. He constructed, from his
youth, a universe which had his own personality as its centre. The need to
distinguish between fact and fiction never concerned Disraeli, whether in his
novels or in his politics. His first novel was reportedly by a man of fashion.
It wasn't, and the discovery of this 'fact' did much to tarnish his reputation at
the time. But contemporary critics missed the point. Disraeli thought he

was a man of fashion and thinking made it so. 'What does Disraeli know of Dukes?' asked his father. Within a few years, there was little he did not know. Indeed, in 1878, he could have become one if he had chosen to. How many aspiring politicians can have written a pamphlet entitled 'What is he?' No clear answer ever really emerged. It is the posing of the question that is significant. The subject of Disraeli's politics was Disraeli. He transcended his environment, bending it to his own requirements, yet always affecting to stand outside, the ironic observer. This was nowhere more apparent than in his use of the Conservative party. He invented his own Tory heritage, attempting to prove to sceptical audiences that the Tories were the true liberals. In his Young England novels, he lampooned the very aristocracy he claimed to be in politics to save. Having broken Peel with the weapon of protection, he cast it aside when its usefulness was done. In the 1850s and 1860s, he sought to educate the Tories in the virtues of *laissez faire* orthodoxy. Well might he reflect to Stanley in the days of Palmerston's ascendancy: 'We are both on the wrong side, but there is nothing for it except to make the best of our position.'[22] In 1867, he first opposed the idea of taking up reform and then pushed through to the cheers of Conservative backbenchers a measure more radical than any wished for by the most advanced Whig, with no thought of what the consequences would be. Under his leadership in the 1870s, the party of Little England became the apostles of Empire. The search for any ideological consistency here is futile; the consistent element was the advance of Disraeli.

What drove him on? He often spoke of power as the true end and goal of politics. But power to what end? It would be tempting to say that for Disraeli the exercise of power was its own reward. But this is true of all successful politicians. A few seek power to implement some ideological programme. This was certainly not true of Disraeli. If it were, his career was a failure indeed. The one fixed point in his ideological horizon was the importance of sustaining the landed ascendancy. But he did little to effect this during the 1850s and 1860s and, when in office, he oversaw with detached fatalism the first real symptoms of its demise. There *was* a consistency in Disraeli's career and one which stretched back to the 1820s. It was his desire for notoriety and social eminence. While he spoke of power as the fitting object of a statesman, he was more candid when, in that late evening of 1852, he told Bright that 'we came here for fame'. If it is doubtful that he spoke for Bright, he did speak for himself. 'How can I help,' asked Stanley in 1861, 'seeing that glory and power, rather than the public good, have been his objects? He has at least this merit, in the last respect, of being no hypocrite.'[23] As a young writer, he had hankered after the literary celebrity of a Byron. Such was never forth-coming. But he found a substitute: the celebrity of political society. 'I am Disraeli the adventurer' he told the sceptical Lord Derby in 1849.[24] It was not the recognition of the populace he craved. That was Gladstone's weakness. It was the attention of landed aristocrats, bejewelled Duchesses, of the Princes of Europe, of Ambassadors and plenipotentiaries, of Courts and Queens that he sought with dogged determination to the very end of his days – 'worn out with age and maladies,' wrote Strachey, 'but moving still, an assiduous mummy, from dinner party to dinner party…'[25] It was, appropriately, in his final novel, *Endymion*, after he had attained to all he had imagined, that Disraeli let his readers into his secret. 'I have finished *Endymion*,' wrote Archbishop Tait in his diary, 'with a painful feeling that the writer considers all political life as a mere play and gambling.' 'The reader,' wrote another contemporary, 'cannot refrain from the disagreeable conclusion that the writer holds the world as a mere plaything, for his special amusement and contempt by turns.' Politics was and remains the greatest of games and Disraeli was one of its greatest practitioners. It was this that makes his career of timeless relevance. He was a politician not of the Victorian age – but of every age.

NOTES

1. Disraeli's Political Career, 1804–1846

1   Smith, 1996, p. 16.
2   Ridley, 1995, pp. 23–4.
3   Schwarz, 1998, p. 45.
4   Curiously, Tita entered the service of Isaac at Bradenham and when his father died, Disraeli secured him a messenger job with the India Office.
5   Blake, 1966, p. 48.
6   Richmond and Post, Chapter Three.
7   Brantlinger, *ibid*, p. 96.
8   Said, 2003, p. 102.
9   Brantlinger, p. 90.
10 Smith, 1946, p. 30.
11 Disraeli, 1833.
12 Disraeli, 1886, p. 16.
13 Smith, 1996, p. 155.
14 *Ibid*, p. 156.
15 Ridley, 1995, p. 155.
16 Vincent, 1990, pp. 23–4.
17 Disraeli, 1833.
18 Disraeli, 1836.
19 Disraeli, 1886, pp. 78–9.
20 Jenkins, 1996, pp. 16–17.
21 *Ibid*, p. 15.
22 Blake, 1966, pp. 165–6.
23 Monypenny and Buckle, 1929, Vol I, p. 523.
24 For a general survey of the Young England movement, see Faber, 1987.
25 Bagehot, 1872.
26 Disraeli, 1845, pp. 68–9.
27 *Ibid*, p. 438.
28 Bentley, 1984, p. 122.
29 Blake, 1966, p. 188.
30 Disraeli, 1844, Book II, ch. v.
31 Machin, 1995, p. 41.
32 Bentley, 1984, p. 122.
33 In the process Disraeli was separated from his old mentor, Lord Lyndhurst, who supported Peel.
34 Blake, 1970, p. 55.
35 Monypenny and Buckle, 1929, Vol I, p. 541.

36   *Ibid*, p. 539.
37   Vincent, 1979, p. 8.
38   Blake, 1966, p. 184.
39   Feuchtwanger, 2000, p. 62.
40   Le May, 1979, p. 39.
41   Machin, 1995, p. 41.
42   Feuchtwanger, 2000, p. 37.
43   Walton, 1990, p. 22.
44   O'Connor, 1878, Chapter 11.
45   Earl of Cromer, 1913, p. 192.
46   Jenkins, 1996a, p. 25.
47   Smith, 1996, pp. 80–2.
48   Machin, 1995, p. 50.
49   R. Aldous, *The Lion and the Unicorn. Gladstone vs Disraeli* (2006), p. 44.

2. The Politics of Opposition, 1846–1866

1   Blake, 1966, p. 260.
2   Vincent, 1990, pp. 31–2; 1978, p. 8.
3   *Ibid*, p. 86. Smith also advances this interpretation in Richmond and Smith, 1998, p. 10.
4   *Ibid*, p. 96.
5   Vincent, 1990, p. 6.
6   Aldous, *Lion and the Unicorn*, pp. 61–2.
7   Monypenny and Buckle, 1929, Vol I, p. 1166.
8   *Hansard's Parliamentary Debates*, 1852, Third Series, Vol. 127.
9   *Ibid*.
10   Vincent, 1978, p. 79.
11   *Diaries of John Bright*, 1930, p. 128.
12   Ghosh, 1984, Vol. 99, p. 276.
13   *Diaries of John Bright*, 1930.
14   Monypenny and Buckle, 1929, Vol I, pp. 1262–3.
15   Blake, 1996, p. 348.
16   Ghosh, 1984, p. 286.
17   Blake, 1966, pp. 395; 1970, p. 38.
18   Vincent, 1978, pp. 167, 173.
19   Blake, 1970, p. 87.
20   Machin, 1995, p. 39.
21   Hawkins, 1998, p. 68.
22   Feuchtwanger, 2000, p. 117.
23   Hawkins, 1998, p. 48.
24   Quoted in Aldous, *Lion and the Unicorn*, p. 60.
25   Monypenny and Buckle, 1929, Vol I, pp. 1558–9.
26   The Whips warned that Gladstone's adhesion would cause a spate of defections, Feuchtwanger, 2000, p. 100.
27   J. Parry, *Benjamin Disraeli* (2007), p. 41.
28   Vincent, 1978, p. 104.
29   *Ibid*, p. 106.
30   *Ibid*, p. 41.

31   Quoted in Aldous, *Lion and the Unicorn*, p. 122.
32   *Ibid*, pp. 238–9.
33   Vincent, 1994, p. 97.
34   Kebbel, 1886, p. 375.
35   Vincent, 1990, p. 47.
36   Bentley, p. 148.
37   Vincent, 1978, p. 90.
38   Vincent, 1990, pp. 46–7.
39   Seaman, 1973, p. 193.
40   Smith, 1996, p. 124.
41   Jenkins, 1996a, p. 55.
42   Blake, 1966, p. 355.
43   Machin, 1995, p. 83.
44   Vincent, 1978, p. 101.
45   *Hansard*, 1854, Vol. 136, p. 210.
46   Vincent, 1978, p. 133.
47   Monypenny and Buckle, 1929, pp. 1382–3.
48   Jenkins, 1996b, p. 50.
49   Vincent, 1978, p. 61.
50   Bentley, p. 92.
51   *Ibid*, 103.
52   Blake, 1970, p. 78.
53   *Ibid*, pp. 58–60.
54   Quoted in Aldous, *Lion and the Unicorn*, p. 67.
55   Vincent, 1990, p. 7.
56   Raymond, p. 165.
57   Machin, 1995, p. 97.
58   Dicey, 1905.
59   Vincent, 1978, p. 155.
60   Jenkins, 1996a, p. 39.
61   Aldous, *Lion and the Unicorn*, p. 127.
62   Vincent, 1981, p. 8.
63   Vincent, 1990, p. 5.
64   Vincent, 1978, p. 140.
65   Hawkins, 1998, p. 179.
66   Walton, 1990.
67   Jenkins, 1996a, p. 61.
68   Smith, 1996, p. 130.
69   Bagehot, p. 502.
70   Vincent, 1981, p. 6.
71   Feuchtwanger, 2000, p. 120.
72   *Ibid*, p. 130.
73   Kebbel, 1886, p. 303.
74   Feuchtwanger, 2000, p. 97.

3. The 1867 Reform Act

1   Cowling, 1967, p. 8.
2   *Ibid*, 69.

3   *Ibid*, 64.
4   Hawkins, 1998, p. 116.
5   Shannon, 1999, p. 24.
6   Cowling, 1967, p. 163.
7   Feuchtwanger, 1975, p. 140.
8   Machin, 1995, p. 111.
9   Blake, 1970, p. 103.
10   Cowling, *1867 Disraeli Gladstone and Revolution*, p. 344.
11   Murray, 1927, p. 186.
12   Blake, 1966, pp. 450–51, 463.
13   Trevelyan, 1922, p. 345.
14   Cowling, 1967, p. 3.
15   Bentley, 1984, p. 182.
16   Murray, 1927, p. 187.
17   Machin, 1995, p. 107.
18   Vincent, 1978, p. 264.
19   Blake, 1966, pp. 464, 476.
20   Cowling, 1967, p. 303.
21   Shannon, 1999, p. 37.
22   Cowling, 1967, p. 161.
23   *Ibid*, p. 47.
24   Hawkins, 1998, p. 119.
25   Shannon, 1999, p. 41.
26   Kebbel, 1886, pp. 337–8.
27   Democratic Tory, *Bull*, 1868, pp. 15–16.
28   Cromer, 1914, pp. 65–7.
29   Bagehot, 1867, p. 491.
30   Jenkins, 1996a, p. 75.
31   *Ibid*, pp. 77–8.
32   Walton, 1990, p. 20.
33   *Ibid*, p. 18.
34   Murray, 1927, pp. 192–3.
35   Parry, *Benjamin Disraeli*, p. iv.

4. Disraeli's Political Ideology

1   Taylor, 1977, p. 118.
2   Matthew, 1997, p. 79.
3   Vincent, 1978, p. 33.
4   Bagehot, 1859, p. 486.
5   Smith, 1996, p. 159.
6   Sichel, 1904, p. 136.
7   Vincent, 1990, p. 27.
8   Blake, 1966, p. 202. This point is acknowledged by Vincent, who notes that race 'justified Disraeli, a converted middle-class Jew, taking his place among the Tory aristocracy on equal terms'; 1990, p. 27.
9   Stapledon, 1943, p. 147.
10   Vincent, 1990, p. 30.
11   Richmond thinks that Disraeli first encountered Bolingbroke's work in 1821 when studying in his father's library; Richmond and Smith, 1998, p. 28.

12 Richard Faber wrote a study on *Beaconsfield and Bolingbroke* (1961), but was unable to demonstrate that Disraeli owed very much to Bolingbroke, beyond the fact that both were 'restorative' thinkers, seeking to reconstruct social systems on the basis of existing structures.

13 Bolingbroke, 1917, p. 77.

14 *Ibid*, p. 79.

15 *Ibid*, pp. 93–94.

16 *Ibid*, p. 54.

17 Leslie Stephen, for instance, concluded his survey of Bolingbroke's thinking thus: 'Yet, of Bolingbroke one can say little, but that he adds one more instance of wasted talents and unaccepted tasks.'; 1902, Vol II, p. 179.

18 Faber, 1961, pp. 29–30.

19 Bolingbroke, 1917, p. 36.

20 Disraeli, 1834, Section 31.

21 Smith, 1996, p. 122.

22 Monypenny and Buckle, 1929, Vol I, p. 1455.

23 *Ibid*, p. 94.

24 Bolingbroke, 1917, p. 93.

25 Richmond dates Disraeli's first reading of Burke to 1825. An inventory of Disraeli's relatively limited London library in 1842 shows that it contained a set of Burke's Collected Works; Richmond and Smith, 1998, pp. 36, 143.

26 Disraeli, 1834, Section V.

27 Burke, 1790, p. 93.

28 *Ibid*, p. 20.

29 *Ibid*, p. 153.

30 Vincent, 1990, p. ix.

31 Disraeli, 1847, Book III, Chapter VIII.

32 Disraeli, Speech at Aylesbury, quoted in White, 1950, p. 107.

33 Disraeli, Speech at Maidstone, quoted in Edwards, 1937, p. 173.

34 Disraeli, 1834, Section I.

35 Interestingly, the young Gladstone was, at the same time, making much of the importance of national character from a religious perspective.

36 Disraeli, 1834, Section III.

37 *Ibid*.

38 Stapledon, 1943, pp. 25–30.

39 Sichel, 1904, pp. 55–56.

40 Disraeli, 1834, Section V.

41 Disraeli, *The O'Connell Letters*, quoted in Edwards, 1937, p. 81.

42 Disraeli, 1834, Section XII.

43 Disraeli, House of Commons speech on the Chartist petition 1839, quoted in Edwards, 1937, p. 194.

44 Blake, 1966, p. 199.

45 Disraeli, 1834, Section XXIII.

46 Sichel, 1904, p. 71.

47 Disraeli, 1845, Book Three, Chapter Four.

48 Smith, 1996, p. 148.

49 Disraeli, 1870, p. x.

50 This aspect of his thought coincides significantly with that of Coleridge and Radical Tories like Oastler and Sadler.

51 Smith, 1996, p. 149.

52   Disraeli, 1845, Book Three Chapter Four.
53   Smith, 1996, p. 126.
54   Pearson and Williams, 1984, pp. 92–3; Blake, 1985, p. 123.
55   Sichel, 1904, p. 204.
56   *Ibid*, p. 205.
57   Monypenny and Buckle, 1929, Vol II, p. 535.
58   Smith, 1996, pp. 163–4.
59   Froude, 1891, II.
60   Eldridge, 1973, p. 177.
61   Vincent, 1994, p. 47.
62   Smith, 1996, p. 164.
63   Blake, 1970, p. 128.
64   Jupp, 1998, p. 151.
65   Disraeli, 1845, Book One, Chapter Three. Niebuhr changed perceptions of Roman history in his *History of Rome*, published between 1811 and 1831.
66   Jupp, 1998, p. 131.
67   Vincent, 1990, p. 21.
68   Stapledon, 1943, p. 25.
69   Jupp, 1998, p. 140.
70   Disraeli, 1845, Book Four, Chapter 14.
71   Vincent, 1990, p. 83.
72   Disraeli, 1844.
73   Smith, 1998, pp. 165–6.
74   Vincent, 1978, p. 90.
75   Blake, 1985, p. 123.
76   Blake, 1966, p. 198.
77   Vincent, 1990, pp. 82–3.
78   *Ibid*, p. 90.
79   Kebbel, 1886, p. 396.
80   *Ibid*, p. 334.
81   Apjohn, 1882, p. 88.
82   Walton, 1990, p. 60–1.
83   Jenkins, 1996a, p. 140–1.
84   Froude, 1890, p. 68.
85   *Ibid*, p. 44.
86   Cromer, 1913, p. 182.
87   *Ibid*, p. 178.
88   *Ibid*, p. 180.
89   Machin, 1995, p. 165.
90   Feuchtwanger, 2000, p. 217.
91   Jenkins, 1996a, p. 30.

5. Opposition Again, 1868–1874

1   Monypenny and Buckle, 1929, Vol II, p. 443.
2   *Ibid*. p. 464.
3   Blake, 1966, p. 519.
4   Froude, 1890, p. 215.
5   Monypenny and Buckle, 1929, Vol II, pp. 509–12.

6   *Ibid*, p. 451.
7   Vincent, 1994, p. 53.
8   Jenkins, *1996a*, pp. 86–7.
9   Disraeli, 1872, p. 18.
10   *Ibid*, pp. 21–2.
11   *Ibid*, p. 25.
12   Eldridge, 1973, p. 176.
13   Monypenny and Buckle, 1929, Vol II, p. 535.
14   Zetland, 1929, Vol I, p. 176.
15   Blake, 1970, pp. 118–9.
16   Monypenny and Buckle, 1929, Vol II, p. 602.
17   Blake, 1966, p. 535.
18   Blake, 1970, p. 114.
19   Monypenny and Buckle, 1929, Vol II, p. 524.
20   Blake, 1966, p. 535.
21   Machin, 1995, p. 125.
22   Jenkins, 1996a, p. 97.
23   Coleman, 1988, p. 144.
24   Kebbel, 1886, p. 356.
25   Walton, 1990, p. 55.
26   Marriott, 1913, pp. 434–5.
27   Jenkins, 1996a, p. 100.

6. Prime Minister, 1874–1880: Domestic Policy

1   Smith, 1996, p. 538
2   Buxton, 1888, Vol II, p. 177.
3   Blake, 1966, p. 538.
4   *Ibid*, p. 543.
5   Clayden, 1880, p. 56.
6   Monypenny and Buckle, 1929, Vol II, p. 639.
7   Bagehot, 1876, in St John-Stevas (ed.), Vol III, p. 503.
8   Monypenny and Buckle, 1929, Vol II, p. 599.
9   Smith, 1996, p. 176.
10   *Ibid*, 651.
11   Buxton, 1888, Vol II, p. 186.
12   *Ibid*, p. 233.
13   Ghosh, 1987.
14   Monypenny and Buckle, 1929, Vol II, p. 717.
15   Zetland, 1929, Vol I, p. 260.
16   Smith, 1996, p. 181.
17   Feuchtwanger, 2000, pp. 168, 172.
18   Monypenny and Buckle, 1929, Vol II, 708–9.
19   Blake, 1966, p. 553.
20   Vincent, 1990, p. 54.
21   Monypenny and Buckle, 1929, Vol II, p. 875.
22   Vincent, 1994, p. 238.
23   Clayden, 1880, p. 138.
24   Bagehot, 1876, p. 503.

25   Ghosh, 1987, p. 74.
26   Smith, 1996, p. 179; Blake, 1966, p. 553.
27   Monypenny and Buckle, 1929, pp. 969, 1175.
28   *Ibid*, Vol II, p. 658.
29   *Ibid*, p. 1342.
30   *Ibid*, pp. 1127, 1178, 1181.
31   *Ibid*, p. 1337.
32   *Ibid*, p. 1335.
33   *Ibid*, p. 1398.
34   Vincent, 1994, p. 202.
35   Monypenny and Buckle, 1929, Vol II, p. 1329.
36   Strachey, 1921, p. 267.
37   Vincent, 1994, p. 421.
38   Stapledon, 1943, p. 75.
39   Monypenny and Buckle, 1929, Vol II, p. 1369.
40   *Ibid*, p. 1371
41   Marriott, 1913, pp. 444–5, 447.
42   Murray, 1927, p. 226.
43   Southgate, 1977, pp. 186–8.
44   Stapledon, 1943, p. 84.
45   Feuchtwanger, 2000, p. 172.
46   Jenkins, 1996a, p. 115.
47   *Ibid*, p. 53.
48   Ghosh, 1987, pp. 69, 72–3.
49   *Ibid*, pp. 76–7, 80–1.

7. Prime Minister: Foreign and Imperial Policy

1   Vincent, 1981, p. 8.
2   Monypenny and Buckle, 1929, Vol II, p. 766.
3   *Ibid*, p. 885.
4   Seton-Watson, 1937, p. 506.
5   Eldridge, 1973, p. 207.
6   Clayden, 1880, p. 159.
7   Vincent, 1994, p. 247.
8   Monypenny and Buckle, 1929, Vol II, p. 897.
9   *Ibid*, pp. 888, 1225.
10   *Ibid*, p. 976.
11   *Ibid*, p. 956.
12   Seton-Watson, 1937, p. 517.
13   *Ibid*, p. 518.
14   Monypenny and Buckle, 1929, Vol II, p. 879.
15   *Ibid*, p. 903.
16   *Ibid*, p. 915.
17   *Ibid*, p. 885.
18   *Ibid*.
19   *Ibid*, p. 920.
20   *Ibid*, p. 925.
21   Blake, 1966, p. 606.

22 Monypenny and Buckle, 1929, Vol II, p. 938.
23 Blake, 1966, p. 601.
24 Clayden, 1880, p. 230.
25 Vincent, 1994, p. 413.
26 Clayden, 1880, pp. 261–3.
27 *Ibid*, p. 298.
28 Vincent, 1994, pp. 392, 465.
29 *Ibid*, p. 418.
30 Blake, 1966, p. 627.
31 Anderson, 1966, p. 197.
32 *Ibid*, p. 196.
33 Monypenny and Buckle, 1929, Vol II, p. 1106.
34 Anderson, 1966, p. 203.
35 Monypenny and Buckle, 1929, Vol II, p. 942.
36 *Ibid*, p. 1163.
37 Blake, 1966, pp. 646–7.
38 Monypenny and Buckle, 1929, p. 1234.
39 *Ibid*, p. 1236.
40 Seaman, 1973, p. 218.
41 Blake, 1966, p. 651.
42 Apjohn, 1882, p. 255.
43 *Ibid*, p. 653.
44 Clayden, 1880, p. 192.
45 Monypenny and Buckle, 1929, Vol II, p. 1239.
46 *Ibid*, p. 1128.
47 Vincent, 1994, pp. 524, 534.
48 *Ibid*, p. 57.
49 *Ibid*, p. 213.
50 Eldridge, 1973, pp. 148–56.
51 S.R. Stembridge, 'Disraeli and the Millstones', *Journal of British Studies*, V (1965), p. 135.
52 Monypenny and Buckle, 1929, Vol II, p. 748.
53 *Ibid*, p. 805.
54 Clayden, 1880, pp. 197–8.
55 Monypenny and Buckle, 1929, Vol II, p. 826.
56 Eldridge, 1973, p. 193.
57 Monypenny and Buckle, 1929, Vol II, p. 1295.
58 Blake, 1966, p. 671.
59 Eldridge, 1973, p. 200.
60 Walton, 1990, p. 41.
61 Monypenny and Buckle, 1929, Vol II, p. 1296.
62 *Ibid*.
63 *Ibid*, p. 1251.
64 Blake, 1929, p. 656.
65 Clayden, 1880, p. 475.
66 Monypenny and Buckle, 1929, Vol II, p. 1253.
67 *Ibid*, p. 1253–4.
68 *Ibid*.
69 *Ibid*, p. 1347.

70   *Ibid*, p. 1348.
71   Clayden, 1880, p. 517.
72   Monypenny and Buckle, 1929, Vol II, p. 1349.
73   Smith, 1996, pp. 202–3.
74   Clayden, 1880, p. 534.
75   Blake, 1966, p. 712.
76   Monypenny and Buckle, 1929, Vol II, p. 1395.
77   Blake, 1966, p. 722.
78   Disraeli to Malmsbury, 1852, in Eldridge, 1973, p. 178.
79   Disraeli to Derby, *ibid*.
80   Bodelsen, 1924, p. 123.
81   Bentley, 1984, p. 224.
82   Stembridge, 1965, V.
83   Eldridge, 1996, pp. 10–11.
84   Feuchtwanger, 2000, p. 161.
85   Jenkins, 1996a, p. 73.
86   Walton, 1990, p. 38.
87   Feuchtwanger, 2000, p. 198.
88   Eldridge, 1973, p. 206.
89   Smith, *Disraeli*, p. 197.

8. Disraeli and the Art of Politics

1   Monypenny and Buckle, 1929, Vol II, p. 1444.
2   Richmond, 1998, p. 41.
3   Monypenny and Buckle, 1929, Vol II, p. 1431.
4   Vincent, 1994, p. 491.
5   Schwarz, 1998, p. 44.
6   Bagehot, 1859, p. 488.
7   Disraeli, 1852, p. 350.
8   Vincent, 1994, p. 315.
9   Feuchtwanger, 2000, p. 177.
10   Richmond and Smith, 1998, p. 14.
11   Vincent, 1981, p. 6.
12   Vincent, 1994, p. 88.
13   Monypenny and Buckle, 1929, Vol II, p. 1475.
14   Bagehot, 1859, p. 488.
15   Blake, 1966, p. 566.
16   William White, quoted in Jenkins, 1996a, p. 62.
17   *Ibid*, p. 567.
18   Lucy, 1919, pp. 30–1.
19   Blake, 1966, p. 764.
20   Monypenny and Buckle, 1929, Vol II, 1505.
21   Apjohn, 1882, p. 293.
22   Vincent, 1978, p. 29.
23   *Ibid*, p. 179.
24   *Ibid*, p. 1.
25   Strachey, 1921, p. 267.

BIBLIOGRAPHY

A Democratic Tory (anon), 1868, *Benjamin Disraeli: The Past and Future, A Letter to John Bull, Esq.*, pp. 15–16.

Aldous, R., 2006, *The Lion and the Unicorn. Gladstone vs Disraeli.*

Anderson, MS, 1966, *The Eastern Question 1774–1923.*

Apjohn, L, 1882, *The Earl of Beaconsfield: His Life and Work.*

Aronson, T, 1977, *Victoria and Disraeli.*

Bagehot, W, 1859, Mr Disraeli, in St John-Stevas, N (ed.), *Collected Works of Walter Bagehot*, Vol III.

Bagehot, W, 1867, Why Mr Disraeli has Succeeded in St John-Stevas, N (ed.), *Collected Works of Walter Bagehot*, Vol III.

Bagehot, W, 1872 Ed., *The English Constitution.*

Bagehot, W, 1876, Mr Disraeli as a Member of the House of Commons, in St John-Stevas, N (ed.), *Collected Works of Walter Bagehot*, Vol III.

Behrens, R, 1987, *Benjamin Disraeli and the Triumph of Imagination*, Warwick Working Paper Number 43.

Bentley, M, 1984, *Politics Without Democracy 1815–1914.*

Blake, R, 1966, *Disraeli.*

Blake, R, 1970, *The Conservative Party from Peel to Churchill.*

Blake, R, 1985, *The Conservative Party from Peel to Thatcher.*

Bodelsen, CA, 1924, *Studies in Mid-Victorian Imperialism.*

Bolingbroke, Lord., 1917 Ed., *The Idea of a Patriot King.*

Brantlinger, P, 1998, Disraeli and Orientalism, in Richmond, C and Smith, P (eds), *The Self-Fashioning of Disraeli.*

Bright, J, 1930, *Diaries of John Bright.*

Burke, E, 1790, *Reflections on the Revolution in France.*

Butler, Lord (ed.), 1977, *The Conservatives: A History from their Origins to 1965.*

Buxton, S, 1888, *Finance and Politics.*

Clayden, PW, 1880, *England under Lord Beaconsfield: The Political History of Six Years from the end of 1873 to the beginning of 1880.*

Coleman, B, 1988, *Conservatism and the Conservative Party in Nineteenth century Britain.*

Cowling, M, 1967, *1867 Disraeli Gladstone and Revolution: The Passing of the Second Reform Bill.*

Cromer, Earl of, 1913, *Political and Literary Essays 1908–1913.*

Cromer, Earl of, 1914, *Political and Literary Essays, Second Series.*

Disraeli, B, 1833, *What Is He?*

Disraeli, B, 1834, *A Vindication of the English Constitution.*

Disraeli, B, 1834, *The Spirit of Whiggism.*

Disraeli, B, 1836, *Runnymede Letters.*

Disraeli, B, 1844, *Coningsby*,
Disraeli, B, 1845, *Sybil*.
Disraeli, B, 1847, *Tancred: or the New Crusade*.
Disraeli, B, 1852, *Lord George Bentinck: A Political Biography*.
Disraeli, B, 1870, *Lothair*, Seventh Ed.
Disraeli, B, 1872, *Speech at the Free Trade Hall, Manchester*.
Disraeli, R (ed.), 1886, *Lord Beaconsfield's Correspondence with His Sister 1832–1852*.
Edwards, HWJ (ed.), 1937, *The Radical Tory*.
Eldridge, CC, 1973, *England's Mission: the Imperial Idea in the Age of Gladstone and Disraeli*.
Eldridge, CC, 1996, *Disraeli and the Rise of the New Imperialism*.
Faber, R, 1961, *Beaconsfield and Bolingbroke*.
Faber, R, 1987, *Young England*.
Feuchtwanger, EJ, 1968, *Disraeli, Democracy and the Tory Party: Conservative Leadership and Organization after the Second Reform Bill*.
Feuchtwanger, EJ, 1975, *Gladstone*.
Feuchtwanger, EJ, 2000, *Disraeli*.
Froude, JA, 1890, *Lord Beaconsfield*.
Froude, JA, 1891, *Short Studies of Great Subjects*.
Ghosh, PR, 1984, Disraelian Conservatism: A financial approach, *English Historical Review*, Vol. 99.
Ghosh, PR, 1987, Style and Substance in Disraelian social reform, c. 1860–80, in Waller, PJ (ed.), *Politics and Social Change in Modern Britain*.
Harcourt, Freda, 1980, Disraeli's Imperialism, 1866–68: A question of Timing, *Historical Journal* XXIII.
Hawkins, A, 1987, *Parliament, Party and the Art of Politics in Britain, 1855–59*.
Hawkins, A, 1998, *British Party Politics, 1852–1886*.
Hansard's Parliamentary Debates.
Jenkins, TA, 1996a, *Disraeli and Victorian Conservatism*.
Jenkins, TA, 1996b, *Parliament, Party and Politics in Victorian Britain*.
Jupp, P, 1998, Disraeli's Interpretation of English History, in Richmond, C and Smith, P (eds), *The Self-Fashioning of Disraeli*.
Kebbel, TE, 1886, *A History of Toryism*.
Le May, GH, 1979, *The Victorian Constitution*.
Lucy, H, 1919, *Men and Manner in Parliament*.
Machin, I, 1995, *Disraeli*.
Marriott, JAR, 1913, *England Since Waterloo*.
Monypenny, W and Buckle, G, (1929 edn), *Life of Benjamin Disraeli*.
Murray, DL, 1927, *Disraeli*.
O'Connor, TP, c. 1878, *The Life of Lord Beaconsfield*.
Parry, J., 2007, *Benjamin Disraeli*.
Pearson, R and Williams, G, 1984, *Political Thought and Public policy in the Nineteenth Century*.
Raymond, ET, *Disraeli: The Alien Patriot* (nd).
Richmond, C, 1998, Disraeli's Education, in Richmond, C and Smith, P (eds), *The Self-Fashioning of Disraeli*.
Richmond, C and Post, J, 1998, Disraeli's Crucial Illness, in Richmond, C and Smith, P (eds), *The Self-Fashioning of Disraeli*.
Richmond, C and Smith, P (eds), 1998, *The Self-Fashioning of Disraeli 1818–1851*.

Ridley, J, 1995, *The Young Disraeli 1804–1846*.

Said, E, 2003 Ed., *Orientalism*.

St John-Stevas, N (ed.), 1968, *The Collected Works of Walter Bagehot*.

Schwarz, DR, 1998, Disraeli's Romanticism: Self-Fashioning in the Novels, in Richmond, C and Smith, P (eds), *The Self-Fashioning of Disraeli*.

Seaman, LCB, 1973, *Victorian England: Aspects of English and Imperial History 1837–1901*.

Seton-Watson, RW, 1937, *Britain in Europe 1789–1914*.

Shannon, R, 1999, *Gladstone: Heroic Minister*.

Sichel, W, 1904, *Disraeli: A Study in Personality and Ideas*.

Smith, P, 1967, *Disraelian Conservatism and Social Reform*.

Smith, P, 1996, *Disraeli: A Brief Life*.

Smith, P, 1998, Disraeli's Politics, in Richmond, C and Smith, P (eds), *The Self-Fashioning of Disraeli*.

Southgate, D, 1977, From Disraeli to Law, in Lord Butler (ed.), *The Conservatives*, pp. 186–8.

Stapledon, RG, 1943, *Disraeli and the New Age*.

Stembridge, SR, 1965, Disraeli and the Millstones, *Journal of British Studies*, V.

Stephen, Leslie, 1902, *English Thought in the 18th Century*, Third Ed.

Strachey, L, 1921, *Queen Victoria*.

Taylor, AJP, 1977, *Essays in English History*.

Trevelyan, GM, 1922, *British History in the Nineteenth Century*.

Vincent, J (ed.), 1978, *Disraeli, Derby and the Conservative Party: Journals and Memoirs of Edward Henry, Lord Stanley 1849–1869*.

Vincent, J, 1981, Was Disraeli a Failure?, *History Today*, October.

Vincent, J, 1990, *Disraeli*.

Vincent, J, 1994, *The Diaries of Edward Henry Stanley, 15th Earl of Derby*.

Walton, J, 1990, *Disraeli*.

White, RJ (ed.), 1950, *The Conservative Tradition*.

Zetland, Marquis of (ed.), 1929, *Letters of Disraeli to Lady Bradford and Lady Chesterfield*.

INDEX

Aberdeen, *Fourth Earl of*, 35, 46, 61, 170

Abyssinia, expedition to, 94

Adderley, *Sir* Charles, 212

Adullamites, 75–77, 80–81, 83, 93

Afghanistan, 169, 183, 189, 193–199, 206

Kabul 194–197

Agricultural Holdings Act (1875), 150, 152

Albania, 172

Albert, *Prince*, 54–55, 64, 122, 156, 204

Aldous, Richard, 33

Alroy (1833), 5

Anderson, M.S., 178

Anti-Corn Law League, 25, 27–8, 45

Apjohn, L., 128

Armenia, 178–180

Arnold, Matthew, 55

Artisans' Dwellings Act (1875), 148, 152

Ashley, *Lord*, 19, 150

Asia Minor, 167, 169, 182–183

Asiatic Mystery, Disraeli and, 5, 97, 116

Athens, 115

Attwood, Charles, 13

Australia, 187

Austria, 166–171, 174–175, 178–186

Aylesbury, 53, 108, 173

Bagehot, Walter, 16, 71, 95, 98, 145, 152, 210, 218

Ballie-Cochrane, Alexander, 15, 18

Batoum, 181, 183

Baxter, Dudley, 79

Beach, *Sir* Michael Hicks, 190

Belgium, 169

Bentham, Jeremy, and Benthamism, xiii, 107, 110

Bentinck, *Lord* George, 27, 36, 38, 49, 157, 210–211, 220

Bentley, Michael, xiv, 26, 63, 84, 205

Beresford, William (Chief Whip), 65

Berlin, Congress of xi, 180–181, 184–186, 197, 202, 209, 220

Memorandum, 168–169, 171

Treaty of (1878), 181–183, 185, 194, 198

Besika Bay, 168, 170

Bessarabia, 168, 175

Birmingham, 13, 62, 78, 83, 89–90

Bismarck, Otto von, 95, 167, 170, 181, 184, 186

Black Sea, 169, 179, 181

Blair, Tony, 104

Blake, *Lord* Robert, 4, 15, 21, 28, 37, 46, 48, 51, 60, 63, 66, 68, 84, 87, 99, 111, 117, 125, 136, 140, 144–145, 151, 153, 161–162, 181–182, 184, 194, 210–211, 218–219

Bodelsen, C.A., 204

Bolingbroke, *first Viscount*, 8, 99–106, 111, 120

Bosnia-Herzegovina, 167–169, 171–172, 174–175, 180–182

Bradford, *Lady*, 138, 157

Brantlinger, P., 5

Bright, John, 20, 43, 45, 50–51, 71, 74–75, 78, 83–84, 218, 221

Buckinghamshire, 2, 8, 36
Budget, (1852) 41–50, 60, 68, 214
   (1858) 47–48 (1861) 69 (1867)
   47–48 (1874) 147, 160 (1876) 146
   (1879) 200–201
Bulgaria, 167, 171–172, 174–175,
   179–181, 184
   Bulgarian atrocities 171–174, 176,
   184, 215
   Bulgarian Horrors and the Question of
   the East (1876), 173
Bulwer, Henry, 5
Burke, Edmund xiii, 99, 104–106, 109,
   112, 122
Bute, *Third Marquis of*, 101, 132
Byron, *Lord*, 2–3, 209, 221

Cairns, Hugh, *first Lord*, 133
Cambridge University, 15, 53
Canning, Charles John, *first Earl*, 28
Canning, George, 41
Cardwell, Edward, 28
Carlyle, Thomas, 88, 122–123, 176,
   218, 220
Carnarvon, Henry, *fourth Earl of*, 79–80,
   176, 178, 187, 190–192
Catholics and Catholicism, 20–21, 37,
   48–49, 53, 69, 130, 132, 138
   Catholic Emancipation, 29
Cavagnari, *Sir* Louis, 196
Cetewayo, Zulu chief, 191
Chamberlain, Joseph, 89, 127
Chancellor of the Exchequer, Disraeli
   as, 40–48, 51, 56, 59–60, 124,
   205–206
Chartism, 13, 57, 114
Chelmsford, Frederick Thesiger, *second*
   Baron of, 158–159, 192
Chesterfield, *Lady*, 138, 157
Church of England 2, 7, 16–17, 20–22,
   37, 49, 51, 53–54, 66, 68, 71,
   92–94, 98, 106–108, 112, 119–120,
   122–123, 128–129, 131–132,
   134–135, 139, 143, 150, 153–155,
   161, 175
Church of Ireland 93–94, 131, 154

Churchill, *Lord* Randolph 216
Churchill, *Sir* Winston 7, 12, 104
Clarendon, George Villiers, *fourth Earl*
   of, 78
Clayden, P., 152, 174, 184, 200
Cobden, Richard, 20, 51, 68
Coleman, Bruce, 141
Coningsby (1844), 17, 22–3, 37, 102,
   107, 111, 120, 122, 128
Conservative party organisation, 40,
   64–66, 90, 141, 202
   Conservative Central Office, 90,
   140–141, 202
   National Union of Conservative
   Associations 90, 136, 140
Conspiracy and Protection of
   Property Bill (see Trade
   Union Legislation)
Conspiracy to Murder Bill (1857), 62
Constantinople 5, 169, 170, 174–179,
   181–186, 195, 197
Contarina Fleming (1832), 5
Corn Laws 8, 20–1, 25–36, 41–42, 51,
   54, 65, 98, 123, 126, 160, 215, 218
Corry, Montagu (Disraeli's Private
   Secretary) 188
Cowling, Maurice 75, 84, 87–88
Cranborne, Robert, *Viscount, see third*
   Marquis of Salisbury
Cranbrook, *first Earl of*, see Gathorne-
   Hardy
Crimean War, 47, 61–62, 169–171, 176,
   178, 181, 185
Croker, John Wilson, 102
Cromer, *Earl of*, 32, 95, 129
Cross, *Sir* Richard, 144–145, 147–150,
   152–153, 161–162, 176
Crystal Palace speech (1872), 113,
   116–117, 126, 136–137, 140, 142,
   187, 205–206
Cyprus, 180–183

Daily News, 152, 171
Daily Telegraph, 175
Dalhousie, *Sir* James Ramsay, 28
Dardanelles, 178, 185

Darwin, Charles, 53
Debts, Disraeli's, 4, 15, 36
Delane, John, 63
Derby, Edward Stanley, *fourteenth Earl of*, xii, 24, 35–36, 39–43, 46–47, 49, 51–52, 55–58, 60–66, 69–70, 72, 76, 78–80, 84–88, 90–91, 133, 157, 216, 218, 221
Derby, Edward Henry Stanley, *fifteenth Earl of*, 39, 48, 51, 53, 56, 60–61, 63–64, 69, 76, 78, 84, 98, 117, 131, 133, 144, 152, 158, 166, 170, 173–181, 184–186, 210–212, 215, 221
Dicey, A.V., 68
Dickens, Charles, xi, 125
Dilke, *Sir* Charles, 157
Disraeli, Isaac, *father*, 2–3, 221
Disraeli, Mary Anne, *wife*, 12, 81–82, 94, 137, 157
Disraeli, Sarah, *sister*, 7, 157
Don Pacifico, 60
Dreikaiserbund, 167, 170, 184
Durham, *first Earl of*, 9

Eastern Question, 167–171, 181–187, 193, 198, 205, 218
Edinburgh, 90, 110
Education Act (1870), 131
Education Act (1876), 150, 154
Edward, *Prince of Wales*, 55, 156, 189
Egypt, 5, 116, 167, 170, 175, 180, 182–184, 187–188, 190
    Khedive of, 187–188
Elcho, *Lord*, 75, 81
Eldon, *first Earl of*, 102
Eldridge, C.C. 166, 182, 190, 205–6
Empire xii, 6, 13–14, 19, 45, 57, 68, 87, 108, 116–118, 123–5, 128–130, 137, 143–144, 155, 157, 159, 165, 169, 170–200, 202, 204–207, 213–216, 219–221
Employers and Workmen Act (see Trade Union Legislation)
Enclosure Act (1876), 150
Endymion (1880), 203, 222

Enquiry into the Plans, Progress and policy of the American Mining Companies (1825), 4
Epping Forest Act (1878) 150
Essay on the Literary Character (1795) 3
Eton 15, 28, 212

Factory Bill (1844), 19
Factory Act (1874), 150, 152 (1879) 150
Falconet (1881), 203
Fenians, 92
Ferdinand, *Archduke*, 182
Feuchtwanger, Edgar, 31, 71–72, 82, 93, 95, 130, 162, 205–206
Fiji Islands, 187, 190
Food and Drugs Act (1875), 148–149
Forster, W.E., 131
France, 43, 62–63, 101, 103, 123, 166–170, 178, 182–183, 187–188
Franco-Prussian War (1870–71), 131
Frere, *Sir* Bartle, 190–192
Froude, J.A., 117, 129

Gallipoli, 178, 185
Garibaldi, Giuseppe, 132
Gathorne-Hardy, Gathorne, 144, 176, 194–195
George I, *king*, 102, 107
George III, *king*, 100–101
Germany 123, 166–167, 169–170, 174, 182–184, 188
Ghosh, P.H., 44, 46, 48, 146–147, 162
Gibson, Milner, 63
Gladstone, William Ewart xii, 2, 21, 23, 28, 30, 32, 35, 39–41, 44–48, 51–52, 54–55, 59–61, 66–70, 73–83, 85–88, 91–94, 96, 98, 104, 122–123, 131–140, 144–146, 149, 153–155, 157, 160, 165, 168, 171, 173–175, 177, 179, 181, 183, 184, 186–188, 191, 197–203, 206, 211, 214–220, 222
Glasgow, 78, 89, 124
Glorious Revolution (1688), 119
Gorst, J.A., 90, 134, 140–141, 202

Graham, *Sir* James, 35, 51, 68
Granby, *sixth Duke of Rutland*, 38
Greville, Charles, 13
Grey, Charles, 8–9
Grey, Charles, *second Earl of*, 9, 203
Grey, Henry George, *third Earl of*, 51
Grosvenor, *Earl*, 76

Harcourt, *Sir* William, 192, 218
Hawkins, Angus 48, 50, 60, 70, 76, 92
Henry VI, *king*, 119
Henry VII *king*, 122
Herbert, Sidney, 28
Herries, John Charles, 38
Hicks Beach, *Sir* Michael, 190, 191–192
High Wycombe, 8–10, 36, 39
History, Disraeli's views on 11, 17–18,
　　99, 118–121, 130
Hodgkinson, G., 82, 86
Holland, 167
House of Commons, xi, 2, 7, 11, 13, 21,
　　27, 29, 36–41, 46–48, 50, 52, 55,
　　57, 61–62, 66–67, 69, 70–71,
　　73–74, 76, 78, 80–82, 86–87,
　　90–94, 96, 102, 108, 111, 114–115,
　　119, 126, 129, 132–135, 145,
　　171–172, 175, 181, 186, 192, 197,
　　199, 204, 211, 215, 218–219
House of Lords, 10–11, 17, 22, 36, 78,
　　85–86, 101, 107, 110, 128–129,
　　133–135, 145, 152, 196, 199, 203,
　　218
House Tax, 44–46, 50
Hughenden Manor, 36, 157–158, 177,
　　204, 217
Hume, Joseph, 50
Hunt, G., 187
Hyde Park, 27, 78, 82

Idea of a Patriot King, The (1738)
　　100–104
India, 47, 57, 61, 79, 116–117, 126,
　　144, 157, 169–170, 174, 179–180,
　　185–191, 193–198, 202, 205
　　Delhi, 174, 189

India Act (1858), 57
　　North West Frontier policy, 193–194
Ireland, 13, 19, 20–21, 25, 35–36, 44,
　　47–49, 54, 92–93, 135–136, 146,
　　172, 201
　　Irish MPs, 13, 38–39, 42, 44, 46,
　　48–49, 52, 66, 69, 76, 134,
　　138–139, 201
　　Irish University Bill (1873), 93, 138
Italy 2, 49, 62, 67, 116, 132, 168, 172,
　　182, 217, 220

James I, *king*, 119
Jenkins, T.A., 32, 58, 71, 95, 128, 130,
　　141–142, 162, 206
Jerusalem, 5
Jews and Judaism, 2, 37, 99, 157
　　Disraeli's Jewishness, xi, 2–3, 5, 8, 20,
　　36–37, 52, 59, 67, 99, 116, 132,
　　174, 181, 212, 217
　　Jewish Disabilities 2, 37–38, 57
Jolliffe, *Sir* William (Chief Whip), 65
Jupp, Peter, 118

Kars, 181, 183
Kebbel, T.E., 72, 94, 127, 141

Lancashire, 134–135, 144, 150,
　　178–179
Leeds, 78, 83
Lennox, *Lord* Henry, 181, 212
Lewis, Wyndham, 12
Lincoln, *Earl of* (later *fifth Duke of
　　Newcastle*), 28, 35, 51
Liverpool, 76, 83
Liverpool, *second Earl of*, 102
Lloyd George, David, 7, 104
Lockhart, J.G., 4
Locke, John, 104
London Protocol (1877), 175
Londonderry, Lady, 61, 157
Longman (publisher), 203
Lord George Bentinck (1851), 36, 49,
　　210–211
Lothair (1870), 132–133

Lowe, Robert, 75
Lucas, Samuel, 64
Lucy, *Sir* Henry, 218
Lyndhurst, *first Earl of*, 9–11, 14, 107, 157
Lytton, Bulwer, 5, 193
Lytton, *first Earl of*, 191, 193–97

MacDonald, Alexander, 149
Machin, Ian, 24, 32, 49, 60, 129, 141
Magna Carta, 118
Maidstone, 12
Malmesbury, *third Earl of*, 69
Malt Tax, 9, 43, 46–47, 50, 160
Malta 179, 185, 194
Manchester, 20, 52, 73, 78, 83, 92, 113, 124, 126, 134–137, 140, 142
Manners, *Lord* John, 15, 21, 29, 144, 176
Marriott, J.A.R., 141, 161
Maynooth College, 20–21, 24, 29, 49
Melbourne, William Lamb, *second Viscount*, 1, 9, 13, 35, 211
Merchant Shipping Act (1876), 148
Midlothian Campaign, Gladstone's, 201
Mill, John Stuart, 115
Monarchy, in Disraeli's thinking, 11, 16–18, 22, 54–55, 57, 102–104, 108, 110–112, 116, 119–120, 128, 134–135, 155–159, 219
Montenegro 167, 171, 172, 174
Monypenny, W., and Buckle, G., 41, 47–48, 117, 132, 140, 143, 151–152, 160, 171, 181–185, 187, 220
Morning Chronicle, 63
Morning Post, 63
Municipal Corporations Act (1834), 9, 120
Murray, D.L., 84, 96, 161
Murray, John, 4, 7

Napoleon, Louis (Napoleon III), 43, 62–63, 95, 101, 192, 220
National Liberal Association, 89
National Reform Union, 73, 82
Nationalism, 171–172, 175, 198, 201

New Poor Law (1834), 13–14, 19, 110, 113, 120
New Zealand, 187
Newcastle, 124
Newcastle, *fifth Duke of*, see Lincoln, Lord.
Newcastle Commission on Education, 57
Newman, *Cardinal* John Henry, 53
Newspaper press, xi, 60, 63–64, 115, 172, 176, 189
Northbrook, Thomas Baring, *first Earl of*, 193
Northcote, *Sir* Stafford, 144, 146, 162, 176

O'Connell, Daniel, 13
O'Connor, T.P., 31
Origin of Species, see Darwin, Charles.
Orsini, G., 62–63
Osborne House, Isle of White, 156
Ottoman Empire, 5, 26, 167–187
Oxford University, 53, 108, 124, 208, 212
    Christ Church, 28
    Oxford Movement, 53, 154

Palestine, 167, 182
Palmerston, *third Viscount*, 37, 39, 41, 51–52, 54, 56, 59–63, 67, 70–74, 76, 89, 131, 145, 165–166, 169, 171, 180, 186, 197–198, 215–216, 221
Paris, Treaty of (1856) 171, 175
Peel, *Sir* Robert, xi–xii, 2, 7, 9–10, 13–16, 18–32, 35–36, 38–42, 46, 49, 51, 54, 56, 59–60, 64–67, 70, 103–104, 106, 120, 122–123, 126–127, 130–131, 134, 140, 143–145, 151, 159, 177, 179, 210, 213–216, 218–221
Peel, *General* Jonathan 51, 79–80, 87
Peelites and Peelism, 22, 35–36, 38–42, 44–46, 51–52, 54, 61–64, 66–67, 69, 75–76, 81, 133, 137

Persia, 116, 169, 183
Piraeus, 115
Pitt, William (the Younger), 7, 102, 120, 152
Plevna, 178, 185
Plimsoll, Samuel, 148, 212
Post, J., 4
Powell, J. Enoch, 97
Press, The, 64, 126
Protectionism, Disraeli and, 24, 27–33, 41–43, 60, 62, 103, 123, 159–160, 215, 221
Protectionists, 27–28, 30, 35, 38–42, 49, 211
Prussia, 131, 165, 168, 188
Public Health Act (1875), 147–148, 152
Public Worship Regulation Act (1874), 154–155, 158, 175

Race, in Disraeli's thinking, 98–99
Radicalism, Disraeli's, 8–11, 13–14, 16, 20, 95, 128, 212
Radicals xii, 8–9, 12–13, 20, 27–28, 38–39, 44–46, 50–52, 57–63, 66–69, 71, 73–76, 78, 81–83, 86–87, 93, 95–96, 132, 134, 172
Raymond, E.T., 67
Reform Acts and Bills, (1832) 7–8, 10–11, 28, 55, 73–74, 77, 88, 106–107, 110, 113, 119–120, 126, 203 (1859) 57–59, 73 (1866) 74–78, 91, 214 (1867) xii, 73–96, 110, 132–133, 135, 140, 145, 159, 214, 216–7, 220–221
  Fancy franchises, 58, 79–81, 114–115
Reform League, 73, 78, 84, 86, 89
Representative, The 4, 126
Revolutionary Epic (1833), 6
Richmond, C., 4
Ridley, J., 3, 9–10
Rivers Pollution Act (1876), 147
Roberts, Frederick, *first Earl*, 196
Romanticism, 2–3, 5
Rose, Philip, 65

Rothschild, *Baron de Lionel*, 37, 188
Royal Titles Act (1876), 158, 174, 188–189, 193,
Russell, *Lord* John, *first Earl*, 26, 36, 38, 40–41, 57–58, 62, 73–74, 76–77, 88, 93
Russia 61, 158, 166–171, 174–186, 189, 193–197

Said, Edward, 5
San Stefano, Treaty of (1878) 179–180
Salisbury, *third Marquis of*, 68, 79–80, 87, 133, 144, 174, 176–177, 179, 184, 186, 193, 195–197, 211
Sandon, *Viscount*, 150, 154
Schumpeter, Joseph, 30
Scott, *Sir* Walter, 4
Seaman, L.C.B., 182
Serbia, 167, 171–172, 174, 182
Shaftesbury, *Seventh Earl of*, see Ashley, Lord
Shannon, Richard, 76, 85, 90
Shelburne, *second Earl of*, 102
Shrewsbury, 14, 28, 112
Sichel, Walter, 117
Smith, Paul, 3, 6, 8, 32, 57, 71, 116–117, 122, 144, 146, 153, 162, 201, 207, 213
Smith, W.H., 176
Smythe, George 15, 17, 21
Social reform xii–xiii, 8, 16, 18, 56, 68, 87, 94, 96, 115–116, 120, 125–127, 129–130, 135.137, 143, 146–153, 160–163, 200, 216, 220
South Africa, 116, 189–193, 199, 202
  Boers, 190–191
  Ishandhlwana, battle of, 191
  Orange Free State 190
  Transvaal 190–192
  Zulus, 158, 190–192, 198, 200, 206
Southgate, D. 161
Spain, 5
Spirit of Whiggism, The (1834), 11
Spofforth, Markham, 65
Stamford, 79

Standard, The, 63
Stanley, Lord Edward George, see Derby, fourteenth Earl of
Stanley, Lord Edward Henry, see Derby, fifteenth Earl of
Stapledon, Sir George, 159, 161
Strachey, Lytton, 158, 222
Straits, The, 170, 175, 179
Strangford, Percy Smythe, sixth Viscount of, 15
Syria, 167, 170, 182
Suez Canal, 126 170, 175, 182, 184, 187–188, 193
Sugar Duties, 19, 29
Sybil (1845), 17, 21, 68, 102, 107, 113, 122, 128, 151, 161
Sykes, Henrietta, 9

Tait, Archibald, Archbishop of Canterbury, 154, 222
Tamworth Manifesto, 19, 22, 30–31, 56, 59
Tancred (1847), 17, 108, 128, 174
Tariffs, 19, 23, 42, 60, 103, 123, 127, 137, 159–160, 200
Taunton, 12
Taylor, A.J.P., 97
Tea Duties, 44
'Ten Minute Bill' (1867), 80
'Territorial Constitution', Disraeli's idea of 17, 27, 31, 51, 94, 97, 112–113, 119, 123, 128–129, 159–160, 200, 202, 212, 219
Times, The, 63–64
Tita (Byron's servant), 3
Torrens Act (1868), 151
Tory Democracy xi, 57–58, 86–87, 90, 95–96, 115–116, 127–129, 151, 160–162, 216
Tory Interpretation of history, Disraeli's, 118–121
Trade Union Legislation, 149–150, 152

Trevelyan, G.M., 84
Turkey, see Ottoman Empire.

University of London 83
Utilitarianism xi, xiii, 16–17, 22, 59, 75, 105, 107, 109–111, 114, 117, 120
Utrecht, Treaty of, 103

Victoria, Queen, xi, 13, 40–41, 54–55, 61–62, 66, 78, 85, 91, 94, 100, 126, 138, 145, 154–159, 168, 170, 174–178, 181, 185–186, 188–189, 191–193, 196, 198, 203–204, 211, 215–216
Vincent, John, 10–11, 30, 37, 40, 46, 56, 67, 69–71, 98–99, 106, 116, 118, 120, 125–126, 133, 142, 152, 165, 213
Vindication of the English Constitution (1835), 10–11, 98, 104, 107, 111, 118, 128
Vivian Grey, (1826), 4–5

Walton, John, 31, 70, 96, 128, 141, 162, 192, 206
Wellington, first Duke of, 9
What is He? (1833), 11, 29, 221
William IV, king, 9, 12
Willyams, Mrs Brydges, 157
Wolseley, Sir Garnet, 192
Working class, 13–14, 57–58, 68, 73–75, 77–80, 82–84, 86–87, 94–95, 106, 110, 113–115, 135, 137, 143, 146–150, 152–153, 160–161, 215–16, 220
Wyndham, Sir William, 8, 102

Young England xii, 15–23, 27, 31–32, 54, 59, 67, 95, 102, 124, 127, 130, 135, 144, 151, 160, 162, 213, 220–221
Young Duke, The (1831), 5, 7

Lightning Source UK Ltd.
Milton Keynes UK
28 October 2010

161990UK00002B/23/P